"This is a book I highly recommend to all Christians as well as to New Age thinkers. It is a giant step taken under the guidance of the Holy Spirit toward a mutual dialogue between New Age thinkers and Christians. Bruce Epperly gives the most balanced critique and appreciation of New Age thinking and practices I have ever seen—without yielding any of the God-revealed elements essential to Christianity.

"The Christian reader is challenged by this work to rediscover insights and practices that have been lost to many Christian leaders and their faithful. New Age readers and other searchers are invited to discover the true power of the Christian cross that brings life out of death and love out of selfishness and greed. They will also discover here Christianity as taught by him who died on the cross for love of us in order to bring about by his resurrection a 'new creation.'"

George Maloney, S.J.
Author, *Mysticism & the New Age:*
Developing a Christic Consciousness for a New Creation

"Old-line Christian churches have responded to New Age movements and ideas chiefly by ignoring them. Fundamentalists, on the other hand, have perceived them as a threatening rival and have attacked them as demonic. Theologian Bruce Epperly points out that neither response is appropriate. New Age ideas and thinkers deserve to be taken seriously, their insights appreciated, and their theological and psychological excesses challenged.

"He believes that a process of critical dialogue between Christians and New Age leaders has the potential of bringing life to the dying bones of the old-line churches as well as helping New Age thinkers to avoid pitfalls that a knowledge of the history of Christian thought make apparent. A Christianity transformed by the dynamism of the New Age experience may be able to respond in a healthy way to the spiritual quest so characteristic of our time. This book points the way."

John B. Cobb, Jr.
Prof. Emeritus
School of Theology at Claremont

"Believing that the Holy Spirit is active always and everywhere and that the New Age movement represents one of the most significant spiritual revolutions of our time, Epperly calls for a serious dialogue with it. Through this dialogue, he hopes that mainline Christianity will be revitalized by recovering an experiential spirituality, the healing ministry of its founder, and belief in life after death. At the same time, Epperly challenges many naive and even destructive beliefs that pervade some New Age communities. This book is a fine example of openness to creative transformation."

Dr. David Griffin
School of Theology
Claremont, CA

"This is a book that was waiting to be written. I am personally indebted to Bruce Epperly for theologically validating much of my own experience of the New Age movement. His work has initiated a very promising dialogue between mainstream Christianity and New Age thought. It is a dialogue that is destined to challenge and enrich all those who are interested in connecting their spirituality with a passion for justice in human life."

Roddy O'Neil Cleary, D.Min.
Interfaith Campus Minister
University of Vermont

CRYSTAL & CROSS

*Christians
and New Age
in Creative
Dialogue*

BRUCE G. EPPERLY, PH. D.

TWENTY-THIRD PUBLICATIONS
Mystic, CT 06355

Twenty-Third Publications
185 Willow Street
P.O. Box 180
Mystic, CT 06355
(860) 536-2611
800-321-0411

ISBN 0-89622-683-2
Library of Congress Catalog Card Number 95-61868
Printed in the U.S.A.

A WORD OF THANKS

The German mystic Meister Eckhardt once said that "if the only prayer you can make is thank you, that will be enough." A number of persons deserve my heartfelt thanks: Professor John Cobb, for his academic and theological mentoring for over twenty years; Father John Breslin of the Society of Jesus, who encouraged me to send this manuscript to Twenty-Third Publications; Dr. Susan Trout of the Washington Institute for Attitudinal Studies for her spiritual support and example of an inclusive new age spirituality; Mr. Dan Connors of Twenty-Third Publications, whose editorial work was graceful and supportive. I am thankful for the spiritual upbringing of my Baptist home and the love of my parents and brother. Most especially, I wish to express my gratitude to my wife, Dr. Kate Epperly, and my son, Matt Epperly, for their love, support, and encouragement, and for the living spirituality of our family life.

CONTENTS

CRYSTAL & CROSS

INTRODUCTION

This book explores one of the most significant personal and corporate spiritual adventures of our time. It is inspired by my own spiritual journey and the spiritual quests of many persons today. For many persons, the new age movement is not a vague, amorphous, superficial, or fringe movement in the North American spiritual smorgasbord; it is a matter of spiritual life and death. Though the new age movement defies exact definition, it is embodied in the lives of many persons. My intention in writing is to provide a bridge for persons who seek to integrate the insights and vitality of the new age movement with the spiritual truths and the tradition of faith embodied by mainstream and liberal Christianity.

Unlike fundamentalists and conservative evangelicals, mainstream and liberal Christians cannot arbitrarily condemn the new age movement as demonic or superficial. At the heart of mainstream Christianity is the affirmation of pluralism and the universality of revelation. Such an affirmation must include the possibility that certain aspects of the new age movement reflect God's revelation for our time. Nevertheless, the rationalistic bias and suspicion of spirituality characteristic of many mainstream churches prevent their members from fully appreciating as well as creatively critiquing the insights of the new age movement.

By their neglect of the spirituality of the new age movement, mainstream Christians may be turning their backs on one of the most active movements of God's Spirit today. At the very least, mainstream and liberal Christians are challenged to approach the new age movement with the same openness that has characterized their encounters with Judaism, Hinduism, and Buddhism. An inclusive church with an open and discerning spirituality has the potential to become a place of dialogue and hospitality for thousands of unchurched new agers in our time.

CREATIVE DIALOGUE AND CRITIQUE

To many persons who read this book, it will seem as if my greatest criticisms are aimed at Christianity, especially mainstream and liberal churches, and that I am overly accommodating of the errors and excesses of the new age movement. Such a critique, however, misses the point of my project. My criticisms of the church are not those of an outsider or an inactive participant in the life of the church, but a son of the church. I grew up in an evangelical Baptist church, the child of an American Baptist minister. As a teenager, I found the narrowness of my church too confining and left it to practice Asian spirituality. In college, I returned to the church, first as an active layperson and later as a pastor and theologian, active in Disciples of Christ, Presbyterian, and United Church of Christ congregations. Yet, like many persons, I often found my spiritual inspiration outside the institutional church: in meditation, in reading the mystics, in spiritual affirmations, and in holistic health and healing. The new age movement inspired me to seek and reclaim the riches of the Christian heritage that have been neglected by a one-dimensional, overly rational church. I am a committed Christian, active church member, and weekly preacher of the gospel. God's presence in Jesus of Nazareth is a matter of life and death to me. But I see God's revelation extending far beyond the visible church in the movements of holistic health, psychic experience, spiritual formation, and human potential as well as in the quest for justice and community.

While I remain skeptical and critical of many aspects of the new age movement, I believe that one of the answers to the spiritual despair and shrinking memberships of mainstream churches is to be found in a creative dialogue with new agers, a dialogue that will inspire the church to reclaim a vision of reality that includes spirituality, healing, and the affirmation of life after death. Mainstream Christianity must become serious about its spirituality if it is to respond to millions of spiritually hungry seekers in our churches and across the country. The church must give seekers the living water and the bread of life.

The church also has much to teach the new age movement. With its emphasis on history, tradition, and social concern, the church can enable new agers to ground their spirituality in the concreteness of the world they live in and help them integrate their quest for personal self-realization with concern for the well-being of others. By transcending the individualism of new age spirituality, the church can help new agers share their own insights with their children and give them the experience of a lively intergenerational community of spiritual seekers.

Although many persons question the use of the term "new age" today, I continue to use it in this book. Some have suggested new religions, alternative religions, or spiritual shamanism as more accurate terms to describe the new age movement. But these terms are equally vague and lack the popular, though ambiguous, identification of the term "new age." In addition, the term "new age" describes the hopeful spirit of personal and global transformation that motivates many seekers. Further, the phrase "new age" has a long history within Christianity and is not a recent addition to our dictionary of popular phrases. The early Christians believed that Jesus Christ initiated the new age, which would be fulfilled at the time of Christ's return. Today, many mainstream Christians and new agers share a common ground: the hope of a new age that will come by transformation rather than the apocalyptic destruction envisaged by fundamentalists.

PERSONS FOR A NEW AGE

In the chapters ahead, I hope to explore this common ground with a sensitive spirit and a critical insight. Chapter One provides a general introduction to the issues at stake in the dialogue between Christianity and the new age. At the beginning of each subsequent chapter, I will point out the salient features of new age insights in areas such as health and healing, survival after death, revelation and channeling, spirituality, and the nature of the Christ. I have singled out many of the most perceptive and popular teachers in the new age movement in North America. In so doing, I hope to dispel the ignorance evident in many Christian understandings of the new age movement. Even as I focus on spirituality in North America, it is clear to me that the new age movement is global in nature and that it embraces the insights of Africa, Asia, and Africa, as well as Europe and North America. In their response to the new age movement, Christians are also reminded of their roots in the Middle East and their need to see Christ's presence in the rituals and faith of non-European peoples.

As I outline the basic beliefs of the new age movement, I will attempt to show how Christians can analyze, critique, and learn from these insights as they discover the new age reminders of their own forgotten truths.

My motive is not merely academic; it is vocational and existential. I have firsthand experience with the movements outlined in this book. As a chaplain at a major university, I am challenged by the diverse belief systems affirmed by my students and colleagues. I seek not only to share the "good news" of God's grace with them, but to listen to the truths they experience. I believe that a new and more vital Christian faith will emerge from a sincere dialogue with the new age movement. What lies ahead in this text and in the Christian-new age dialogue is a voyage in search of a truth, light, and love that will transform our lives and our planet at this most critical juncture in history. It is an adventure awaiting us all.

Let me conclude by sharing three encounters that inspired me to write this book. The first was with an active layperson in a mainstream Protestant denomination. Throughout her life she has sought to experience Christ's presence through prayer and Scripture. Recently, she encountered the popular writings of Shirley MacLaine, actress and new age evangelist, and Dr. Jerry Jampolsky, the popularizer of attitudinal healing. This woman's studies of the new age movement introduced her to the use of visualizations, affirmations, and energy work as vehicles of spiritual transformation and physical well-being.

These new experiences became an important part of her faith and self-nurture, but whenever she mentions her interest in spirituality, healing, and new age thought to her pastor and church friends, they respond with raised eyebrows and jokes about the eccentricities of California spirituality. Although she continues to be active in her home church and still studies new age literature, she is unable to find a bridge between the rationalism of her church and the expansive spirituality of the new age movement. As a Christian she feels uneasy with some of claims of new age spirituality, especially its understanding of the omnipotence of the mind and the insignificance of evil, but she also feels alienated from the rationalism of her church, which neglects the dimensions of spirituality, healing, and survival after death. Daily she prays for direction, guidance, and the ability to integrate her two, apparently conflicting, worlds.

Representative of other seekers in our time is a former Roman Catholic layperson. He, like many persons today, has become alienated from the church of his baptism and childhood. When he thinks of the Christian God, he responds with feelings of guilt and anger. He can no longer believe in a god of vengeance who punishes without mercy those who doubt their faith or miss worship services. After leaving the Catholic church, he drifted briefly into an evangelical denomination, but he found its wrathful God and concept of original sin further destructive of his faith and self-confidence. In this church, those who questioned a literalistic understanding of the Bible were deemed heretical. Rather than keeping silent, he migrated to a mainstream church. At first, everything seemed perfect: the church affirmed the role of women and even had a woman pastor; questions were encouraged; and God was portrayed as a loving parent. But something was lacking. There was little spiritual fire and emotional fervor in the church. He wanted to discover a way to experience the inclusive God of Christian liberalism directly.

Eventually, he left the mainstream church and became involved in personal and group study of *A Course in Miracles*, one of the most popular channeled writings of the new age movement. Today, he attends church only at Christmas and Easter. Although he is content with the spirituality of *A Course in Miracles* and the seminars in visualization and attitudinal healing he often attends, he misses the sense of community and the celebration of the Lord's Supper. He dreams of a Christianity that would combine an inclusive and robust theology with a lively and adventurous spirituality. He also is searching for a place where his young children can find a supportive community, with a loving theology to match the love of its members.

A third group that has inspired this book are the pastors I have encountered at conferences and church gatherings. At a recent conference, a pastor shared her concern about an unexpected phenomenon. Persons influenced by the new age movement are beginning to come back to her church. Her church's liberalism, interest in social action, and inclusive Christian education program are appealing to them. But they and their young children enter the church with a different language and set of preconceptions about faith and spirituality than most of her traditional parishioners have. As we talked, she shared her concerns about ministering to her new parishioners and their children. "How can I respond to their spiritual needs when I barely understand their religious background? I want to be able to meet them in the middle and to help them integrate their spirituality and understanding of Christ with the tradition of the church, but sometimes we seem to speak two different languages and mean two different things when we speak about God, Christ, or spirituality." She also worries that some of the more conservative members of the church will see this influx of new members as a Satanic conspiracy to take over their church. "How can I interpret the spiritual common ground we all share when I hardly understand the spirituality of the new age?"

Today, a growing number priests and ministers are trying to be bridge builders between Christianity and the new age movement. They see the possibility of a Christianity creatively transformed and spiritually energized by its encounter with new age thought. But there is much work to be done both within mainstream Christianity and in dialogue with new age believers.

As you read this book, I invite you to embrace the spirit of transformation. I believe that Christ is present in every movement of truth and spiritual growth and that in these final years of the twentieth century we are called to a renewed and transformed vision of God, ourselves, human possibility, and Earth. Despite the real and apparent differences between mainstream Christianity and the new age movement, we are all, in our various ways, seeking to be new persons for a new age.   •

QUESTIONS FOR REFLECTION AND DISCUSSION

1. Where have you encountered the new age movement? What is your response to the new age movement?

2. Is the church responding to the spiritual hungers of persons today? In what areas, if any, is the church's response insufficient to meet contemporary spiritual needs?

3. What is your image of God, or the ultimate reality? Has this image supported your spiritual growth process? What spiritual practices have nurtured your faith?

Chapter One

Christianity and the New Age

An Unlikely Birthplace

We arrive in Findhorn on a misty day in July. It is typical Scottish weather. In contrast to the glamour and glitz of many of today's new age centers, Findhorn is unpoetic, unpretentious, and nondescript. As we follow the signs leading to the Findhorn Foundation, we are greeted by a stark, weather-beaten trailer park and the roar of low-flying military planes from the nearby Kinloss Air Force Base. The atmosphere of the community itself is reminiscent of a haphazard new age boutique or a stroll down San Francisco's Haight-Ashbury during the "summer of love." Medallions, crystals, long hair, and long dresses adorn persons of all ages and nationalities as they meander through the lush green of well-tended organic gardens. The Findhorn we witness is a place for new alternatives, a place for persons exploring a new vision of themselves and the world.

The story of Findhorn is a parable of the new age spiritual journey. One would hardly expect a great spiritual adventure to have had its beginnings here.

In 1962, Peter and Eileen Caddy and their three children settled in the modest Findhorn trailer park, nestled between a torpedo dump and an air force base. Jobless and penniless except for welfare checks, they saw Findhorn as a place of last resort. They perceived themselves to be spiritual seekers, venturing beyond orthodox Christianity in search of the God within. Yet, their search seemed to have come to an impasse. It had yielded no clear answers and had led them from comfort to poverty. They had sought to put God first in their lives, but now their lives were disintegrating.

For Eileen Caddy, who later became the spiritual leader of Findhorn, the spiritual journey had begun years earlier in a small chapel in Glastonbury, England. In the quiet of the chapel, she heard the voice of God whispering to her the words of Psalm 46, "Be still and know that I am God." From that moment on, she discovered that if she were still enough, she would hear God's voice and find God's guidance for her life. The voice within had promised her that if she and Peter sought God above everything else, they would have an important role in the emergence of God's new age.

In those first few winters, when they lived on simple meals of vegetables from their garden, God's promise seemed like a cruel hoax. How could such unlikely circumstances bring forth ministers of the new age? How could this dismal and unpromising environment become a sanctuary for persons seeking the light? Yet, in the spiritual journey, things are not always as they seem. From barren Sarah and aged Abraham, a great nation arose. A lowly stable was the birthplace of the Messiah. Beneath its barren facade, Findhorn proved to be an energy point, a place of spiritual and ecological intensity, a holy spot and place of growth for persons as well as for the over-sized vegetables and flowers for which it was to become famous. In a vision received in 1975, Eileen Caddy was told the deeper meaning of Findhorn: "What is Findhorn? It is a state of consciousness, and that consciousness is of Love, Peace, and Joy. Those are the seeds that are to be sown all over the planet, and the harvest will be tremendous."[1]

Today, Findhorn is still known for its lush gardens and the penetrating beauty of its flowers. Although the vegetables no longer spring forth from the sandy peninsula in unlikely proportions, Findhorn is still a place of paradoxical beauty and inspiration. It is an international beacon of hope for those seeking physical and spiritual wholeness. Findhorn attracts persons disillusioned by the ways of death and competition and the shallowness of Western spirituality. It is a place where God is sought not just as a word or a ritual but as each person's guiding, inner spirit. During even the briefest visit, one experiences Findhorn as a place where the spirits of nature and humankind dwell in harmony. Though it is now world renowned, Findhorn still lives by its founding principles: that divinity is accessible to each of us at all times, and that nature, including the planet itself, has intelligence and is part of a much larger plan. Although Findhorn has no formal creed, the community is based on the belief that "an evolutionary expansion of consciousness is taking place in the world, creating a human culture infused with spiritual values."[2]

Findhorn, like many other new age centers, owes its existence to the spiritual courage and insight of a woman. Eileen Caddy's books and conversations are filled with a deep awareness of God's presence. God speaks to her in language reminiscent of the mystic or the charismatic Christian. To her, the words "god," "prayer," and "healing" are living realities. In language similar to that of conservative Christians, Eileen Caddy speaks of the Second Coming of Christ. But her words have a different tone from the doomsaying pulpit thumpers who capture the media's attention with their constantly updated reports on the fulfillment of biblical prophecy. To Eileen Caddy, Christ is the spirit of the new age. "The Christ is a very powerful transforming and transmuting energy that is within and around each one of us."[3] The Christ she hopes for is not restricted to one person, such as the historical Jesus, or one religious tradition, such as Christianity or Judaism. Like the leaven in bread or the imperceptibly growing mustard seed, Christ is emerging slowly but powerfully in all living things. "To me," she says, "the return of the Christ is not as one single Messiah but as the recognition and nurturing of the Christ spirit in all men and women everywhere."[4] Caddy sees the task of Findhorn and her own task as awakening persons to their role as partners and cocreators with God in the birthing of the new age.

The witness of Findhorn is like that of the humble manger in Bethlehem. God's revelation does not always occur among the powerful and well-known, but in unexpected, lowly, and unpromising people and places. God is revealed in the lives of women as well as men. The quiet spirit of Findhorn is a far cry from America's opulent publicity-hungry channelers and celebrities, who have come to represent the new age movement in the public eye. Findhorn reveals the deeper truth that God may be most fully present in the ordinary and the everyday cycles of personal growth and natural harmony.

As we departed from Findhorn, our minds filled with questions and our car loaded with books and artifacts, we knew that we had been to a holy place. We felt it as we gazed at the luminous flowers and as we meditated in the chapel. Yet as we drove toward our next destination, the Isle of Iona, we pondered how we as Christians might fully affirm both the magic of Findhorn and the mystery of our own faith. Is the Christ of Findhorn and the new age it proclaims also the Christ of Christian faith?

THE NEW AGE: DIVINE OR DEMONIC?

The new age movement has captured the popular imagination. Johnny Carson and Jay Leno joke about Shirley MacLaine's past lives, crystal power, and the harmonic convergence. New age bookstores and newspapers are found in nearly every major city. Suburban bookshops market the channeled sayings of spirits such as "Lazaris" and "Ramtha." Books on self-help through crystals or past life therapy, and the latest new age evangels of luminaries such as Louise Hay, Shirley MacLaine, and Stephen Levine continue to sell well. James Redfield's *The Celestine Prophecy* has reached the top of the best-seller list and has inspired discussion groups in mainstream churches. New age music has become a billion dollar industry, its soothing melodies enjoyed even by those who would be scandalized if they discovered the spirituality reflected in the music. Even Native American religion and its rituals have been rediscovered and transformed by spiritual seekers in the new age movement.

At first glance, the new age seems to be so inclusive and amorphous that it lacks any significant defining characteristic. Just leaf through the pages of *Pathways*, a resource guide to personal and social wellness published in the Washington, D.C., area. Between articles on life after death, environmental transformation, the men's movement, and how to enjoy the holidays, the reader is confronted by an amazing array of advertisements and workshops, all suggesting that they are part of the new age movement: martial arts, psychic readings, meditation, yoga, holistic dentistry, tarot cards, colonics, reiki, body work, herbs, wiccan goddess worship, and astrology. The only thing held in common by these new age groups and practices is that they are self-proclaimed alternatives to our society's established and institutional streams of education, medicine, religion, and psychology, and that they promise to help persons find spiritual and physical wholeness. There is no hierarchy, central office, credentialling process, or institutional network. Further, its leaders are more likely to be women than men.

New agers affirm a personal religion whose individualistic bent is tempered primarily by common reading lists, shared workshops, and informal networking. If there is any mecca for the new age, it is found in "energy centers" such as Findhorn, Scotland; Taos, New Mexico; Sedona, Arizona; and Glastonbury, England; in conferences such as "Common Boundary" and "Heart to Heart," both held in Washington, D.C.; and in centers such as Esalen in Big Sur and the Omega Institute in upstate New York. New age churches are virtually nonexistent. Although many new agers may belong to Unity, Religious Science, or even mainline churches, the typical new age gathering is a workshop, conference, or a short-term study group.

The new age movement is, as Marilyn Ferguson suggests, a "conspiracy" of persons with a common purpose, the aspiration to transcend the alienation, violence, and materialism of the current Piscean Age in preparation for the coming of the Aquarian Age of light, love, and peace.[5] Accordingly, any definition of the new age risks confusing the forest with the trees. Perhaps there is no forest or kernel to the new age movement, but rather a vague, unbounded, and undefined movement toward spiritual growth and adventure that has directly or indirectly touched millions of persons in our time. One mainstream pastor goes so far as to suggest that "if New Ageism were a denomination, it would be the third largest in the United States."[6] A California pastor asserts that the new age is "an indigenous movement in California . . . as common as going to the supermarket. It's like getting a tan."[7] While such comments may exaggerate the impact of the new age movement, they reflect the deep spiritual hunger, unmet by church and synagogue, that is addressed by the various new age and alternative religious movements of our time.

The new age has even penetrated the church. For the past few years,

I have taught lay education classes on topics such as death and dying, healing, and the new age movement at Wesley Theological Seminary in Washington, D.C. My students have been typically middle-aged and upper middle class Methodists, Presbyterians, Congregationalists, and Baptists, active in the lay leadership of their churches. To outward appearances, they are quite conventional people. Yet I have found that virtually every one of my students has encountered the new age in one of its many forms and has been attracted by its mystery, its spirituality, and its promises of health and personal transformation. For more than a few, a new age book on spiritual healing or Shirley MacLaine's autobiographical journey has meant the difference between spiritual or physical life and death. Some seminarians have been inspired to enter the ministry not by their pastor or religious upbringing but by an encounter with a psychic or a study group on creative visualization, tarot cards, or *A Course in Miracles.*

Many persons have integrated crosses and crystals in their personal jewelry and household shrines. But almost every Christian I have encountered still wonders, "How can I integrate the experiences and insights I have found in the new age movement with my life as a Christian?" Or, as a soon-to-be-ordained United Methodist seminarian confessed, "I study tarot cards and have heard the voices of spirits, but I don't think I could ever share this with my congregation or district superintendent. Would they ordain me if they knew about this?"

Sadly, Christian seekers have received few answers from their pastors or spiritual leaders. Equally disappointing is the fact that few new agers have been welcomed in mainstream churches. The church often acts as if the new age is unimportant or does not even exist. Yet, the new age has made a difference to the church, not only in terms of the greater frequency of practices such as guided meditation, affirmations, and holistic health practices within Christian spiritual formation and worship, but also in terms of the migration of young people and adults from the church to new age movements in search of a spiritual vitality they assume is lacking in their own churches. A Baptist observer of contemporary religious movements reflects that the new age is especially attractive to those for whom "the dominant Christian worldview has broken down, or the church as they have known it has disappointed them."[8] In a time when the outer journey has exceeded inner growth, when churches are often more concerned with institutional survival and social justice than with spiritual growth, the new age promise of spiritual nourishment and vital personal experience provides a vision of hope and a pathway to transformation for seekers both within and outside the church.

Interpreters of the New Age Movement

The new age movement is one of the most significant contemporary challenges to the church. The issue is not only "whether we can be both Christians and new agers," but also, "can the church once more become a place in which the lively, unfettered and always new spirit of God is found?"

One of the most articulate voices of the new age movement is David Spangler. Indeed, Spangler is one of its few authentic theologians or philosophers. Currently residing in the Pacific northwest, Spangler was once a leading spiritual force in the growth of the Findhorn community. According to Spangler, the new age represents a new level of religious experience, neither Eastern nor Western, but planetary in nature.[9] In his recent reflections on the new age, Spangler admits that he has been distressed with the media's focus on the exotic practices and miraculous claims that are now being identified with the new age. Whereas channeling, crystals, UFOs, prosperity consciousness, and harmonic convergence have always been part of the new age, they are now often seen as its defining elements.[10] Spangler contends that the new age is much deeper than these external trappings. In an age of crisis, the new age is "a way of talking about our relationship to the future and our creative capacity for transformation."[11] According to Spangler, the new age is "the myth of the Golden Age, of Utopia, of Progress, and the creation of a more Perfect and Just Society."[12] The new age is, in fact, ancient. It is a return to the spiritual roots of humankind. "It draws many of its values from the essential spiritual teachings of all the world's great religions."[13] In the spirit of Isaiah's vision of the messianic age in which "the lion and the lamb dwell in peace" and humankind will "beat its swords into plowshares," Spangler believes that the myth of the new age is:

. . . the myth of the sacred world. Such a world is one in which

there is communion and harmony between humanity, all creatures, and God. It is a world in which society and culture on the
one hand and ecology and nature on the other are mutually
empowering. It is a world in which actions and decisions are
based on a deep recognition of the interdependency, the inter-
connectedness, and the sacredness of all things organic and inor-
ganic.[14]

Spangler suggests that the new age paradigm includes the following elements:

We are each accountable for the world we experience. We are all
participants in a living, interconnected, interdependent universe
in which the actions of one affect the wellbeing of all. Our consciousness is not confined to the physical world but at its highest
levels is co-extensive with the universe and one with God. Our
task is to awaken to these higher levels of awareness and bring
their perspective and energy to bear on the healing and unfoldment of ourselves, our societies, and of the world. In so doing, we
must learn to express our compassionate and co-creative wills
more powerfully and effectively to shape our future and also be
more receptive to the reciprocal will of life as a whole and of
God.[15]

This vision of the new age is much more than a solitary individual,
such as Shirley MacLaine, running along the beach shouting, "I am
God, I am God." While personal empowerment is an important part of
the new age agenda, the quest for personal self-realization is rooted in
the commitment to protect and enhance the sacredness of all things.
Spangler believes that the new age goes astray when it forgets the
rich historical foundation (including Christianity and Judaism) upon
which its best insights are based. Hand in hand with the tendency to
downplay the importance of the past is the temptation among some
new agers to affirm novelty merely for its own sake and to be indis-
criminate and uncritical in their quest for wholeness and communion.
Unfortunately, some new agers have confused "psychic phenomena
with wisdom . . . channeling with spirituality, and the New Age per-

spective with ultimate truth."[16] Tragically, the quest for a new world has often degenerated into narcissistic grandiosity and magical thinking.

In words reminiscent of process theologian John Cobb's understanding of Christ, Spangler claims that "the New Age is a metaphor for the act of creative transformation."[17] It is present everywhere. Indeed, Spangler believes that the most powerful vehicles of transformation may be found in the forgotten, yet still vital, wellsprings of traditional spiritual experience.

> New Age spirituality is not a teaching unto itself, some kind of new revelation; rather it finds its fuller strength when expressed in context with existing spiritual traditions. . . . To me, the New Age is not a new religion. Instead it is the bringing of some fresh perspectives and practices to the traditions we already enjoy for the benefit of both the emergent and the established. It is simply a further expression of an age-old human quest for inner wholeness and completeness and oneness with the sacred. . . . It is about deepening more than it is about change. It is at heart about spiritual unfoldment.[18]

From Spangler's vantage point, there is no ultimate chasm between Christianity and the new age. The cross and the crystal can mutually nurture one another. Whereas Christianity provides tradition, structure, and critical reflection, the new age movement provides vitality and new direction to Christianity's ancient path.

Marilyn Ferguson, author of the widely read *Aquarian Conspiracy*, is one of the most sought after interpreters of the new age movement. Ferguson believes that the interplay of the social activism of the 1960s and the "consciousness revolution" of the 1970s is moving humanity toward "a historic synthesis: social transformation resulting from personal transformation—change from the inside out."[19] The new age, described by Ferguson as "the Aquarian Conspiracy," is a powerful and unprecedented network whose goal is to bring about radical change in the United States and across the globe. Grounded in the recognition that our pathology is our opportunity, the Aquarian conspiracy seeks to transform our culture through the integration of the insights of modern science and ancient religion. This transformation can arise only from a new way of experiencing the world, which will then be reflected in new ways of living and shaping the world. Human consciousness is on the verge of a new threshold, bringing together ancient wisdom, global spirituality, and modern technology for the good of the whole Earth.

At the heart of the new age is what Ferguson describes as a "paradigm shift," or a radical transformation in the way we perceive the world.

> The paradigm of the Aquarian Conspiracy sees humankind embedded in nature. It promotes the autonomous individual in a decentralized society. It sees us as stewards of all our resources, inner and outer. It says that we are not victims, not pawns, not limited by conditions or conditioning. Heirs to evolutionary riches, we are capable of imagination, inventions, and experiences we have only glimpsed.

> Human nature is neither good nor bad but open to continuous transformation and transcendence. It only has to discover itself. The new perspective respects the ecology of everything: birth, death, learning, health, family, work, science, spirituality, the arts, the community, relationships, politics.[20]

More than anything, the new age represents a conspiracy of hope that invites us to move from despair to transformation. Despite the glowing words of Spangler and Ferguson, Christians must still ask if there is a point of contact between the hope of the new age and the Christian hope that all things will be made new through the grace of God in Jesus Christ.

Critical Dialogue
Few theologians or church leaders have attempted to address the insights and attraction of the new age movement. Some, no doubt, see only the glamorous or eccentric aspects of the new age and judge it as an irrelevant and narcissistic trivialization of spirituality. Others may be genuinely frightened of the new age and its emphasis on alternative

forms of spirituality. Still other mainline pastors and leaders see the new age concern with spiritual transformation as peripheral to the political, social, and ecumenical mission of the church.

Despite their critiques of the new age movement, this amorphous movement of seekers still remains a challenge to mainstream Christianity in the last decade of the twentieth century. Although Christianity has its roots in the unexpected life, death, and resurrection of Jesus Christ and the pervasive experience of "signs and wonders" in the early church, few pastors are successful in nurturing such experiences in their own parishes. Many fail to realize the biblical connection between spirituality, healing, and political liberation.

For example, a pastor in Virginia carefully encouraged the initiation of a healing ministry in his church until a number of laypeople learned Dolores Krieger's practice of "therapeutic touch." He later confessed to me that while it was all right to pray for the sick or do the traditional laying on of hands, "manipulating energy fields a few inches above the body was just too weird." He proceeded to shut down the healing ministry without any further discussion.

Other pastors and church leaders have succumbed to the ministry of "works righteousness." Like Martha of the gospels, they are so busy going about doing good that the graceful silence of meditation frightens them. The new age appropriation of the biblical injunction to "be still and know that I am God" (Psalm 46:10) has no place in their concept of worship, personal growth, or service to neighbor. They have little to offer those persons who come seeking a deeper sense of God's presence in their lives. Nevertheless, despite mainline Christianity's uneasiness with healing and spirituality, it is imperative that Christian leaders and laypersons dialogue with the new age movement. If the church is to be relevant to the current revolution in consciousness and spirituality, it must awaken from its slumber and find new ways to provide spiritual sustenance for its own spiritually malnourished multitudes.

Jesuit George A. Maloney is one of a small but growing number of Christians who has seen the new age as both a gift and a challenge to contemporary Christianity. We live in an exciting time, Maloney exclaims, in which "there is an upheaval of the habitual ways we consider ourselves, the world, God, science, politics, and economics."[21] A

new picture of the cosmos is emerging that challenges centuries-old
assumptions of who we are and what we are called to do. Maloney
believes that Christians "can and should accept [much of new age
thinking], insofar as it is compatible with the basic truths of Christian
revelation."[22] Indeed, Maloney believes the new age is ancient as well
as novel. Our openness to it may be the prelude to a powerful inbreak-
ing of God's Holy Spirit within Christian consciousness. Maloney
maintains that although

> the seeds of such a holistic, planetary thinking have been plant-
> ed within the revelation of Jesus Christ . . . many of the valuable
> and seemingly revolutionary insights coming from the "new
> thinking" all too often have been lost in Christianity, especially in
> its Western form of scholastic theology, in its "masculine" legal-
> ism and organizational power.[23]

Christians are called to reclaim for their own religious tradition the
insights of the new age by nurturing a spirituality of Earth and a
"logos mysticism" that sees God's presence in all things. In so doing,
Christians will find themselves in partnership with other seekers of
truth in the quest for a new age of planetary spirituality.

Maloney's attitude toward new age spirituality has recently been
affirmed by the Thirty-fourth General Congregation of the Society of
Jesus. This international gathering of Jesuit leaders asserts that the
gospel "resonates with what is good in any culture." To those who see
the contemporary world as a spiritual wasteland, the General
Congregation notes that "peoples' spiritual lives are taking place outside the church" and that Christians need to "listen carefully when people say the Gospel does not speak to them."[24] While not explicitly speaking about the new age movement, the Congregation's assertion that
Christ "makes his presence felt in the diversity of human cultural experiences" surely applies to the spirituality of the new age movement.[25]

In the section on "Our Mission and Inter-religious Dialogue," the
Congregation affirms the Vatican II emphasis on dialogue with other
faiths and contemporary religious movements by positively noting its
challenge "to acknowledge, preserve, and promote the spiritual goods
found in other religions" and "to join hands with them to work toward

a world of peace, liberty, social justice, and moral values."[26] In the spirit of these documents, therefore, Christians encountering new agers must be willing to listen as well as to critique. Perhaps mainstream Christians, Catholic and Protestant, will deepen their own spirituality by encounters with the new age movement in the same way that they have experienced spiritual growth as a result of their dialogues with Jews, Hindus, Muslims, and Buddhists.

Ted Peters, a Lutheran minister and a professor of theology at Pacific Lutheran Seminary and the Graduate Theological Union in Berkeley, California, has also sought to dialogue with the new age movement. Peters maintains that in its attempt to integrate East and West and ancient and modern, "the new age is a phenomenon of cultural synthesis that is attempting to recover a religious grounding for understanding ourselves and the cosmos that is our home."[27] Peters perceptively notes that one of the most salient and attractive characteristics of the new age is to be found in its inclusive spirit.

> New Age practitioners have discovered the secret of religious success in America. The secret is this: you can ask Americans to convert to a new set of beliefs, but do not ask them to give up their previous affiliations. . . . Americans can affirm almost any new idea—no matter how preposterous—as long as they are not required to abandon earlier commitments.[28]

According to Peters, the new age inclusiveness and quest for harmony make room for virtually any viewpoint, including contradictory viewpoints such as an interest in reiki or natural foods—which affirm the importance of bodily well-being—and adherence to the principles of *A Course in Miracles*—which denies that we have bodies.

The new age movement, Peters believes, is part of a cultural spiritual quest, arising from mainline Christianity's inability to meet persons' deepest spiritual needs. In light of the popularity of the new age movement, Christians are called to "test the spirits" in order to determine what is healthy and unhealthy in the movement. Accordingly, Christians must critically evaluate the teachings and practices of the new age. What is at stake is "the spiritual health of individuals and groups. To get at this spiritual health we need healthy theology."[29]

According to Peters, we need to evaluate the new age in terms of the Christian vision of human existence and the God-world relationship. Peters recognizes that "modest dabbling" in new age spirituality may be helpful and that the new age vision is a noble and edifying one. Nevertheless, he cautions that its tendency toward a "gnostic monism [that is, the belief in the unity of all things and salvation through higher knowledge] is dangerous because it leads to naivete and to a denial of God's grace."[30] In its optimism about human potential, the new age is often blind to the shadow side of human existence. Consciousness raising alone cannot save us from evil. Its very denial of evil is its own undoing. Further, although God is present in our lives, neither we nor the world is divine. The very presumption of our divinity, assumed by some new age teachers, may blind us to the grace that truly transforms the human spirit. In his challenge to the new age, Peters proclaims:

> We have divinity within us, to be sure. But it is an alien divinity. It does not belong to our nature. It has come into us from the outside. It is a gift of grace. The Holy Spirit dwells within us, empowering us toward renewal, toward transformation. . . . What this means theologically is that I cannot equate God with myself. . . . You and I, along with the rest of everything that exists, belong to what we call "the creation." We have been created. We are creatures . . . in the ongoing movement of the cosmos, we are co-creators with God. But in the initial and definitive sense we are creatures, totally and completely dependent on the free and loving act of God by which we were brought into existence out of nothing. We are created co-creators.[31]

While I do not share Peters's radical distinction between God and the world and his notion of grace as "alien," Peters correctly points out some of the primary issues between mainstream Christianity and new age thinking. Persons certainly need a healthy theology, as Peters contends, but I would add that they also need a healthy spirituality. While the church can educate the new age in realism, the church must be willing to reappropriate its own spiritual roots in dialogue with the spiritual and healing practices of the new age movement.

Spiritual Warfare

Not all Christians are open to the new age movement. For some, even the critical dialogue that Maloney, Peters, and I propose is a dangerous expedition into enemy territory and an enterprise that compromises the saving message of Christian faith. While evangelical and fundamentalist critiques of the new age vary in insight, they share one thing in common—they believe that there is no point of contact between the teaching and spirituality of the new age movement and orthodox Christianity.

The most radical denunciation of the new age comes from Constance Cumbey, a Michigan attorney. To Cumbey, the new age truly is a conspiracy in the worst sense of the word, a subtle and destructive weapon of the demonic. Like the legendary Trojan horse, the new age hides the reality of evil itself beneath its pleasant images of the rainbow, the loving insight of spirit guides, and the luminous beauty of crystals. Cumbey believes that the new age fits the prophetic requirements of the Anti-Christ and can be described as a subterranean Nazism.[32]

Likening the new age movement to the serpent of the Genesis story, Cumbey asserts that it 1) denies the authority of the Bible, 2) denies the reality of death through its belief in reincarnation, and 3) claims falsely that humans are divine. Cumbey asserts that the new age is identical in belief and cosmology to the Nazism of Hitler. In the spirit of Nazi philosophy, the new age affirms a neo-paganism that deifies the Earth and suggests that the truth of Christian faith is found in the secret doctrines of an esoteric Christianity. Further, Cumbey notes many new agers speak of a "cleansing" of the Earth, a destruction of reactionary or unenlightened people, before the new age emerges.[33]

While the wildness of many of Cumbey's claims discredits her position, she is not alone in her denunciation of the new age movement. Ron Rhodes, in his *Counterfeit Christ of the New Age Movement,* suggests that the new age emphasis on the cosmic Christ rather than on the historical Jesus is "an old lie in a new package . . . one of the most comprehensive attacks against the deity and uniqueness of Christ ever launched by the kingdom of darkness."[34] Rhodes believes that Christians must be especially vigilant of the new age, because the new age has appropriated much of the traditional language of faith—belief in God, Christ, soul, prayer, and life after death—but with very different meanings.

In the judgment of these critics, new age spirituality and theology is at the very least heretical and quite possibly demonic. The "poisonous teaching of the new age," identified by Rhodes and others, challenges the Christian vision of reality through its heretical doctrines: 1) the impersonality of God, 2) the focus on ignorance rather than disobedience as the primary problem of human life, 3) the denial of the uniqueness of the historical Jesus, 4) reincarnation, and 5) the relativity of truth and morality. For Rhodes and other conservative Christians, our very salvation and the survival of authentic Christianity are at stake in the conflict with the new age. Participation in the new age movement can only lead us astray since it is "a counterfeit theology that centers on a counterfeit Christ who proclaims a counterfeit gospel, thus yielding a counterfeit salvation."[35]

Unlike most of their liberal and mainline contemporaries, evangelical and fundamentalist theologians and religious leaders take the new age quite seriously. Some of their better critiques of the new age reflect serious study not only of the Bible but of the new age sources they oppose.[36] To these Christians, the only possible attitude toward the new age should be one of spiritual warfare. The battle lines are drawn. The forces of good and evil are mustered. "The new age is a viable contender to both secular humanism and the Jewish-Christian tradition" for the hearts of human beings.[37] If Christians do not challenge the new age, they will implicitly welcome this "spirituality of the serpent" and its belief "that we can be as gods."[38] Even the apparently "good works" of the new age must be condemned, according to some opponents. New age critic Douglas Groothuis maintains:

> If someone is healed of cancer through the laying on of hands by biblically discerning Christians, this is a sign of the kingdom. Yet, if a psychic healer heals a person of cancer, this is not from God, although the result—in the short run—is similar.[39]

Fundamentalist critics believe they must oppose even the most innocuous and helpful manifestations of the new age—affirmations, guided meditations, positive imaging—whether they are employed in the classroom, workplace, or church.

In many ways, the fundamentalist critique of the new age parallels its critique of the theory of evolution and contemporary science. Conservative evangelicals and fundamentalists affirm that Scripture alone is the source of God's guidance to humankind. Any revelations or spiritual experiences not explicitly grounded in the Scriptures are, by definition, false and misleading.

While the inclusiveness of the new age movement may tend to obliterate significant moral and theological differences, the excessive narrowness of fundamentalism limits God's presence to a solitary stream, made available only to the favored few. Fundamentalists forget that although Jesus Christ is "the way, the truth, and the life" (John 14:6), Christ is also the living presence who "enlightens everyone coming into the world" (John 1:9). Paul's sermon to the Athenians recognizes that even though they are not fully aware of the one true God, the Athenians are, nevertheless, aware of the divine reality "in whom we live and move and have our being" (Acts 17:22–31). In their desire to make an exclusive claim to truth, fundamentalists forget that Christianity, from its very beginning, has lived in dialogue with its cultural environment and has always articulated its message in terms of the philosophy and symbols of its age and culture. While new agers may believe "too much" in terms of the nature of spiritual reality, fundamentalists believe "too little" in terms of God's saving presence in the world.

A more moderate critique of the new age movement comes from Jesuit Mitch Pacwa. Pacwa believes that Catholic interest in the new age movement is grounded in people's ignorance of their own spiritual tradition. Catholics must oppose the infiltration of new age ideas such as astrology, crystals, and the enneagram into Catholic parish and educational life. The Catholic approach to the new age movement should not inspire study or spiritual appropriation of new age ideas. Rather, encounters with the new age should be motivated by the desire to identify the threats the new age movement poses to orthodox Catholicism. Instead of learning from the new age movement, Catholics should immerse themselves in the historic teachings of their church.

CHRISTIANITY AND THE NEW AGE: THE JOURNEY AHEAD

A few days after our adventure at Findhorn, we journeyed to the western coast of Scotland. After skirting the shores of Loch Ness and venturing over the narrow, sheep-filled roads of the Isle of Mull, we caught a glimpse of the ancient Isle of Iona. While new agers speak of Findhorn, Iona, and Glastonbury as the three primary energy points in the British Isles, this solitary emerald island off the coast of Scotland is also known as the birthplace of Celtic Christianity in Scotland. The ruins and the ancient crosses testify to a tradition of faith that goes back to the voyage of Columba in the sixth century. Iona was a place of solitude and spiritual renewal for the Celtic saint. But it was also the place from which he ventured to spread the gospel to the Druids and Picts of ancient Scotland. Columba's faith and the faith of the Celtic church was that of an earthy spirituality. Christ was truly incarnate and God was present in their lives and in the mysterious, beautiful, and sometimes frightening world of nature. Like St. Paul before him, Columba recognized that the rituals and beliefs of the pagans pointed to the one true God. Columba used the insights of the pagan faith to express the dynamic vitality of Christianity. Columba is noted for proclaiming in the language of the non-Christian natives that "Christ is my druid," that is, my teacher and protector. In the spirit of Columba, this isolated island became the radiating center of the Christian mission in England and Scotland.

Over the centuries, the vitality of Iona was forgotten. The attacks of Vikings, the Reformation abolition of the monastic life, and its own isolation from the world left it in ruins until a Scottish minister, George MacLeod, began the work of transformation. In the late 1930s, MacLeod concluded that only a radical reformation of the church's life and work could make it relevant once more to the needs of spiritual leaders and working people. From the wreckage of the ancient community, a new community emerged at Iona, built on the principles of prayer, Bible study, and the stewardship of time and money. Like Findhorn a quarter of a century later, Iona was called to be a "beacon," a place of light, manifesting in new ways the presence of God in the modern world. Today, seekers flock once more to Iona in search of the refreshment of spirit that will enable their lives to radiate Christ's love to the world. In the seclusion of Iona, pastors and laypersons find refreshment through silence, Scripture, and study that will enable them to share God's love in their everyday routine.

Iona, like Findhorn, presents us with a vision of the new age. For Christians, it reveals the power of the ever-present and radically historical Christ, which embraces and sanctifies the whole Earth. The Christ of Iona, like the Galilean teacher who inspired its founding and renewal, reaches out to embrace the alien and unexpected, and invites his followers to do likewise. Like Findhorn, Iona is a symbol of the new age, of birth amid the ruins, of the rebirth of the ancient wisdom in our times, and of an open-hearted spirituality that embraces ordinary life. The vital and inclusive spirit of Iona is a symbol that motivates my own ministry and my own concern with the Christian-new age dialogue.

The new age presents a significant and creative challenge to Christian faith. Today, Christians are called to listen prayerfully to the voices of truth and love within the new age movement and to hear in these strange and alien tongues messages that have been forgotten or repressed in our own heritage. We are called to listen and to learn. But we are also called to speak from our own truth and our own experience of the good news of Jesus of Nazareth that liberates and transforms persons and institutions alike. If Christ is "the way that excludes no ways," as theologian John Cobb suggests, then Christians must embrace the truths of the new age in the spirit of the living Christ, the Galilean teacher, whose light "enlightens all persons."

QUESTIONS FOR REFLECTION AND DISCUSSION

1. Where do you experience God's revelation in your life and the world today? Is it possible for God to be present in the new age movement?

2. How do you respond to Eileen Caddy's encounter with God?

3. How do you respond to the statement, "The cross and the crystal can mutually nurture one another"? Do you think Christians can learn from the new age movement?

4. Both Marilyn Ferguson and Constance Cumbey use the word "conspiracy" to describe the new age movement. How do their uses of the term differ?

5. What is the primary focus of the fundamentalist objection to the new age movement? Do you find their arguments convincing?

6. What does it mean to say "Christ is the way that excludes no ways"?

7. How do the Catholic responses of Maloney and Pacwa differ? Which seems most in agreement with contemporary Catholic teaching?

CHAPTER TWO

FINDING GOD IN A TECHNOLOGICAL AGE

I will pour out my spirit upon all flesh, and your sons and daughters shall prophesy, and your young men shall see visions and your old men shall dream dreams; yea, and on my manservants and my maidservants in those days I will pour out my Spirit, and they shall prophesy. And I will show wonders in the heaven above and signs on Earth beneath.

SIGNS AND WONDERS?

These words of Peter's Pentecost sermon in Acts (2:17–19) summarize the experience of the early Christians. In the days following the ascension of Christ, the disciples prayerfully waited for the promise of God's Spirit. It came upon them unexpectedly—a mighty wind and tongues of fire—enlightening and enlivening every soul. Miraculously, men and women spoke in foreign tongues and heard the good news of salvation in their own tongue.

In describing the early church, the author of Acts proclaims that "awe came upon every soul, and many signs and wonders took place through the apostles" (Acts 2:43). While the letters of Paul suggest that these accounts of the early church are somewhat idealized, they depict a church far different from most mainline churches today. Compelled by their encounter with God, the early Christians lived in the expectation of signs, wonders, healings, and conversions. Dreams and visions were embraced as acts of God and means of spiritual guidance. Healing and prophetic utterance reflected the presence of the Holy Spirit. Worship was lively, spirit-filled, and adventurous. Although the believers could never predict which way the winds of the Spirit would blow, they eagerly anticipated their movements.

In those early days of the church, the good news of God's grace was unfettered. Despite resistance from traditionalists, God's grace could not be contained by the clear-cut boundaries of geography, race, gender, ritual, or theology. Like the mustard seed of Jesus' parable, the church grew unexpectedly and exponentially. Lives and life-styles were transformed as persons encountered the lively and iconoclastic Spirit of God. Faith and action, spirituality and social concern, were united in the church of the Pentecost. As the author of Acts proclaims (2:44–47):

> And all who believed were together and had all things in common; and they sold their possessions and goods and distributed them to all, as any had need. And day by day, attending the temple together and breaking bread in their homes, they partook of food with glad and generous hearts, praising God and having favor with all the people. And the Lord added to their number day by day those who were being saved.

Today, such passages are, at the very least, an indictment of the spiritual vacuum characterizing many mainline and liberal churches. When most Christians attend church in the 1990s, they don't expect surprises and they seldom desire miracles. Worshipers don't expect the world within worship to differ markedly in quality, emotional fervor, or insight, from the secular world of jobs, television, and politics.

In a time of great spiritual hunger, the malnourished receive words and tasks, but often fail to find the bread of life. In describing her departure from a mainline church, one self-described new ager recounts that all she received from her church was "words about God and forgiveness, but never the real thing. Everything seemed to be in the head, while what I wanted was a religion of the heart."

Many ministers are also dissatisfied and frustrated by the spiritual atmosphere of their worship and study groups. Still other pastors avoid contemplation and prayer altogether. Mainline Christianity has emphasized an extroverted, action-oriented, world-changing religion. Without a doubt, the world has been positively changed by the deeds of mainline Christians. Yet their approach often has been one-sided in its neglect of the inner life. Although many pastors and lay leaders ceaselessly remind their congregations of the good works characteristic of the Christian life-style, they seldom give them the spiritual guidance necessary to perform these tasks in Christ's name and with Christ's spirit.

Like Martha of the gospel story, mainstream Christians are anxious about many things. They seek peace among the nations, but have little peace of mind. Burnout is epidemic among those who seek to do God's will in the world. United Church of Christ theologian Gabriel Fackre notes that "we've been so preoccupied with our social agenda and institutional survival that we have failed to deal with basic human hungers . . . about life, death, and human destiny."[1] In their own fatigue and spiritual hunger, clergy and religious leaders often feel that they have little to give their parishioners. They know there is something more, but the path to the more abundant life eludes them.

Despite the challenges of modern science and secularity, people are still fundamentally, if not institutionally, religious. The Gallup Poll confirms that 94 percent of Americans believe in God. The baby boomers came out of the 1980s and into the 1990s discovering that consumerism is a poor substitute for community, love, or inner peace. At the edges of life, persons are discovering that modern medicine can neither defeat death nor ease the suffering of the human spirit. Face-lifts, health clubs, organic vegetables, and liposuction cannot nurture experiences of meaning and inner beauty. There is a quest for something more than materialism and technological control.

In spite of the pervasive spiritual hunger of North Americans, fewer and fewer persons find personal meaning within the vaguely defined and rationalistic spirituality of mainstream religion. The same Gallup Poll that notes the increase in belief in God also notes that 59 percent of Americans believe that churches and synagogues are "too concerned with organizational as opposed to theological or spiritual issues."[2] While fundamentalist, evangelical, charismatic, and new age groups have flourished, mainstream Christianity has, for the most part, been left out of the spiritual revival of the 1980s and 1990s.

Although some mainstream Christians believe that spiritual revival depends on a return to the "faith of the fathers" and narrow denominational searches for self-identity, such retreats into the past are neither theologically healthy nor spiritually advisable, since Christian faith is about new creation. Fidelity to God today calls us to go forward into an unknown and uncertain future—to embrace diversity and welcome the possibility of a new and startling revelation of God's presence in mainstream Christianity. As Hoge, Johnson, and Luidens suggest in their study on the declining membership of mainline denominations,[3] the membership crisis mainline churches are facing today is ultimately a challenge to discover a vital spirituality and authoritative theology in a culture of pluralism, individualism, and denominational weakness.

A creative dialogue with the new age movement may be the catalyst for the spiritual revival mainstream Christianity so critically needs. In the remainder of this chapter, I will address this issue by exploring the causes of mainstream Christianity's spiritual and theological crisis and by suggesting a constructive remedy in the context of a dialogue with new age spirituality and metaphysics.

NEW AGE OR NEW REFORMATION?

What has gone wrong in mainstream Christianity? In his influential study of the American spirit, Robert Bellah notes that mainstream Christianity has historically sought to avoid the individualism characteristic of both mysticism and fundamentalism. The god of mainstream Christianity is neither the "wholly other" authority figure of fundamentalism nor the "higher self" of transcendentalism, mysticism, and the new age movement. In seeking to address the needs of a broad spectrum of Christians, mainstream Christianity has nurtured an encounter with a god who is typically undramatic and this-worldly. Mainstream Christianity, at its best, for example, has sought to relate biblical faith to contemporary life by "steering a middle path between mystical fusion with the world and sectarian withdrawal from the world."[4] Accordingly, mainstream Christianity has sought to be inclusive not only of religious diversity but of culture itself. In so doing, it has profoundly shaped the mores of our culture and greatly contributed to the ecumenical spirit characterizing most denominations today. It has been a home for all peoples.

There has, however, been a cost to this inclusivism and openness to culture. Mainstream Christianity's emphasis on the horizontal dimension of life, reflected in its commitment to social concern and cultural pluralism, has eclipsed the encounter with the vertical dimension of life, reflected in moments of spiritual transcendence, passion, and illumination. In its attempts to be inclusive, mainstream Christianity has often sacrificed its spiritual core and theological uniqueness. Even the social impact of mainstream Christianity has been weakened by its lack of spiritual vitality and theological insight.

Today, theologians, pastors, and laypersons are calling the church to a new adventure. Theologian John Cobb speaks of his longing for the renewal of a passionate, progressive faith.[5] Cobb asserts that if

> . . . Christ is the savior of the world, then why do we not make that clear in our weekly preaching and church pronouncements? Why do we continue to describe that from which Christ saves us in such ways that few see the need for such "salvation"? If we convincingly showed how Christ can save us, individually and corporately, from the utterly critical problems we all face, then the church would once again be looked to with expectancy for leadership. There would be authentic excitement among its members.[6]

Cobb maintains that the current malaise of mainstream Christianity finds its source in its failure to think creatively about Christian faith in our time. In words that echo the dissatisfaction of today's spiritually malnourished people, Cobb states that the church's "ministers and bureaucratic leaders are too busy with 'practical' matters to engage in profound reflection. So the church grabs at quick fixes, catchy phrases, and public relations to resolve the pervasive malaise that all are forced to recognize."[7]

The failure of the church to respond to today's theological questions and spiritual yearnings has left the church far behind the new age movement, popular psychology, and evangelical Christianity in addressing two of the most basic spiritual needs of many persons today: a coherent understanding of God's presence in the world and an experience of holiness in the everyday. In this time of crisis among mainstream Christians, the church must once more present the world with a vision of God that enables persons to experience God's saving presence in their everyday lives, in the struggle for justice, and in the encounter with the nonhuman world.

If Christ is to become good news again in mainstream churches and in the world beyond the church, we must, first, identify the bad news that has led to our current malaise. Why has mainstream Christianity lost much of its theological insight and spiritual vitality?

One of the primary reasons is to be found in mainstream Christianity's theological and experiential accommodation to the modern worldview. Put briefly, the scientific worldview maintains that humans can neither know nor experience what lies beyond the five senses. Reality is ultimately biological and physiological in nature. From this perspective, dreams, visions, and mystical experiences—the signs and wonders of Pentecost—are merely subjective states of mind that give no evidence as to the nature of things. In the strict "closed system" cause and effect world of Newtonian science and Darwinian evolution, there is no room for God, immortality, mysticism, or healing. To those who see the world as one-dimensional, the biblical accounts of Jesus' miracles and the mighty acts of God are myths that have no place in a coherent understanding of reality. Stripped of the outmoded and irrelevant worldview of the Scriptures, Christians can focus on issues of existential meaning and social concern in this world.

Yet the "enlightenment" viewpoint of scientists and theologians has proven to be a prison. In banishing the encounter with God and the spiritual world from human life, the modern worldview has robbed persons of two of their greatest needs—spiritual nourishment and a framework by which to understand their place in the world. In absolutizing the scientific and humanistic worldview, theologians, scientists, and educators failed to recognize the deeper dimensions of life now being rediscovered by quantum physicists, scientists studying the effects of prayer and meditation, researchers in near death experiences, and ordinary persons who suddenly find themselves in the presence of the holy.

In light of new scientific and psychic discoveries, the church must learn again to think adventurously and creatively. It must also explore the realm of the spirit with humility and without embarrassment. If it is to become a guiding presence in the spirituality of our time, the church must break free of the shackles of the now outmoded modern view and position itself at the frontiers of spirituality and theology. When the church closes its doors to the deeper movements of God's Spirit, be they political, intellectual, or spiritual in nature, God's Spirit breaks through somewhere else. Despite its vagueness, imperfection, and occasional excesses, the new age movement may very well be a vehicle for spiritual awakening not only for the secular culture but also for the church. Accordingly, dialogue with the new age movement is as important for the church today as dialogues with Buddhists, Hindus, feminists, and social critics have been in the past. The church needs to encounter the spiritual vitality and metaphysical exploration of the new age movement, and the new age movement needs to hear the graceful, liberating, and socially sensitive message of those who follow Christ.

In the remainder of this chapter, I will outline the essential features of the new age movement as these relate to a transformed Christianity of the future. I will point out some of the insights as well as the over-sights of new age spirituality.

NEW AGE SPIRITUALITY: AN OVERVIEW

The new age movement is countercultural in spirit. Dissatisfied with materialism and institutional religion, its spiritual seekers are looking for something to believe in as well as a means to experience inner peace and spiritual transcendence. In a world of fragmentation, new agers are seeking unity and wholeness. But the religion they seek is profoundly personal and pragmatic in nature. Even though it has spawned a variety of metaphysical visions, the new age movement emphasizes experience over abstract doctrinal positions. In contrast to the Christian focus on doctrine as fundamental to religious experience, many new agers see beliefs as tools that help us shape reality and enhance our personal experience. Reality is created by our thoughts, and not vice versa. Accordingly, the value of a belief system is judged not by its consistency but by how it manifests itself in a person's life.

"This is my truth" or "this is my reality" are common expressions in the new age movement. In this regard, new age religion resembles Robert Bellah's use of the term "Sheilaism" to describe the individualism characteristic of the American religious spirit. In the words of Sheila Larson, a person who typifies this individualistic spirituality, "my faith has carried me a long way. It's Sheilaism. Just my own little voice."[8] While the fundamentalist Christian denounces new age individualism as evidence of pride, relativism, and self-idolatry, new agers see religion as primarily a personal and subjective matter. There are potentially as many truths and religions as there are personal perspectives.

Amid the variety of new age spiritualities and metaphysical systems, however, there are common threads of belief and practice that characterize the new age movement: 1) the unity of all life, 2) the divinity of each person, 3) the power of the mind, and 4) the focus on spiritual technologies for personal growth and transformation. We need to understand these essential threads of new age spirituality as they relate to the spiritual concerns of mainstream Christians.

1. The Unity of All Life

The new age understanding of the unity of all life ranges from the belief that all life is interrelated to the affirmation that there is but one reality: God, Love, or universal mind. In new age thinking, the unity of all things stands in sharp contrast to the compartmentalized and dualistic worldview of the philosophical and scientific followers of Newton and Descartes. In new age thinking, pain and separation are not the result of the sins of pride, passivity, or disobedience, as mainstream Christianity might suggest, but find their basis in ignorance and egocentricity. Psychiatrist Jerry Jampolsky, noted for the use of "attitudinal healing" as a technique of responding to critical illness in children, states that "love is the only reality there is. Anything that we perceive that doesn't mirror love is a misperception."[9] While we are always united in love, fear creates a world of separation and death.

Susan Trout, the Director of the Institute for Attitudinal Studies in Washington, D.C., states that "there is a Divine Source, an Eternal, a

Higher Power, a God, a Goddess, All that is. Each of us is part of this Source like a droplet of ocean water, while not being the ocean, is part of the ocean."[10] Echoing Jampolsky, Trout contends that "the basic problem in our lives is that we have forgotten our Oneness with the Divine Source. The basic solution is remembering our true identity."[11]

In her description of the nature of spirituality, Charlene Spretnak, ecological activist and pioneer of the Green political movement in the United States, suggests that the destruction of the ecosphere arises from the failure of modern persons to perceive the interrelatedness of life. Our experience of separation from nature is an illusion. When we look deeper into reality, we discover the true nature of things: "All is One, all forms of existence are comprised of one continuous dance of matter/energy arising and falling away, arising and falling away."[12] Ecological wisdom and spiritual insight are interrelated. The experience of "grace" or "God consciousness" involves living "with a deep awareness of the elemental Oneness of all creation."[13]

David Spangler, like Spretnak, sees this basic unity of life as physical as well as spiritual. Spangler describes the new age in terms of the myth of the sacred world in which "there is communion and harmony between humanity, all creatures, and God."[14]

Alternative physician Larry Dossey enthusiastically embraces the unity of life suggested by the relativity physics of Einstein and his followers. According to Dossey, the fact that there is some unity of perception in the interplay of the five billion minds inhabiting planet Earth gives reason to affirm the existence of one universal mind that shapes the data perceived by each individual mind. Dossey approvingly quotes physicist Henry Margenau's belief that "each individual is part of God or part of the Universal Mind . . . each of us is the Universal Mind but infected with limitations that obscure all but a tiny fraction of its aspects and properties."[15] Dossey finds further support for the unity of all minds in the "holographic" theory of British physicist David Bohm. Bohm has stated that each part of the universe reflects the totality of the universe. The part contains the whole, and the whole embraces each part. As Bohm maintains, "the entire universe . . . has to be understood as a single undivided whole, in which analysis into separately and independently existing parts has no fundamental status."[16] The unitary visions of reality, suggested by

Spangler, Dossey, Spretnak, and Bohm, challenge the atomistic and compartmentalized worldview of the Newtonian-Cartesian paradigm as well as the focus on individual salvation and damnation emphasized by fundamentalist Christianity.

While physicists and ecologists see unity as including and affirming the interdependence of diverse life forms, *A Course in Miracles,* one of the most influential "channeled" texts of the new age movement, holds that there is only one reality, the divine mind, and that all else is an illusion, born of our fearful misperceptions. Recalling the Gnostics of the first century after Christ, *A Course in Miracles* states that we have fallen from our essential spiritual unity into a material world of our own creating. As pure thought, God has nothing to do with the illusion of physical existence. "The world is false perception. It is born of error."[17] As commentator Kenneth Wapnick notes, "God and Christ alone are real."[18] Our separate personalities and centers of consciousness, our bodies and our relationships, are a dream that blinds us to the only reality that exists, the mind of God.

Despite the vast philosophical differences between the spiritual monism of *A Course in Miracles* and the abundant interrelated cosmos of the "deep ecologists" and "new" physicists, both reflect the new age assertion that unity is prior to individuality. Both assert that our salvation arises from seeing the world with new and different eyes. To be spiritually free we must identify ourselves with the whole, the divine, rather than the apparently separate parts.

2. The Higher Self

A legend of India tells the story of a lion who was raised by goats. Although he was a lion, he acted and felt like a goat. When the great lion, the king of the jungle, approached the herd one day, the young lion cowered and ran like all the others. The great king grabbed him by the neck and carried him to a pond, where he forced him to see his own reflection. "You are not a goat," roared the great king. "See who you are. You are a lion. Roar, and eat meat!" While vegetarian new agers might shudder at the lion king's carnivorous advice, new age thought agrees that we are all stronger and more perceptive than we think we are and that we are divine beings who have forgotten our true identity.

From the dawn of time, some humans have performed miraculous feats of physical activity and spiritual discipline. Persons like Jesus and Buddha have awakened their followers to an abundant life and a healed vision of themselves. They have called us to be more than the bumbling, frightened, and hateful mortals we sometime see ourselves to be. Today, psychologists note that most humans use less than 10 percent of their brains. We are discovering the vast, untapped power of the mind to influence health, personal success, and spiritual growth in a positive way. The mind and spirit are now the new frontiers of human experience. New age leaders hope to guide us forward into this unknown, promised land.

The call of the new age is to spiritual transformation and to the rejection of all that would limit human existence. For new agers, negativity, sin, and guilt have no place in the future adventures of humankind. We are not material beings, but reflections of the divine mind, which reveals itself to us if we but listen for its voice. Jerry Jampolsky proclaims that when we realize that the essence of our being is love, we will "say goodbye to guilt" and self-limitation. Jampolsky asserts that we "do not have to reach for guidance outside to find out what to do."[19] Susan Trout adds that an inner voice within us speaks from the divine source of all things. "Each individual is a spark from the universal light; this spark is our essence."[20]

In his work with critically ill persons, Jampolsky counsels his clients to eliminate any form of negativity from their language and thoughts. "Our thoughts make up the world . . . if we change our thoughts, our world will change automatically."[21] Since growth arises from creativity rather than negativity, Jampolsky suggests that we eliminate words such as "impossible," "can't," "should," "but," and "try" from our vocabulary. We are already healthy, successful, and at peace; we are just unaware of it.

In its optimism, the new age movement reflects a kindred spirit to the "human potential movement" of recent psychology and the "positive" and "possibility" thinking movements of Norman Vincent Peale and Robert Schuller. For the new ager, such optimism is grounded in the affirmation of our oneness with divinity and the existence of the higher self within each person. We all participate in the divine, whether we call it the collective unconscious or psyche (Jung), a peak experience (Maslow), the soul (Christian mysticism), or the Atman (Hinduism). Indeed, many new agers would affirm with Swami Muktananda that our divinity compels us to love and nurture ourselves—"Kneel to your own self. Honor and worship your being. God dwells in you as you." While some new agers would wince at the apparent narcissism of Shirley MacLaine's exuberant proclamation, "I am God, I am God," most would affirm her more modest statement that the higher self is "our personalized reflection of God, our link to divine energy, which enables us to learn why we are here and receive guidance for our actions."[22]

In its affirmation of the higher self as the presence of God within us, new age thought reflects the nineteenth-century Transcendentalist critique of a Christianity that focused on human sinfulness and divine otherness. Over 150 years ago, Ralph Waldo Emerson reacted to the Puritan notions of original sin and total depravity by asking, "In how many churches, by how many prophets, is man made sensible that he is an infinite soul, that the earth and heavens are passing into his mind; that he is drinking forever the soul of God?"[23] To the young ministers of his day, Emerson counseled, "yourself a newborn bard of the Holy Ghost,—cast behind you all conformity and acquaint yourself first hand with Deity."[24] Such words scandalized the Puritans of Emerson's time and they may scandalize many Christians today. But the message of our inner divinity must be heard, proclaim the apostles of human possibility.

Larry Dossey describes the higher self in terms of the "nonlocal" mind. Whereas the "local" mind is hemmed in by time and space and is doomed to death and destruction, the nonlocal mind is unlimited in time and space. In its universality, the nonlocal mind cannot be fully identified with the particular brain or body with whom it is most intimately related. While the illusory local mind is separated from God by its sinfulness and individuality, the nonlocal mind is a reflection of the universal mind. Accordingly, "if minds cannot be bound in space and time, we must be prepared to admit. . .that we are endowed with the godlike characteristics of immortality, omniscience, and unity."[25] We must recognize our own inner divinity as we cast off the shackles of those religious traditions that overwhelm us with the message that we are "despicable, unworthy creatures with no redeemable qualities of our own."[26] We must, Dossey advises, recover the Christ as a power within ourselves rather than as the judge outside ourselves. At stake is our personal destiny and the destiny of the planet. In words sounding almost apocalyptic, Dossey challenges his readers:

> In the end we can choose to continue to believe that we are local, isolated, doomed creatures confined to time and the body and set apart from all other human beings. Or we may elect to open our eyes to our immortal, omnipresent nature and the One Mind of which we each are a part. If we choose the former, nothing will save us. If, however, we choose to awaken to our divine Self, we face a new dawn.[27]

In his optimism, Dossey, like many new age devotees, rejects any ultimate ambiguity in our essential human nature. Beneath the apparent brokenness of everyday experience, each of us is a perfect representation of the divine, each of us is in contact with the universal. There is no room for sin, for humankind in its essential nature has never really left the garden. Indeed, the traditional Christian understanding of sin is itself a reflection of the ignorance and ego attachment from which we need to be liberated. Those who see themselves as sinners are like the lion who thinks he is a goat. If we awaken from the dream of a lonely, limited, sinful self, we will discover our true reality and full potential and be the spiritual lions we are meant to be.

3. *The Power of the Mind*

The spirit of new age optimism is captured in Richard Bach's *Jonathan Livingston Seagull*. Dedicated "to the real Jonathan Seagull, who lives within us all," Bach's novel challenges us to affirm the unlimited power of the human mind. "We can be free! We can learn to fly."[28] In his struggle with the limitations of the flock's worldview, Jonathan learns that mind is the only reality and that he can fly as fast as thought. "I am a perfect, unlimited gull!" proclaims Jonathan.[29] Once imprisoned by the limitations of his mind and his culture's expectations, Jonathan now becomes a messiah, guiding others to limitless horizons, and sharing the message that "each of us is in truth an idea of the Great Gull. . . . Your whole body, from wingtip to wingtip . . . is nothing more than your thought itself, in a form you can see. Break the chains of your thought, and you break the chains of your body, too."[30] To soar into the heavens and to fly at the speed of thought, we only need to change our level of consciousness.

In the spirit of Jonathan Livingston Seagull, the new age movement proclaims that transformation is possible for every person. United with the one reality, the divine mind present as our higher self, we can, to use the words of the apostle Paul, "do all things" (Philippians 4:13). Echoing Paul's letter to the Romans, the new age proclaims, "Be not conformed to the world" and its limitations of vision and possibility, but be "transformed by the renewing of your mind" (Romans 12:2).

In its emphasis on the power of the mind, the new age movement is reclaiming for our time the New Testament concept of life-changing faith. To the woman who touched his garment, Jesus proclaims, "Your faith has made you whole" (Luke 8:48). This same insight, reframed in more idealist terms, reemerged in the nineteenth- and twentieth-century precursors of the new age movement: New Thought, Christian Science, Science of Mind, and Unity. Based on the belief that "as a man [or woman] thinketh, he [or she] is" (Proverbs 23:7), these movements emphasized the infinity of God, the divinity of humankind, and the infinite possibilities that arise from the power of positive thinking. Like earlier Christian reformers, these nineteenth-century visionaries felt that they were restoring Christianity to the vitality of its origins.

Ernest Holmes, the founder of the Science of Mind movement, expresses the foundational ideas of the power of the mind in his description of the spiritual practices of Science of Mind:

1. We are completely surrounded and permeated by Universal Mind. We are finite expressions of the infinite.
2. The mind is always creative and manifests what we believe in our experiences.
3. Universal Mind creates for you according to the pattern of your thoughts.
4. You can choose to remain in poverty or sickness, health or prosperity.[31]

Within the mind is the power of prosperity, healing, love, and success. All we need to do is to unblock the flow of this limitless energy and the power of the God or the higher self will flow through our lives. This release of energy is an act of faith, but it is faith in the divine within rather than any external or transcendent source of power.

In new age thinking, the power of the mind is grounded in the recognition of our unity with the divine and the presence of the divine as the higher self within us. David Spangler notes that "the agenda for the New Age is based on the premise that both as individuals and as a species we use only a tiny fraction of our inherent creative and spiritual potential."[32] Like the movements of possibility thinking and positive thinking within mainline Christianity, "the New Age appeals to people because it is an empowering vision at heart; it speaks to our need for a frontier and for the possibilities of new unfoldment and growth."[33] In this spirit, Jerry Jampolsky's practice of "attitudinal healing" with critically ill children is motivated by the belief that our minds are only limited by our thoughts and that "if we change our thoughts, the world will change automatically."[34] While many of the children Jampolsky works with eventually die from cancer, he asserts that their openness to the infinite power of love heals their spirits even when their bodies are dying.

In its emphasis on the power of the mind, the new age inspires a spirit of self-responsibility. According to many new age thinkers, each person is not only responsible for her or his perceptions of the world, he or she is also responsible for the world that is perceived. Shirley MacLaine states that "the new age is all about self-responsibility. New age thinking asks each person to take responsibility for everything that happens in life."[35] New age healer Louise Hay adds that "we are each 100 percent responsible for everything and for all of our experiences."[36] Hay asserts that we not only create every physical and mental illness, we also "create our experiences, our reality, and everyone in it."[37] Rather than inspiring guilt, Hay believes that such affirmations encourage us to take control of our lives and become catalysts in our own healing.

Here I must part company with MacLaine, Hay, and others who suggest that the mind is all-powerful in the shaping of our reality. While I recognize the importance of the power of the mind in transforming our perceptions of the world, it is my contention that the mind's power is relative rather than absolute. We live in a world of shared experience and shared power. To assume that each mind is omnipotent in the creation of its reality not only makes each being a demigod, it also undercuts the affirmation of the wholeness so important to new age thinking. If the world is really a projection of the individual mind, with each self projecting its own reality, then relatedness is an illusion and community an impossibility. The many reflections of the one divine mind are divided by their own personal thought projections. This tendency toward personal omnipotence and isolation is revealed in Shirley MacLaine's assertion that "reality is basically what each of us perceives it to be; what may be real to me is not necessarily real to a friend, much less a stranger. We each live in a separate world of reality." MacLaine's views reflect an extreme instance of the radical individualism characteristic of the American ethos and new age metaphysics: "My world is uniquely mine and only I can do anything about it."[38]

While new age thinking correctly encourages persons to move from victimization to power, I believe that the dark side of this mental omnipotence and cosmic individualism is revealed in the tendency toward the conflicting emotions of grandiosity, guilt, and isolation that infect many new agers. As the creators of our destiny, we are responsible for poverty as well as prosperity, failure as well as success. The otherwise gentle spirit "Lazaris," channeled through Jach Pursel, expresses the absoluteness of cause and effect in the mental sphere: "Those who are suffering tragedy did create their own reality."[39] In our cosmic destiny, we are the prisoners as well as the beneficiaries of our thoughts. Apartheid, cancer, AIDS, and infant mortality are not accidents, but reflect the choices of the self in this life and previous incarnate lifetimes.

It is ironic that the spiritual individualism of new age thought intersects with certain popular myths of "old age" capitalism and Christian fundamentalism. If prosperity is the result of positive thinking, then the poor must be either ignorant or lazy. If positive affirmations can cure illness, then those who remain ill must suffer from a lack of faith!

The emphasis on the power of the mind often tends to neglect the impact of the wider environment within which persons live. Positive imaging can bring prosperity, but cycles of poverty and unstable households limit one's initial options and future choices. Visualization can provide relief from cancer, as Bernie Seigel and O. Carl Simonton have demonstrated. But a carcinogenic environment contributes to occurrences of cancer. While the godlike status of self-responsibility affirmed by new age thinking may empower some persons in their medical treatment and personal growth, it also may leave the chronically broken and sick isolated in a graceless world. Similar to the positive thinking movements in Christianity, new age optimism has little to say to those who are troubled by chemical imbalances, depression, and serious personality disorders, that is, those who, despite their efforts, may never get well.

A member of a Religious Science congregation once confided, "We aren't very good at asking for help. We think we can solve our problems on our own." Many new agers unconsciously and consciously avoid persons who are ill or who think negatively, in part because such negativity might challenge their own peace of mind, on the one hand, and, on the other hand, because they believe sickness is a choice that must be worked out completely by the individual involved.

The new age movement is right to emphasize the significance of the mind in health and illness. As I suggest in Chapter Four, the mind and body clearly influence one another. Yet, in its emphasis on individualism and personal power, the new age movement leaves those who are failures in their own eyes feeling ashamed, guilty, and alone. There is no room for the relational faith expressed in the popular poem "Footprints." Later in this chapter, I will expand on the notion that truly holistic spiritual power has its ultimate basis in the community, described by Paul as the "body of Christ." In such a community, we are called to share pain and brokenness as well as success and joy.

4. Spiritual Technologies

The new age movement is, by definition, eclectic and pragmatic. Any technique or belief that enables a person to find peace of mind or healing or experience their higher self is embraced. The relativity and fluidity of the new age is at the opposite extreme from the rigid dogmatism of fundamentalism and secular humanism. Within the new age movement almost any belief system or spiritual technology is affirmed as long as it promotes self-actualization.

Beneath the collage of new age technologies lies a basic metaphysical assumption: although the divine is one, there are as many paths to
god as there are persons, and each person is invited to take the path or
paths most suitable to her or his needs at a particular time. The universe, or divine mind, is abundant in providing means for spiritual
transformation. Although the critical mind counsels "let the buyer
beware," new age optimism contends that eventually every path, even
those that appear to be misdirected or inauthentic, will lead the seeker to her or his goal.

Like the storefront preachers of our cities, the new age movement
grounds authority in the personal call of the practitioner as much as in
the process of accreditation. With its workshops and psychic fairs, the
new age deserves the humorous epithet, "spiritual smorgasbord." Its
journals provide the opportunity to find spiritual nourishment for virtually any hunger. In two years of training at the Washington Institute
of Attitudinal Studies, I experienced the eclecticism of the new age
movement first hand. I had the opportunity to explore chanting,
bioenergetics, Jungian psychology, psychosynthesis, meditation, guiding visualization, communication skills, *A Course in Miracles*, and the
use of affirmations.

Among the many paths available, the most popular new age practices involve the use of affirmations, visualization, and meditation for
personal growth. The new age sees itself as a "science of mind," using
the universal laws to contact the higher self and experience healing
and prosperity. Ernest Holmes, founder of the Science of Mind movement, employs a technique of "spiritual mind treatment" that is common to many new age spiritual technologies. After a time of quiet
focus upon the power of the divine mind, the participant affirms the
perfection of life and the goodness that is coming to them. Part of the
spiritual treatment includes affirmations such as: "My body is a manifestation of the living spirit . . . that power is flowing in and through
me"; "I am one with the infinite rhythm which flows through me in
love, in harmony, and in peace"; "There is one life, that life is God, that
life is perfect, that life is my life now."[40] Next, one uses an affirmation
relating to a particular need. For example, as a writer, I might affirm,
"God's wisdom permeates my mind and I express myself creatively"
or "Good ideas come easily to me." If I am seeking to lose weight, I

would affirm the beauty and health of my body as a *present reality*—"I am slender and healthy"—even if this seems to contradict my current waist size. We are already perfect manifestations of the divine spirit. We need only to realize our perfection for it to come to pass.

In my training course in attitudinal healing, I daily affirmed one of the twelve principles of attitudinal healing, such as "I am not a victim of the world I see," "Forgiveness is the key to happiness," or "All that I give is given to myself." The use of affirmations serves not only to refocus and retrain the mind, it also releases destructive patterns of thought that have characterized our conscious and unconscious perceptions of reality. In changing our perceptions, it is believed that we can change the world—even our bodies—for all things reflect the orientation of the mind.

In contrast to the positive direction of affirmations, Holmes counsels the explicit denial of every thought that would challenge these affirmations. In the context of the use of affirmations, these denials serve to convince the mind to accept the verdict of perfection. The principle of conscious denial, while not present in every new age use of affirmations, reveals an important characteristic of new age metaphysics. Evil is ultimately an illusion or a lack of good. By changing our minds, we gain a larger vision of ourselves and the world in which what we call evil becomes merely an expression of our thoughts or a learning experience, and not an objective, external reality. Holmes concludes his "mind treatment" with another affirmation: "It is now done. It is now complete. There is one life, that life is good, that life is perfect, that life is my life now."[41]

Most contemporary teachers of affirmations follow some variation of the basic principles articulated by Ernest Holmes. Shakti Gawain, who has been the leading new age figure in the use of visualization techniques, writes that, "Creative visualization is the technique of using your imagination to create what you want in your life."[42] Based on the belief that the mind is always creating pictures of the world, creative visualization invites persons to use their imagination to bring about positive results. By regularly holding on to an image in our mind, one gives it positive energy, which eventually manifests itself in the world. The practice of creative visualization is as follows: after a moment of relaxation, one imagines whatever seems best for them, for example, a new job or car, a better relationship, spiritual insight. After several minutes of imaging, one closes with an affirmation and a statement such as: "This or something better, now manifests for me, in a totally satisfying and harmonious way, for the higher good of all concerned."[43]

Virtually all new age practices include a component of meditation or silence. Practitioners are invited to share in a wide range of approaches, such as breathing exercises, mantras (the repetition of special words often of a Buddhist or Hindu origin), or imageless meditation. In silence, one opens to the voice of the higher self within. Most new agers use Hindu and Buddhist forms of meditation, primarily because the Christian churches of their origin have only recently returned to contemplation and meditative prayer as authentic forms of spirituality.

At the heart of new age spirituality is the belief in the potential of the human mind to awaken to the higher self. New agers typically do not expect a helping hand in their spiritual quest, for there is no external grace or personal god to aid the seeker. The help we need is already embedded in the self. Like a gold miner, each person must uncover what is already there or find directions from a book or workshop. The grace of god for the new ager is the eternal, yet impersonal, energy of the universe, which propels us forward if we approach it wisely. In contrast to the Christian notion of the unmerited and freely given grace of God, new age spirituality typically claims that by our own efforts we are able to save ourselves and evolve into higher beings. As reflections of the divine, we are unlimited. All we need to do is wake up, for our salvation is here if we are willing to explore the power that created us and the power we are.

New age spirituality is a challenge for spiritual reformation. While it lacks the "fear and trembling" of Paul's advice to the Philippians, it concurs that we must "work out our salvation" (Philippians 2:12–13). While Christians need not follow new age practices and may challenge new age beliefs, we must take seriously the insights of the new age movement in terms of human possibility and spiritual development. Pastors and active laypersons must nurture their own hunger for spiritual vitality as a prerequisite for their mission to the Christian community and the secular culture.

CHRISTIAN SPIRITUALITY FOR A NEW AGE

In his reflections on character development, organizational trainer Stephen Covey points out the significance of the paradigms, or maps of reality, by which we live. Covey notes that even with the best attitudes and behaviors, we will still end up being lost in Chicago if all we have is a map of Detroit.[44] Recently, the new age movement, along with evangelical Christianity and Asian spirituality, has challenged mainstream Christianity to reform and transform its theology and spirituality, that is, to reflect on its map of reality and the path it needs to find its way. Mainstream Christians are challenged to listen to the insights of the new age movement not only because the new age brings fresh perspectives to spiritual practice and metaphysics but also because some of Christianity's brightest young people have found their spiritual nurture in the new age movement rather than in the church.

The dialogue is reciprocal. As I will show throughout this book, the new age movement will also benefit from a dialogue with Christian faith. Christianity provides a reality check and a historical background for the ungrounded assumptions of some new age thinkers. Further, the new age movement is enriched by Christian insights into the significance of service and social justice as well as the role of sin and grace in human life.

As they listen, analyze, and critique the new age movement, Christians today need to recognize that the new age may be the most recent of many reformation movements that have arisen within the context of Christianity. In the midst of the errors as well as the insights we find in the new age movement, we may intuit the Spirit of God, who emerges in the most unlikely places. Accordingly, it is my belief that Christian theology and spirituality in our time must address and dialogue with the new age movement in the four areas of new age spirituality discussed in the previous section: the unity of life, the higher self, the power of mind, and the technology of spiritual transformation. While new age language is not commonplace in most Christian communities, I believe these four areas correspond to the traditional Christian affirmations of the body of Christ, the Christ within, the process of sanctification, and spiritual formation.

Area 1: The Body of Christ, or Divine Unity

Unlike the new age focus on the inner divinity, Christian theology begins and ends with God, who is both intimate and transcendent to the human self. The self and its possibilities find their meaning and energy in their relationship to a living and personal God, who is the creative ground, the inner voice, and future hope of all things. While new age thought tends to focus on the journey of the higher self, Christian thought sees companionship with God as the ultimate reference for the human adventure. As Roman Catholic mystic Thomas Keating maintains, "Salvation is fundamentally the realization of oneness with God."[45]

Yet, the existence and character of God has been a problem for many Christians. God has been pushed out of the modern world not only by science and psychology but by outdated and dysfunctional theology.

Many new agers have left the church because God was presented to them as masculine, judgmental, angry, and jealous of human potential. The God they identify with the church and Sunday school is a cosmic policeman whose omniscience leads to feelings of guilt rather than comfort. Sadly, many new agers exiting the church have failed to hear the message of God's love. This exodus of spiritual seekers from the church to individualistic and noninstitutional forms of spirituality is a call for Christians to rethink their images of God in terms of omnipresent and everlasting love rather than coercive power.[46]

Many persons within the church are also struggling to find a healthy, creative, and life-supporting image of God. Many "new age Christians" have remained in the church and have honored the faith of their fathers and mothers and the gifts of their denominations. But they hunger for a vision of God that will enable them to integrate their own spiritual frontiers with the faith of their childhood. The church must boldly proclaim creative and lively images of God if it is to minister to the needs of those who search for new directions within its precincts as well as to those who have been disenfranchised by dysfunctional and oppressive images of God.

I believe that a vision of God for the new age must find its basis in a lively and creative personal and corporate experience of Jesus Christ. Historically, Christian faith has proclaimed that Jesus Christ is the ultimate revelation of God's true nature. In Christ, Christians have affirmed that "God so loved the world that God gave us [God's] only begotten Son" (John 3:16). In Christ, God's nature is revealed in terms of love, relationship, and unity. While Christians believe that the fullest revelation of God is found in the particular person Jesus of Nazareth, they also maintain that the power and wisdom present in Jesus is universal in scope and impact. As the first chapter of the Gospel of John asserts, the creative word incarnate in Jesus is present in all things.

Like reformers past and present, Jesus of Nazareth sought to transform the religious tradition he had inherited. Jesus proclaimed in word and deed that fidelity to God means both to cherish the wisdom of the past and to embrace the adventure of the future. Jesus invited the least likely, and most antagonistic, persons in his time to become his followers—strangers, oppressors, the uneducated, the elite, unclean, poor, foreigners, and women. To the outsiders, he promised comfort and acceptance. But he also challenged them to transformation—to see themselves and the world in a new way, to see the world as God's world and to see themselves and all others as beloved and empowered children of the loving God. To the comfortable, Jesus spoke a word of judgment, but also a message of repentance and transformation. In language that resonates with the ideals of the new age, Jesus preached companionship and unity with God and the glorious potential of human life.

In contrast to the ideals of many new agers, however, the God Jesus revealed is a personal being who is known more by love than by thought. To an age in which God was often viewed as distant and demanding, Jesus spoke of God as "Abba," or "Daddy." God is not only the creator of the universe but the lover of all creation. Like a loving mother or father, God seeks after each child until he or she is found.

Our relationship to God can be described in terms of the vine and its branches. Each of us, Jesus claimed, has the possibility of claiming our role as a branch of the divine vine (John 15:1–11). Although we are rooted in God and Christ, our fruitfulness and spiritual well-being depend on our willingness to let their power flow through us. Our turning away from God has serious consequences for ourselves and the world. But, despite our waywardness, in God's eyes we are still

God's own children, able to reach out to the love that is seeking us.

Although my brief description of Jesus as the revealer of God's nature hardly expresses the fullness of the incarnation, it is clear that the God revealed in Jesus' life differs markedly from the God many new agers have rejected. The God reflected in Jesus is personal and vulnerable. The cross reveals God's own willingness to bear our burdens and share our suffering. God is neither aloof nor absent, but is, as Alfred North Whitehead notes, the "fellow sufferer who understands."[47]

In contrast to the tendency of many new agers to identify salvation with self-awareness, the New Testament picture of Jesus portrays salvation in terms of relationship, connectedness, and personal communion with God and neighbor. Although humankind has lost the fullness of relationship and communion, God is still seeking to bring us back into partnership and unity.

As contemporary Christians explore lively images for God's relationship to the world, one of the most powerful images they will discover is that of the body of Christ. In many ways, it parallels and expands the image of the vine and branches. This image sees God as the spirit of the universe, the mind of the world's body, and the love that courses through all of life. Contemporary images of the mind-body relationship illuminate this close communion of God and the world. Holistic medicine sees the body and mind as dynamically interrelated. Our thoughts influence our physical well-being, and our physical well-being influences the quality of our spirituality. Contrary to Descartes' dualism of spirit and flesh, holistic understandings of reality proclaim that the mind permeates the body and that each cell reveals the movements of the mind and contributes to the life of the mind. Interdependence rather than independence or fusion describes the relationship of God to each creature and the totality of things.

The metaphor of the body of Christ as the primary image for the relationship of God and the world expresses three characteristics of reality and the divine-human relationship—communion, differentiation, and subjectivity. First, God and the world are essentially related to one another. The world—both as a totality and in every part—arises from divine creativity, expresses divine wisdom, and contributes to the divine experience. God is the sap that nurtures the branches and the intelligence that guides the body. Without the vine, the branches would wither. Without the spirit, the body would be lifeless. As the English mystic Julian of Norwich proclaims, "Everything has being through the love of God."[48] We reflect the influence of God in the same way as the body reflects the mind. As the body of Christ, the universe, both part and whole, is enchanted and divinized—the heavens declare God's glory and each cell radiates the light of the world.

The unity of all things in the body of Christ, however, reveals abundant diversity rather than impersonal homogeneity. Although Jesus proclaims, "I and the Father are one" (John 10:30), neither God nor Jesus loses individual uniqueness as a center of experience. Within the body, communion requires differentiation and uniqueness. Indeed, in contrast to the monism and pantheism of much new age thinking, the Hebraic-Christian God brings forth multiplicity and pronounces it good. In his description of the body of Christ in 1 Corinthians 12, Paul states that although the body is one, each of its many members expresses the wisdom of God in its own unique way. While no part of the body can proclaim "I am God," every part reveals God's presence to a greater or lesser degree.

Communion and differentiation ultimately imply both subjectivity and relationship. Contrary to Gnostics and materialists who see the physical world as mindless and valueless, the image of the world as the body of Christ envisages a universe that is enchanted, lively, and dynamic. All things uniquely reveal God, and God has a unique relationship with each thing. As the cells of the body reflect the presence of the mind, each entity reveals God from the inside as well as the outside. While no cell can claim to be the mind, each cell is influenced and permeated by the mind. As the body of Christ, the universe, in all its varied parts, is a revelation of God. From this perspective, my awareness of my own experience as well as my experience of the world beyond me expresses and reveals an aspect of God's own experience.

The divine unity is the source of all creaturely unity. As the source of all things, God is also the spirit that joins all things in a dynamic sympathy. From this perspective, one of the primary creaturely sins is the refusal to be part of the body or the rejection of community.

Life in community involves sorrow as well as joy. God's own sympathy with the world is the model for creaturely relations. In a shrinking planet, we can easily recognize the wisdom of Paul's theological affirmation that in the body of Christ, "if one member suffers, all suffer together; if one member is honored, all rejoice together" (1 Corinthians 12:26). Christian thought maintains that God not only loves the world, but also suffers with it. While the new age movement and Eastern religions often suggest that ultimate reality is impersonal, impassive, and eternal, the deepest insights of Christianity see the ultimate reality as a passionate personal center of experience that embraces all things.

As Christians claim the metaphor of the body of Christ for their vision of the new age, they will overcome the disastrous dualisms of mind and body, spirituality and everyday life, and humankind and nature. Relatedness and sympathy are the gifts of a new age Christianity to a planet torn apart by the fragmentation of the modern worldview.

Area 2: The Higher Self

Christians seldom use the term "higher self" in describing God's presence and guidance in human life. Instead, they have traditionally used terms such as "the Christ within," "the inner light," "the kingdom within," and "the soul." While these terms do not imply that God's fullness dwells in any particular human being or that there is a strict identity between God and the creature, they point to the belief that the Spirit constantly addresses each person and guides all those who seek its wisdom.

The Christian understanding of the Christ within or the higher self is portrayed in a incident in life of the sculptor Michelangelo. One afternoon, the sculptor was chiseling on a gigantic boulder. When a curious neighbor asked him what he was doing, Michelangelo replied, "There is an angel inside and I'm trying to set it free."

Christian theology affirms the wonder and beauty of the human self—there are truly "angels" within each one of us. In contrast to those who have preached a spirituality of weakness, guilt, and passivity, the authentic teachers of the Hebraic-Christian tradition have proclaimed that humankind is created "in the image of God" (Genesis 1:26). While no creature can claim to be of the same nature as God, every creature is, in its most essential character, a revelation of God.

The wonder of human existence is portrayed in Psalm 8. In the midst of his reflections on the grandeur of God, the immensity of the universe, and the finitude of humankind, the psalmist also discovers that humankind is made a "little less than God . . . crowned with glory and wonder" (Psalm 8:5). The Prologue of the Gospel of John proclaims that "the true light . . . enlightens everyone" (John 1:9).

Although each of us is a reflection of God, Christian theology maintains that we have forgotten our essential nature. We have turned from God and, in so doing, have become alienated from ourselves and our neighbors. This is the personal as well as theological meaning of sin. The angel, hidden within the boulder, cannot liberate itself on its own, especially when its actions and omissions have debased and disguised its own inner beauty. Indeed, the boulder doesn't see itself as incomplete—it is happy in its isolation, pain, and alienation. Like the lion who thinks itself a goat, it assumes that such incompleteness and forgetfulness is normal. It neither sees nor expects any significant change in itself or human nature. The Christ within, or the higher self, is hidden as well as tarnished by sin and can be set free only by the dynamic and liberating grace of God.

Whereas the higher self of the new age is almost godlike in its eternity, perfection, and freedom, Christianity sees the image of God in humankind as utterly dependent on the grace of God for its existence and well-being. Sin is not merely a result of ignorance or failure to recognize one's divinity, as some new agers assert; it also arises from our own actions and choices. Sin, accordingly, makes a difference in our own lives and in the life of the cosmos. By ourselves, as the twelve step programs point out, we cannot escape the bondage either of our own actions or of actions inflicted upon us by others. The recognition of our brokenness and dependence on our relationship to a power greater than ourselves is not, however, a call to passivity or victimization, but a challenge to open ourselves and then respond creatively to God's movements in our lives. It is a challenge to repent, forgive, and immerse ourselves in God's transforming love.

The messages of channels and the exploration of intuition in the new age movement challenge Christians to reappropriate the spiritual insights of our own biblical heritage. Too often, we as Christians have shrunk our understandings of self to the images of the secular world or the emotionally high-powered "hellfire and brimstone" preachers. We have forgotten Jesus' promise that God and his followers would be one in the spirit (John 17:22–23). The inner voice of God, revealed in the dreams, visions, and insights of the early church, has often been silenced within mainstream churches. Yet, whether or not we listen, the voice of God speaks to our particular condition. While Romans 8 is a testimony to the all-pervasive wisdom of God in the natural world as well as in human experience, it also portrays the voice of God that speaks from within us as our deepest reality. "Likewise the Spirit helps us in our weakness; for we do not know how to pray as we ought but the Spirit intercedes for us with sighs too deep for words" (Romans 8:26).

Today's Christian is challenged by the new age movement to reclaim the long tradition of Christian mysticism and prayer within Christianity, as it has been exemplified by spiritual movements such as the Quakers, who proclaim that God is present as the inner light or Christ within each person. The Quakers teach that all those who seek God will experience the divine wisdom flowing from their own souls. While neither the Quaker nor the mystic proclaims "I am God," both recognize that when grace breaks down the walls of sin and selfishness, God appears as the most significant reality within a person's life.

In the area of spiritual growth, new age thinking can learn much from a healthy Christian understanding of sin and grace. New age perfectionism, reflected in its image of the higher self as all-wise and omnipotent, often encourages the denial or repression of human negativity and limitation. Used all by themselves and apart from personal introspection and the life of a community, affirmations retrain the mind, but they often leave deeper pockets of pain untouched. Affirmations and creative visualizations work more effectively for personal healing when they are accompanied by the recognition of the totality of one's experience—fear and negativity as well as the possibility of personal transcendence—and the ongoing accountability which arises from commitment to a spiritual community.

Apart from a realistic vision of one's present as well as ideal self, one is often left feeling guilty or impotent when one does not immediately achieve success or peace of mind through visualizations or affirmations. Repression of negativity and obsession with the ideal self imprison the self within its own experience and create an unbridgeable chasm between the perfect, higher self and the constantly egocentric and harried everyday self.

In Christian thought, the movement of God's Spirit within one's self exposes as well as heals our wounds. The message of the cross is that healing and forgiveness come from facing the pain and negativity rather than avoiding them. Even as it reminds us of our divine destiny as partners of God and members of the body of Christ, Christian thought constantly invites us to recognize the gap between our ideals and our actions. We need God and one another to be whole. While we are to "work out our salvation with fear and trembling," we are also constantly reminded that "God is at work within us, both to will and to work God's good pleasure" (Philippians 2:12–13). In contrast to the naive idealism that often characterizes the new age movement, a transformed Christian spirituality recognizes both the weakness and grandeur of humankind and reminds us that spiritual achievement is not a solitary process but the result of graceful relationships.

Area 3: The Power of the Mind

In many ways, the positive outlook of new age thinking finds its origins in the historical consciousness of Christianity and Judaism. While Christianity and Judaism do not claim that history and human existence are perfectible, they assert that, as a result of God's presence, unexpected and novel events occur and that history is progressing toward a divinely initiated goal.

The new thought movements of the nineteenth century and the science of mind movements of the twentieth century grounded themselves in a spiritual interpretation of the life and ministry of Jesus. Advocates of the power of the mind such as Mary Baker Eddy and Ernest Holmes saw their work as a revival of a lost dimension of Christian thought: the power of faith and a transformed mind.

The biblical tradition proclaims the presence and power of a God is who always doing new things. From the time of Abraham and Sarah to the present time, God has called unlikely people to embark upon journeys of the faith and geography. History and human life are the stage to which God is always inviting humankind to achieve far more than it can imagine, spiritually, politically, and intellectually. The heart

of the biblical vision of human potential can be found in Paul's affirmation: "The secret is simply this: Christ in you! Yes, Christ in you, the
hope of all the glorious things to come" (Colossians 1:27).

The call of the sixth-century prophet Jeremiah epitomizes the
adventure of faith and human potential. When God calls Jeremiah to
be a prophet to Judah, Jeremiah protests his youth and experience:
"Ah, Lord God, I do not know how to speak, for I am only a youth."
God replies (Jeremiah 1:6–8) with words of promise and possibility:

> Do not say, "I am only a youth"; for to all to whom I send you,
> you shall go, and whatever I command you shall speak. Be not
> afraid of them, for I am with you to deliver you.

The New Testament witness is a testimony to the transformation
that occurs when persons dedicate their lives to God. Simple men and
women, Jesus' first disciples, triumphed over doubt, despair, and sin
to become the proclaimers throughout the known world of the gospel
of the risen Lord. Men and women who marveled at Jesus' miracles
themselves became wonder workers. Through dreams, visions, and
healings, the disciples became channels of the divine. God constantly
pushed them beyond their self-imposed limits—in their understanding of God's power, their own abilities, and the scope of salvation.
With Paul, Christians can affirm, "I can do all things through Christ
who strengthens me" (Philippians 4:13).

Faith, as the acceptance of God's grace, is not only the experience of
forgiveness, it is also the openness to new dimensions of reality and
oneself. Faith is the affirmation that, in spite of my present experience,
I am a child of God and the recipient of God's promises of greatness
and adventure. If God is truly the spirit of the body and the sap of the
vine, then divine inspiration is constantly nurturing us, even when we
are unaware of it.

Today, the new age movement calls mainstream Christians to
explore the frontiers of spiritual experience in terms of healing, prosperity, and human potential. Like Jonathan Livingston Seagull, the
new age promises that if we can dream it, we can do it! From new age
philosophies today's Christians can learn the meaning for our time of
the biblical promises that God's Spirit "will guide us into all truth"

(John 16:13) and that "all things are yours, and you are Christ's and Christ is God's" (1 Corinthians 3:21, 23). As Justin Martyr, an early leader of the church, proclaimed, "Jesus became what we are that we might become what he is."[49] God constantly calls persons to new adventures of faith, wisdom, and love.

The power of the mind, in Christian thought, is ultimately rooted in God's action. While Christians may appropriately use visualizations and affirmations, they are called to remember that empowerment is not ultimately a matter of hard work or mental focus but the grace of God and dynamic Christ within. In contrast to many new agers who place the limits of human possibility entirely in their own hands, Christian thought sees the power of the mind in terms of the interplay of the body of Christ and the power of God. As a Christian, I am not 100 percent responsible for my life, nor do I completely create my own reality. Rather, I receive the gift of life from God's constant creativity and from the cosmic community within which I live. My relations with this larger cosmic environment both enhance and limit my possibilities. Healing of the spirit and the body, the quest for justice, the experience of new life, all occur within a matrix that includes not only my own choices and mental power, but the impact of my past, the environment supplied by the human and nonhuman world, and the loving care of God.

The power of the mind, left to itself without the presence of divine love and wisdom, leads to the collapse and ultimate isolation of our own personal towers of Babel. In its quest for personal power, the point of Christian existence is not success, prosperity, or personal accomplishment but loving faithfulness to God and one's companions in the world. When we are tempted to focus only on the power of the mind and what we can achieve for ourselves and by ourselves, Paul's words to the Corinthians remind us that "if I have prophetic powers and understand all mysteries and all knowledge, and if I have all faith, so as to remove mountains, but have not love, I am nothing" (1 Corinthians 13:2).

Area 4: The Spiritual Path

After many years of neglect, mainline Christians are once more exploring the spiritual disciplines. In their interchanges with Hindus,

Buddhists, and new agers, Christians are discovering the unique wealth of their own tradition.[50] In the spirit of Paul's counsel to the Corinthians, all spiritual disciplines are lawful to Christians. It is not improper for a Christian to practice Zen meditation, transcendental meditation, creative visualization, or affirmations as long as he or she remembers that prayer and meditation are a gift of grace rather than a solitary work. The point of prayer and meditation is found in the words of the psalmist: "Be still and know that I am God"(Psalm 46:10). Communion with God and obedience to divine guidance are the ultimate aims of Christian spirituality. Accordingly, the focus of spirituality is not to contact the higher self or "spiritual guides" from another dimension but to experience oneself as being known, loved, and guided by God.

Christian spirituality is profoundly relational. Contemplation joins us with the body of Christ in its unity and diversity. Moments of silence drive us back into the world in acts of love and witness. As Thomas Merton counsels, "Prayer does not blind us to the world, but it transforms our vision of it, and makes us see it, all [people], and all the history of [humankind], in the light of God."[51]

Any form of prayer that deepens our awareness of God, the Christ within us, and our neighbor, is an appropriate form of Christian spirituality. Today's Christians, then, can practice a variety of methods of prayer and meditation, ranging from the silence of a Quaker meeting and the use of imagination in the *Spiritual Exercises of St. Ignatius* to the chanted prayers of Orthodox Christianity and the Taizé community. Yet, all Christian spirituality is "body prayer" since its goal is to awaken us to our life within the body of Christ.

The popularity of Maharishi Mahesh Yogi's transcendental meditation has led many Christians to rediscover the use of mantras, or words, as a means of focus in prayer and meditation. The use of a particular prayer word focuses the mind and allows a person to experience God's presence in deeper levels of the self. Basil Pennington has emphasized the use of "centering prayer," an ancient Christian prayer form that bears a great resemblance to transcendental meditation. Centering prayer involves the following technique:

1. Taking a moment to relax in a comfortable position.

2. Opening oneself in faith and love to God's presence in the center of one's being.

3. Focusing on a "love word" (for example, God, Jesus, light, love).

4. Bringing oneself gently back to the love word, whenever the mind wanders.

5. Concluding with the Lord's Prayer.[52]

Similar to centering prayer is the "Jesus Prayer," described in the Orthodox classic, *The Way of the Pilgrim*.[53] This prayer involves the simple repetition of the words, "Lord Jesus, have mercy upon me, a sinner." Through the recitation of this prayer throughout the day, a person discovers her or his ultimate dependence on the graceful love of God. My own personal meditations often involve the repetition of a phrase such as "God's light" as a means of becoming aware of the constancy of the divine presence within me.

In recent years, Christians have rediscovered Scripture as a source of spiritual affirmations. Countless affirmations arise from an intuitive reading of Scripture. I have found the following biblically based affirmations helpful in my own spiritual life: "Christ within me, the hope of glorious things to come," "God's light shines through me," "I am a child of God," "I give Christ to and receive Christ from everyone I meet," "Nothing can separate me from the love of God," "I can do all things through Christ who strengthens me." I preface my use of affirmations with a prayerful recognition of my need for God's grace and guidance. I recognize that I am not in full control of my life and that I am ultimately unaware of what I really need. In prefacing my affirmations with an openness to God's guidance, I affirm my own possibilities and insights in light of my willingness to follow God's greater power and wisdom as it is revealed in Scripture, inspiration, community, and the events of my life.

The goal of Christian prayer and spirituality is worship, love, and the attunement to God's will, that is, willing participation as healthy members of the body of Christ. Such commitment to God unifies the human spirit and makes every moment, even the negative and painful, a moment of praise and prayer. The totality of my life, including the negative, is to be embraced in my journey with God, who knows and accepts my real self and not an idealized or perfect projection of my desires. In this way, we learn what it means to "pray without ceasing" and to bring holiness to each day.

A CONCLUDING WORD

In many ways, the Christian encounter with new age spirituality resembles the current Jewish-Christian dialogue. As products of the Western world, the new age and Christianity are spiritually connected. In many ways, the new age is a lively younger sibling to more traditional Christianity. As such, it lacks the structure, discipline, and maturity of the older sibling. No doubt many Jews of the first century looked at youthful Christianity in the same way that today's Christians look at the new age movement. Some early Christians, conversely, tried to avoid the structure and tradition of their Hebraic roots by eliminating the Hebrew Scriptures from their worship and devotion. The separation of the church and the synagogue is one of the painful tragedies of both Christianity and Judaism.

From the same perspective, it is clear that the new age movement can learn the importance of ritual, history, community, and social concern from mainstream Christianity. As a younger sibling, the new age can bring fresh vitality to mainstream Christian spirituality. In its exuberance, the new age challenges lifeless traditions and dysfunctional theologies. In its freedom, the new age resembles the "Jesus movement" of the sixties and the charismatic movement of the contemporary church.

As they dialogue with persons in the new age movement, mainstream Christians must listen as well as witness. We must not forget that the greatest gift we can bring to the dialogue is our experience of God's graceful and embracing love.

In the following chapters, I will continue the dialogue of Christianity and the new age movement in terms of the more specific topics of revelation and channeling, health and healing, the nature of Christ, and the reign of God in this world and the next. In this time of global crisis and spiritual malnourishment, I am convinced that mainstream Christianity and the new age movement can mutually nurture each other in the quest for a transformed and healed planet.

QUESTIONS FOR REFLECTION AND DISCUSSION

1. What has led to the current malaise in mainstream and liberal Christian spirituality?

2. How do you understand and evaluate the new age idea of the higher self or inner voice?

3. What is your response to new age slogans such as "You create your own reality" or "If we change our thoughts, the world will change automatically"?

4. In what ways do Christian images of the self and techniques of self-discovery differ from new age ideas and techniques? How are they similar?

CHAPTER THREE

REVELATION AND CHANNELING

AN EVENING WITH A CHANNEL

I arrived at their home on a stormy July evening. With the rumble of thunder and flashes of lightning in the distance, the atmosphere seemed right for a seance. For a number of years, I had studied channeled materials and had found many parallels between new age channeling and biblical revelation. I had always found the popularity of channeling among new agers amusing. It seemed that most of the spirits had theatrical names such as "Ramtha," "Lazaris," "Mafu," and "Orin." It amazed me that people would spend hundreds of dollars to hear a person apparently talking in their sleep. Over the years, I had noted that while most new agers ridicule the notion of the verbally dictated and inerrant Scriptures claimed by Christian fundamentalists, many of these same persons would spend small fortunes on workshops, tapes, and books originating from the revelatory utterances of disincarnate beings.

Still, my response to channeling had not been entirely skeptical or condescending, because, in contrast to many Christians, I had found certain channeled materials helpful in my own spiritual development. Over the course of a year, I had integrated the exercises of *A Course in Miracles*, a three-volume set of materials claimed to have been channeled from Jesus Christ, into my morning spiritual discipline of prayer and scriptural meditation. I could attest to the effectiveness of the *Course*'s affirmations in nurturing a sense of the divine in my everyday experience. My study of the *Course* had helped me improve my spiritual health and family relationships.

But that evening as I pulled into the parking lot of a typical suburban apartment complex in the Washington, D.C., metropolitan area, I felt quite ambivalent. On my drive over, I had pondered Jon Klimo's definition of channeling as:

> . . . the communication of information to or through a physically embodied human being from a source that is said to exist at some other dimension of reality from the physical as we know it, and that is not from the normal mind of the channel.[1]

Reading about the messages of disincarnate spirits was one thing, but encountering such a spirit was another! I was unsure whether I would meet "Casper the Friendly Ghost" or the demonic spirit of *The Exorcist*. While I wanted to maintain an attitude of openness to whatever I observed, a war was going on in my mind: the liberal rationalist saw channeling as, at best, nothing more than information from the unconscious mind and, at worst, a theatrical sham; the conservative faith of my childhood memories worried about encountering a demonic spirit; and the mystic within me saw channeling as a means by which God might enter my own human experience in a new way.

I was met at the door by Russ and his wife, Kris. The atmosphere of their modest apartment was a far cry from the glamour of channeling celebrities such as J.Z. Knight, who channels "Ramtha," and Jach Pursel, who channels "Lazaris." For the past few years, Russ had been channeling "Samuel," a soul he claims exists in a higher dimension. By day, Russ works as a human relations officer at a suburban Washington, D.C., bank. On evenings and weekends, Russ and his wife, a graduate student at a major university in Washington, D.C., open their lives to "Samuel" through workshops and private consultations. Russ and Kris impressed me as simple, unpretentious, down-to-earth, and friendly people—the sort of people I would choose for neighbors. Yet, beneath the appearance of normalcy, Russ and Kris

were animated by the influence of a mission greater than themselves—
sharing the truths of a deeper dimension of reality to persons on the
spiritual journey.

Raised in a devout Roman Catholic home, Russ found that by the
time he had reached college the church and its teachings no longer met
his spiritual needs. In his quest for spiritual insight, Russ studied
metaphysical literature, astrology, and the well-known channeled
materials of "Seth" as received by Jane Roberts. Although he had
received guidance from a channel that he ought to think about channeling himself, Russ was apprehensive at first. He was afraid of losing
control of his rational mind.

In early 1988, Russ decided that he would make a serious attempt at
contacting a higher being. Using relaxation and centering exercises
developed by Sanaya Roman, a well-known channel, Russ asked for
"the highest possible source to come to him." At first, he experienced
only a vague image, blending with his own personality. It was not
until he surrendered completely to the wisdom of this higher power
that Russ fully encountered his own spiritual guide. Then, as Russ
relates, "a voice started pouring out of me." When asked who he was,
the voice replied, "I go by many names, but to you I am Samuel."

For a number of years, "Samuel" has been a regular companion to
Kris and Russ. During the first few years of their spiritual partnership,
Russ channeled "Samuel" for only a select group of friends. In the last
year or so, Russ and Kris have been widening the circle of "Samuel's"
acquaintances by offering workshops, private readings, and tapes.
Although he still works at a local bank, Russ hopes eventually to turn
his energies and time to channeling on a full-time basis. While many
channels have achieved wealth and fame, Russ maintains that he is
more interested in sharing the truth and experiencing the joy of his
new vocation than in making large sums of money. Just to channel for
"Samuel" gives Russ a feeling of "fantastic joy" that he would like to
share with others.

For Russ, the process of contacting "Samuel" is quite straightforward: he simply takes a few moments to relax and blend his energies
with those of "Samuel." Although some channels fall into a trance-like
state when they mediate disincarnate spirits, Russ never loses consciousness. He is aware of what is occurring, and yet he feels both

relaxed and detached. He describes himself as a distant observer, sitting "at the top of the bleachers, far away from the playing field" while "Samuel" is in the spotlight.

When I asked who he thought "Samuel" was, Russ described him as "other than me," a being who has insights I would be unaware of. From the channeled conversations, Russ believes that "Samuel" is a soul, who is more highly evolved in its experience than we are. "Samuel" is a member of a group of eight souls, known as "the council of the learned," who are supplemented in their work by four other disincarnate consultants. (Kris, Russ, and I thought it humorous that there are consultants even in the spirit world, or at least, among those spirits that communicate in the vicinity of our nation's capital.)

Kris and Russ believe that persons come to hear "Samuel" for a variety of reasons: to find their spiritual gifts, to integrate their inner and outer lives, to find healing, and to improve their relationships.

In line with his own personal humility, Russ added that "anyone can channel, the ability is not unique to me." In this regard, it is evident that although the channeling movement has its luminaries, it is highly democratic in its approach to spiritual gifts: everyone has the capability of contacting their spiritual guides or higher intuition.

After about an hour's conversation, Russ asked me if I'd like to meet "Samuel." Still somewhat skeptical and a bit apprehensive, I replied in the affirmative. Russ closed his eyes, took some deep breaths, and scrunched up his face as if in pain. As he tilted his head back, Russ appeared to take on a new character. Leaning forward, a bit stoop-shouldered, avuncular in voice and demeanor, "Samuel" greeted me, "Ah, yes, yes. Blessings to you. I am Samuel. I bring you blessings." Appearing to be educated, friendly, with a bit of an accent and rather theatrical in his movements, "Samuel" began what was to be an hour's conversation on Jesus, the meaning of life, and metaphysics.

In the following paragraphs I will describe some of the highlights of my evening with "Samuel." Indeed, the evening was anything but spooky or frightening. Conversation with "Samuel" reminded me of the first meetings I've had with other wise women and men—comfortable, insightful, and humorous.

My first query was simply, "Who are you?" "Samuel" responded by saying: "I am a soul, no greater than or less than you. I am energy. . . . I am not expressing my soul in a physical body other than through Russ's body and voice, which express my energy." "Samuel" claimed to have only occasionally taken on physical existence, most recently in the lost civilizations of Atlantis and Lemuria, although he had also communicated as a spiritual guide to humans in Egypt. While "Samuel" is not omniscient, he asserts that he perceives reality from a wider dimension than most humans, his vantage point being from the eternal soul rather than the temporal body. Although he prefers the nonhierarchical term "spiritual guide" to describe his vocation, "Samuel" admits that his characteristics and mission closely resemble those beings who have traditionally been identified as angels. "Samuel" sees his mission as twofold: 1) to encourage persons to seek a deeper understanding of their divine selves and 2) to be a catalyst of spiritual change in this critical and dangerous time in earth history.

When I asked "Samuel" about Jesus, he responded that Jesus is known in his dimension as "Yehosah," the great one, and that he has a vast devotion, love, and honor for Jesus. According to "Samuel," Jesus is a very evolved expression of God. Although we are also manifestations of God, Jesus is immensely closer to the totality of God and experiences a deeper oneness of God than we are currently experiencing. "Samuel" claims that we are all connected with Jesus. In many ways, Jesus' mission paralleled that of "Samuel's" own: 1) to raise the personal and planetary consciousness of the divine and 2) to make a significant change in his time, which like ours was fraught with danger and hatred. Yet, while "Samuel's" mission is similar to Jesus', he does not claim equality with the great one. "Samuel" admits that "my knowledge and my energy are not as vast as that of Jesus, my connectedness does not express God as deeply as Jesus did and continues to do." Yet, "Samuel" insists that there is a continuity between Jesus and ourselves. "Samuel" believes that "given enough time and experience, we could attain the same type of gifts and oneness with God" as Jesus expressed.

When I asked about the nature of God, "Samuel" paused and shook Russ's head vigorously as if to open himself to greater energy and insight. "Samuel" explained that "God is the totality of all that is, an infinite expression of love and forgiveness, an infinite energy evolving across the cosmos. The soul is part of God, but God is apart from each soul. You are one with God, yet apart from God." Our task as souls is to seek to know God more fully. "Samuel" concluded his remarks on God's nature by stating that "God is so much greater and more loving than you can imagine."

In response to my comment that fundamentalist Christians might think that channeled spirits like himself are demonic, "Samuel" replied that not all spirits are highly evolved. What we would call demonic spirits do exist and are, in fact, self-centered beings who evidence little evolution or spiritual experience. The key element in discerning the quality and intent of spirits involves the element of choice and the spiritual energy they radiate. "Both Russ and I are choosing to participate in this relationship," he said. "Samuel" noted that the encounter with lesser spirits, or demons, reflects the level of our own consciousness, that is, we attract the spirits we desire. As if to respond to the fears of fundamentalists, "Samuel" stated that "those who see channeling as a concern feel a weakness in their own ability to love. If you believe God protects you, how can you worry about being possessed by something negative?"

When I asked "Samuel" about the relationship between evil and responsibility, he reminded me that there are two ways of looking at any situation, from the level of the mind, which focuses on a particular event, and from the level of soul, which sees the wider perspective of that event in terms of a person's spiritual journey. In its desire to know God better, the soul takes on many births in order to learn particular lessons. Each birth reflects the soul's choices and is a means to experience God more directly. For example, a seemingly negative birth, such as being born into slavery, may mean that the soul "needs to learn issues around power. By being a slave, it will learn that power is not meant for oppression or manipulation, but that power is really love, forgiveness, and compassion." A child who dies of starvation may sacrifice itself so that a compassionate global consciousness may emerge.

In "Samuel's" understanding of reality, our births are not accidental, nor are they singular. While, on the whole, "Samuel's" philosophy resembles the cosmic individualism I described in chapter two, "Samuel" also notes that our spiritual journeys are interconnected and that the experiences of one soul are lessons for all the other souls. In the context of the soul's journey, my primary responsibility to my brother or sister is, first of all, "to know and love myself in the greatest way possible." Self-knowledge enables each person to connect with God and with her or his neighbor in compassion and forgiveness.

"Samuel" concluded the evening with a few personal remarks and a review of his perception of the points of agreement between Christian theology and the new age. While "Samuel" noted that his views would not be embraced by every Christian or new ager, he maintains that Christianity and the new age share a common understanding of: 1) the nature of the soul, that is, there exists an infinite soul that transcends the physical world; 2) the oneness of God, who is the totality of love, joy, and energy; 3) the true teachings of Jesus, which are love and forgiveness; 4) the unity of all persons in God's eyes; 5) the respect for all life. "Samuel" closed our conversation with a blessing, which reflected the traditional trinitarian formula of Christianity and bestowed upon me God's grace.

As I left Russ and Kris that evening, I was still uncertain as to "Samuel's" identity. On the one hand, it was clear to me that "Samuel" represented something authentic in Russ's experience. I felt no reason to believe that Kris and Russ were attempting to deceive me or that "Samuel" is merely a character in Russ's theatrical repertoire. At the very least, he is an expression of what the psychologist Jung would call the "collective unconscious," or what Roberto Assagioli, the originator of psychosynthesis, would call a "subpersonality." While some psychiatrists suggest that channeling may be a subtle form of multiple personality disorder, I did not observe any form of possession or pathology in my encounters with Russ and "Samuel." Indeed, on the whole, Russ appeared quite normal and ordinary in his demeanor. Another possible explanation, both comforting and disturbing to Christians, is that "Samuel" may, in fact, be exactly what he says he is, an "angel" or spirit communicating from another level of reality.

While "Samuel" stressed the continuity of his message with that of Christianity, his understanding of the soul and the relationship of Jesus to humanity would hardly be accepted by an orthodox Christian. To an orthodox or fundamentalist Christian, "Samuel's" guidance would be just another example of new age heresy, especially in terms of its concept of reincarnation, the potential divinity of each person, and its easy dismissal of the demonic.

"Samuel's" words would also leave some mainline Christians uneasy. While "Samuel" recognizes the importance of social concern, he sees apartheid, hunger, and poverty as examples of the soul's choices rather than this-worldly injustice. In contrast to the social teachings of liberation theologians and social activists, "Samuel" believes that ultimately there is no injustice in the world. While compassionate responses to evil are appropriate, the evils we crusade against are ultimately of little importance either to the sufferer or the oppressor, except as lessons their souls must learn. Our own efforts to ease the suffering of others are the means by which we respond to our own suffering and ignorance.

In spite of the questions and controversy that channeling raises among Christians of both the right and left, I contend that the channeling phenomenon challenges Christians to reflect on the meaning of divine revelation in our time. While concern for the spiritual world may appear absent in many churches, the spiritual world seems to be quite active among the mediums and channels of the new age. In the next few sections, I will explore the significance of channeling in our time by considering: 1) the nature of channeling, 2) its points of contact with biblical revelation, 3) the problems created by restricting divine inspiration solely to Scripture, and 4) a theology of inspiration. Following the style of the second chapter, I will allow the channels and spiritual beings to speak for themselves before I interject my own Christian interpretations and analysis. Like all religious phenomena, channeling must first be understood before it is criticized.

THE SPIRIT OF CHANNELING
The Call of the Channel
In contrast to Ted Peters and David Spangler, who see channeling as a peripheral element of the new age movement, I contend that channeling is an essential factor in the spread of new age spirituality. For many persons, their first encounter with the new age movement came through reading channeled material. For others, the experience of channeling or counsel from a channel is a reminder that the spiritual world is as real as the world of the five senses.

Channels and their spiritual guides have become media figures, and channeling has become big business. Channels such as Jach Pursel, J.Z. Knight, and Kevin Ryerson have appeared on national television and are even lampooned in "Doonesbury." Lesser known channels appear on the radio or public access television. Thousands of people each year spend expensive weekends with "Lazaris," "Ramtha," and other channeled beings.

The channeling phenomenon is another instance of new age ability to attract persons whose needs have not been met by institutional religion. The video tapes of "Lazaris," the books of "Seth" and "Emmanuel," and the three-volume *A Course in Miracles* have taken the place of the Bible in the lives of many. Some have even relocated to be near such luminaries as Elizabeth Clare Prophet and J.Z. Knight. Their workshops and tapes provide the sense of community and guidance that many persons fail to find in the church and synagogue. Through a relationship with a channeled being, who promises to accept them and be available for them in times of need, some even experience the acceptance and friendship that elude them in everyday life.

Despite its current notoriety, there is nothing new about channeling or encountering higher beings and disincarnate spirits. Within ancient and traditional religions, shaman and shamanesses, prophets, apostles, and mystics often have claimed to encounter a higher dimension of reality than the everyday world of the five senses. The fundamentalist Christian assertion that the Bible is the very word of God, verbally transmitted to its recorders, would qualify the Bible as channeled material. Muslims claim that the Koran originated from Mohammed's encounter with Allah through dreams, waking visions, and spoken words. In charismatic Christian churches, persons receive prophecies and words of knowledge from the Holy Spirit. The existence of channeling in our time opens up the possibility that the divine may still be speaking to humankind and that the closing of the scriptural canon was premature and, quite possibly, spiritually disastrous.

Although channeling, like virtually every other new age phenomenon, is vague and amorphous in composition, some of its basic characteristics can be outlined. David Spangler, who himself channeled the entity "John" during his years at Findhorn, defines channeling as a phenomenon in which a physical person enters an altered state of consciousness and lends his or her mind and/or body (depending on the technique employed) to be used by a non-physical entity in order to communicate from its level of experience to ours.[2]

Researcher Jon Klimo describes channeling as a process in which "otherwise ordinary people seem to let themselves be taken by, or in other ways receive messages from, another personality who uses them as a conduit, medium or channel for the communication."[3] Klimo adds that these personalities claim to be from a "higher," "more evolved" dimension of reality. Accordingly, their words take on significance that would otherwise be absent from normal communication. William Kautz, of the Center for Applied Intuition in San Francisco, identifies channeling with nonconscious, intuitive experience. Channeling is "a mental process in which the individual [the channel] partially or totally sets aside waking consciousness, to allow knowledge that lies beyond conscious awareness to flow into the mind."[4] Whether or not one claims that channeling involves spiritual entities, the phenomenon of channeling reflects and undergirds the new age belief that reality is multidimensional and that humans may encounter their own higher selves as well as beings from the spiritual world.

Channeling receives a mixed, albeit ultimately negative, reaction from today's fundamentalist Christians. Strangely enough, these fundamentalists—unlike the rationalists of liberal Christianity—freely ascribe to the notion of communication with disincarnate entities, based on scriptural evidence. But their scriptural interpretations depict these entities as deceptive and malevolent surrogates for Satan.

While the current phenomena of channeling bears some resemblance to the prophetic utterances of charismatic Protestants and Catholics, the most recent predecessor of today's channeling was the spiritualist movement of the nineteenth century. What is described today as channeling was known as mediumship during the spiritualist era, and those we call channels today were once known as mediums. Jon Klimo notes that whereas mediums sought contact with deceased human beings, contemporary channels communicate with entities from many levels of reality, some of which have never entered physical existence.[5] Further, as parapsychologist D. Scott Rogo notes, while "mediumship is the art of bringing through the spirits of the dead to communicate with their relatives," channeling "brings forth some sort of intelligence...whose purpose is to promote spiritual teachings and philosophical discussions."[6]

While the more theatrical channels share a common ground with the rappings, knockings, and shaking furniture of their nineteenth-century predecessors, the information that is sought is often either more philosophic or more personally relevant to the life of the seeker than detailed information about the "whereabouts" of a deceased aunt and uncle. Yet, channels and the mediums both affirm eternal life and communication with different levels of reality.

At first glance, there are many similarities among the process of channeling, charismatic prophecy, the Marian apparitions at Lourdes and Medjugorje, and biblical inspiration. Although some channels eagerly seek encounters with the spiritual realm, most channels (persons who receive messages from disincarnate spirits) initially feel an ambivalence about their experiences similar to that of the Hebraic prophets. A common characteristic of the Old Testament prophets and spiritual leaders was the experience of awe, unworthiness, and ambivalence in the presence of the divine. Moses protests his inexperience and inability to speak with clarity (Exodus 3:1–12, 4:10–17), Jeremiah points out his youthfulness (Jeremiah 1:4–10), and Isaiah recognizes his sinfulness (Isaiah 6:1–8). While today's channels seldom focus on their sinfulness, they often experience a deep initial reluctance to hear the messages from beyond. For example, Russ, who channels "Samuel," notes his fear of letting go and falling under the control of higher beings.

This reluctance is illustrated in the initial encounters with the spiritual world of two noted channels, Helen Schucman and Ron Scolastico. Helen Schucman, the transmitter of *A Course in Miracles*, felt great ambivalence and fear when she first heard the voice of Jesus speaking to her. Although she had been raised in a family influenced by metaphysical writings, she had become an atheist. As a psychology professor, Schucman found herself embroiled in the competitiveness and hostility of her academic department. In a department meeting one day, when a colleague, Bill Thetford, announced that there must be a better way of dealing with departmental politics and that he was determined to find it, his words struck a resonant chord in Schucman's heart. From that day on, the two became partners in a quest for a new way to live their lives.

A few months later, Schucman began to have visionary and psychic experiences, which frightened and repulsed her. A voice kept saying to her, "This is a course in miracles. Please take notes." At first Shucman questioned her sanity. Despite her misgivings, Shucman, with Thetford's help, eventually began to transcribe the messages she received virtually every evening. For seven years, she transcribed the messages that resulted in the three-volume, 1200-page book called *A Course in Miracles.* Throughout the process, she experienced a great deal of uneasiness, in good measure because of her resentment at the supposed author, "Jesus." When she asked the channeled voice, "Why me? I'm not religious; I don't understand these things; I don't even believe them. I'm about the poorest choice you could make," the inner voice responded, "You are an excellent choice . . . because you'll do it."[7] Today, *A Course in Miracles* is studied by thousands of Christians and non-Christians in solitude, in small groups, and at programs offered in Unity, Metaphysical, and Science of Mind churches. It has become one of the bibles of the new age, and thousands of lives have apparently been transformed by its teachings.[8]

Ron Scolastico, a channel from California, experienced a similar ambivalence when he first encountered his "Guides." For years, Scolastico had pursued an academic interest in spirituality and psychic explorations. Following the completion of his Ph.D. at the University of Iowa, Scolastico found himself penniless, with educational debts of over twenty thousand dollars. He was eager to find a teaching job. Yet, just as he was being offered an opportunity to interview for an excellent position at a major university, Scolastico heard a strange voice speak for him. Scolastico recalls the experience clearly. In response to the offer of an interview, Scolastico first replied, "Wonderful. . . . I'm very interested, and I'll fly out right away." Then, to his horror, he heard a voice that sounded different than his own saying, "I want to thank you very much, but I'm seriously considering another offer, and I'm just not able to respond to yours right now."[9] Although he did not know it at the time, this was his first "channeled" experience and it profoundly changed his life.

After much soul searching, Scolastico discovered that he really didn't want to teach in his discipline—humanistic psychology and communication theory—but he did want to teach spiritual truths. His search for a spiritual vocation led him to a psychic trance reader. Although he had read many of the well-known early channeled materials from Edgar Cayce and Jane Roberts, Scolastico generally considered persons involved in psychic pursuits to be intellectually naive "thrill seekers" in the realm of human consciousness. Despite his reservations and amusement at the strange voice emitting from the psychic, Scolastico was amazed when it told him, "You have followed many pathways with your mind, but you have followed none with your heart." In a later reading, another psychic asserted that Scolastico had promised in an earlier life to be a trance medium in this lifetime. "Wait a minute," Scolastico thought, "you've got the wrong person." Although he felt continuing skepticism and embarrassment, Scolastico allowed himself to be "coached" by a trance channeler. His first full-fledged channeling experience was with a spirit, speaking in an Irish brogue.

After months of practice, Scolastico began to trust his experience and to share the wisdom of the voices with other spiritual seekers. Scolastico claims to channel the "Guides," a group of spiritually advanced souls, who after many lifetimes on earth, "now exist in a non-physical realm of beauty and life that lies beyond the physical world." From his own Guides, Scolastico has heard that each person has their own spiritual guides, which Scolastico's Guides and other guides can contact to give persons advice, counsel, and nurture. In his description of the source of his guidance, Scolastico states that "it appears that the non-physical realm where the guides exist stands as a vast pool of knowledge that we can tap into by attuning to our own spiritual guides."[10] Scolastico describes his own experience as a channel in words that echo those of Russ, the channel I visited.

During the readings, I continue to experience the most beautiful feeling of love and truth that I can imagine, and the intensity of the experience grows with each passing year. Yet, the words spoken during the readings still appear as if by magic, without any perception of the source of the knowledge. I only feel the source. I feel it as a deep, unlimited love. I think of the source of the readings as *the Guides* because I believe that such guides exist, even though I have not directly perceived them.[11]

In an era in which channeling is often seen as theatrical and exotic, the experiences of such channels as Russ, Ron Scolastico, and Helen Schucman attest to the fact that common persons, seeking higher knowledge, encounter *something* that provides them with the assurance that their lives are meaningful, that the eternal soul is real, and that they no longer need to be afraid of life. Indeed for these channels, the experience of channeling came as an answer to their spirits' deepest desires, and has, in turn, been a gift of guidance and comfort to many others. While they do not claim to channel the Holy Spirit as Christian charismatics claim to do, they find both authority and insight in the messages they receive.

The Message of the Spirits

Jon Klimo describes the essence of channeled material as a positive message, "stressing the reality of a larger, spiritual universe and our own creative self-determination in this lifetime."[12] In many ways, the message of "Samuel" and other channeled beings reflects and exemplifies the new age philosophy discussed in Chapter Two. While the spiritual beings freely dispense metaphysical information, their counsel is, above all, practical. In this lifetime, our soul is challenged to awaken both to its essential unity with God and to the particular tasks the "schoolroom" of life is giving us through the seemingly "accidental" circumstances of life. Channels such as "Samuel" and "Emmanuel" even provide their students with guided meditations to enable them to claim their spiritual and material power.

Essential to virtually every new age channeled message is some form of the doctrine of reincarnation. In contrast to the often dismal accounts of karma and rebirth detailed in Buddhism and Hinduism, the channeled version of reincarnation gives a positive image of growth and spiritual adventure. The pain we feel in this life is, in fact, the result of our soul's particular "curriculum" in this life. In line with Western optimism, rebirth is one more graceful opportunity to find out who we are.

While few channeled entities are as extreme in their understanding of the consequences of one's behavior as J.Z. Knight's "Ramtha," his radical counsels capture the essence of new age optimism in its most radical form. According to this 35,000-year-old warrior, "Everything you have ever done, however vile or wretched, has enhanced life by the wisdom you have obtained by doing it."[13] "Ramtha" continues, in words that echo the messages of credit card companies, "As long as you forgive yourself, you never have to pay for anything in this life or the next."[14] According to "Ramtha," in the soul's journey, good and evil are relative judgments, which may, in fact, slow down one's spiritual progress.

While I believe that both the experience and the message of channeled beings reflect a deep spiritual hunger, it is equally clear that today's channels omit the ethical and social proclamations characteristic of the message of Jesus and the biblical prophets. Seldom do they challenge personal behavior or social practices, and only occasionally do they address current global historical situations such as hunger, international conflict, and racism. The political and historical concreteness of biblical prophecy is absent from channeled writings. If the channeled beings speak for the spiritual realm, the spirituality they represent demonstrates little interest in politics, hunger, or social welfare. The transformation of the individual is their primary concern. Indeed, the optimism and individualism of today's spiritual guides have led Harvard theologian Harvey Cox to note that "They're cuddly and friendly. They seem to be yuppified versions of the demons and spirits of another time."[15]

The messages of the most popular channels differ radically from the "thus saith the Lord" of an earlier time. They lack the holistic spirituality, embodied in the integration of person, community, and planet, found in the divinely inspired insights of the ancient Hebrew prophets, Jesus of Nazareth, and contemporary Christian mystics such as Thomas Merton, Mother Teresa, and Howard Thurman.

The Source of the Messages

There is much speculation as to the origin of channeled messages. On the one hand, the fundamentalist Christian, whose metaphysics embraces a spiritual world populated by angels and demons, holds that channeled beings may be substantially real and not merely unconscious projections. To the fundamentalist, channeling is "not God's designated and approved means for communication between his realm and the earth."[16] Fundamentalists would say that although the spirits channeled today may present themselves as benevolent and helpful, their ultimate aim is to deceive persons and lead them away from the message of Jesus Christ. Fundamentalists cite scriptural prohibitions of spiritualism as evidence that Christians should in no way follow or study channeled material, except to challenge its veracity. Rather than seeking the advice of spirits, the fundamentalist counsels persons to denounce them and place themselves obediently before the Bible, God's only means of channeled revelation.

> And when they say unto you, "Consult the mediums and spiritists who whisper and mutter," should not a people consult their God? Should they consult the dead on behalf of the living? To the law and the testimony! If they do not speak according to this word, it is because they have no dawn. (Isaiah 8:19–20)

According to the fundamentalist critique, to seek the messages of mediums and spirits is to forsake the word of God, which comes only through prophetic revelation and the orthodox written Scriptures. The admonition against spiritualism is as old as the Hebraic conflict with the religions of Canaan (Deuteronomy 18:9–12).

> When you enter the land which the Lord your God gives you, you shall not learn to imitate the detestable things of those nations. There shall not be found among you . . . a medium, spiritist, or one who calls up the dead. For whoever does these things is detestable to the Lord.

To the fundamentalist, the experience as well as the messages of channeling are demonic. Truth, maintains the fundamentalist, can only be found in the verbally inspired word of God, the Bible.

The fundamentalist affirms that the canon is truly closed. We cannot expect to hear any other revelation from God apart from the witness of Scripture. Spirituality must cling to and be judged by a literal understanding of Scripture, as initially and uniquely "channeled" by God through the King James version of the Bible.

In contrast to the fundamentalist position, many commentators on channeling suggest that its ultimate source is to be found in the "higher self" rather than in the words of disincarnate spirits, be they good or evil. The messages from beyond are really messages from within, from the presence of God deep within our own experience. From this perspective, the phenomenon of channeling is a particular manifestation of the experience of human intuition or unconscious inspiration, present in and available to all human experience.

Still others explain channeling in terms of a person's encounter with the universal mind or collective unconscious. Popularized by the psychologist C.G. Jung, the collective unconscious is the dynamic stream of symbolic experience shared by all humankind. Rather than being a primitive vestige of a bygone era, the collective unconscious, like the higher self, is the source of the creativity and growth we experience in conscious life. Whereas the collective unconscious most often emerges through dreams, rituals, and religious symbols, it is also expressed in ecstatic experiences such as mystical visions, speaking in tongues, prophetic utterances, and channeling. From this perspective, the conscious mind is but a small portion of human experience, merely the tip of an iceberg that embraces the angelic as well as the demonic. What people channel are messages from their deeper selves or from the divine that speaks through the unconscious.

David Spangler also affirms the origins of channeling within the unconscious. In reflecting on his own experience as a channel, Spangler believes that channeling should be understood as a performance not unlike a concert or a painting, in which the unconscious mind of one calls to the unconscious mind of another.

> Like all art forms, it has the ability to reach us at a deep unconscious level and to stir up forces in our psyches, much as art can do, precisely because, to a greater or lesser degree, channeling is acting as a conduit for the evocation of the energies of the unconscious. Channeling is a performance of the powers of the unconscious, raised to a conscious level. It is a performance of myth, imagery, metaphor, and story in the form of a transmission of information and guidance.[17]

Accordingly, channeling, like all other experiences of the unconscious mind, such as dreams, requires symbolic as well as personal interpretation. Channeled beings exist. Yet, their existence finds its basis in the projections, creativity, and spiritual movements of the unconscious mind. Spangler asserts that the current popularity of channeling arises from its usefulness in awakening people to their own spiritual depths.

A variation on the Jungian understanding of channeling comes from the practice of psychosynthesis, popularized by psychiatrist Roberto Assagioli.[18] Each person, Assagioli suggests, has in her or his unconscious many subpersonalities, reflecting the many dimensions of human experience. Like the Jungian archetypes, these subpersonalities constellate around certain images such as "wise old man," "teacher," "spiritual guide," or less socially approved images such as "the murderer," "complainer," "seducer." When these are repressed, they may come out unexpectedly in strange behavior or projections on other persons. Channeling, from this perspective, may be a process of encountering certain of one's own many subselves and projecting them onto the external world as independent entities. Accordingly, channeling reveals the nature of the cosmos and the spiritual journey as certain parts of our unconscious self understand it.

Finally, the channeled beings may be exactly what they claim to be: spiritual beings who have made contact with humanity in order to hasten our personal and collective spiritual transformation. In this regard, "Samuel" is representative of such spiritual entities. While he is not all-knowing or divine, "Samuel" claims to experience reality from a higher vantage point and is willing to share this experience so that we might gain a wider perspective on our own lives. Implicit in such a view is both an affirmation and a negation of physical existence. While channeled beings must use physical bodies as mediums of communication, they supply a wisdom that is usually missing in embodied experience. The messages of such entities become problematic when they seem to contradict the traditional Christian affirmations of bodily existence, morality, the incarnation, and the suffering love of God.

Reflections on Channeling
However we explain it, channeling is one of the most significant

spiritual expressions in our time. It represents the perennial hunger to experience life more deeply and to discover the meaning of our personal lives. It also reflects a hunger for spiritual guidance, which has been lacking in institutional religion. On the one hand, mainstream religion's preoccupation with the therapeutic and nondirective approach to spiritual growth has left persons without any clear guidance in the formation of character and spirituality. On the other hand, the autocratic directives of fundamentalist preachers have neglected the particular uniqueness of each person's spiritual quest. By contrast, the channeling experience is real and life-changing for many of those who encounter it.

Like all human experiences, channeling is ambiguous. On the one hand, it may empower persons to seek their own spiritual growth. On the other hand, it may become another addictive and authoritarian form of religious experience when persons fail to integrate it with their own broader life experience and wisdom or follow uncritically the advice of channeled beings. Further, it must be remembered that neither the projections of the unconscious nor the manifestations of the spiritual world are entirely benevolent. They can represent the "shadow" as well as the "light." "Samuel" notes the existence of "mischievous" and "egocentric" spirits. Steve Woods, a metaphysical minister in the Washington, D.C., metropolitan area, notes that most of the entities being channeled today are spiritually immature and egocentric.[19] He suggests that the fact that channeled beings collect followings as well as money is a sign of their lack of spiritual depth. An example of the dark side of channeling is revealed in the migration of scores of persons to the Pacific Northwest in order to be guided personally by "Ramtha," channeled by J.Z. Knight, rather than follow their own inner guidance.

The Bible speaks of "powers and principalities," evil spirits, and demons as well as angels and divine messengers. Biblical spirituality rightly observes that disincarnate existence does not necessary imply benevolence or enlightenment. In the biblical vision, Lucifer and the fallen angels are also spiritual beings. One must cultivate the gift and discipline of spiritual discernment in any encounter with the spirit world.

Channeled communications, like all revelatory experiences, are concrete, limited, and perspectival. Broad though their perspective may appear, spirits do have a limited perspective and this perspective is shaped by the conscious and unconscious values and needs of the receiver or channel. In biblical religion, only God is all-wise and all-knowing; angelic beings may share in God's wisdom, but they, too, are finite and, as the myth of Satan's fall suggests, subject to temptation.

Oftentimes, when we hear the message of the Bible or other spiritual guides, we hear only what we want to hear or what justifies our current practices. Quite often the spirit beings simply echo the beliefs of their receivers. Their words seldom challenge their hearers to self-sacrifice or downward mobility. One can have everything and spiritual evolution as well.

The fact that the spirits are disincarnate may, itself, be a handicap in their understanding and guiding of embodied human life. In contrast to timeless metaphysical speculation, the wisdom of the incarnation and the concreteness of biblical prophecy are found in the concern for the temporal as well as the eternal and the body as well as the spirit.

Just as sermons and inspirational books vary in quality, the messages of channeled beings are sometimes insightful and other times trivial and banal. David Spangler suggests that one should always ask "How would I evaluate a given channeled message if an ordinary person had said it?"[20] From my perspective, we must evaluate channeled messages on the basis of their concern for justice and fairness in personal and social life, their insight into the complexity of human life and decision making, their affirmation of freedom and responsibility, and their affirmation and respect for the unenlightened, poor, and disenfranchised. Any channeled advice that minimizes human suffering or suggests that injustice is an illusion or part of the soul's educational journey must be seriously challenged.

While channeling responds to a deep spiritual hunger, it cannot provide by itself the spiritual nutrition that persons truly need. Channeling in and of itself lacks the accountability and personal interaction necessary for spiritual growth. Although the channeled beings speak of themselves as friends, they are no substitute for the "real presence" of "in the flesh" spiritual friendship which, in a community of faith, challenges as well as supports us on a regular basis. Despite the wisdom they may give us, channeled entities seldom demand anything of us. We cannot hurt them, nor do they seem to be bothered by our spiritual shortcomings or ethical backsliding. Their workshops and publications are no substitute for the sharing of joys, sorrows, and mutual accountability present in the body of Christ at its best. In this regard, the spirit of channeling differs greatly from the prophetic messages of Scripture. When the prophet asks, "What does the Lord require of you?" his words center around commitment, relationship, responsibility, and community. Prophetic utterances challenge us to a changed life-style as well as a transformed inner life. To the prophets, what we do in our soul's journey truly matters not merely in terms of our growth but in terms of the health of our community and our relationship to God.

It is my hope that the new age will discover its deepest expression in the context of committed and open-minded communities of faith. Listening to a tape, reading a book, or going to a workshop may indeed enhance our spiritual journeys. But these journeys need to be grounded in the day-to-day practical spirituality of committed, embodied, and imperfect relationships within the context of a spiritual community, be it a church or gathering of spiritual seekers. A truly holistic spirituality combines the inspiration and focus on personal experience characteristic of the channeling phenomenon, with the accountability, support, and social consciousness found in vital communities of faith and action.

A Theology of Inspiration

Biblical Background

The Hebraic-Christian tradition finds its spiritual vitality in the communication between God and the world. God speaks the world into existence (Genesis 1:3–2:3), and the divine word or logos is the maker of all things (John 1:1–5). From the beginnings of human history, God communicates to humankind, first, in words of guidance and protection, and, later, in words of challenge and reconciliation. Encounters with God are pivotal in humankind's understanding of itself and its purpose in history. These encounters are never abstract; they address the specific needs of persons and communities in words of guidance, judgment, deliverance, and promise. Though such encounters seem anomalous in our age of science and reason, virtually every Christian remembers the strange encounters of Abraham, Sarah, and the angelic visitors (Genesis 18:1–15), Moses and the burning bush (Exodus 3:1–12), the giving of the ten commandments on Mount Sinai (Exodus 19:16–20:20), and the calls of sleeping Samuel (1 Samuel 3:1–14), reluctant Jeremiah (Jeremiah 1:4–10), and sinful Isaiah (Isaiah 6:1–13). While God speaks directly to people, revelation also comes from angels, strange visitors, and even animals who speak on behalf of God. In the biblical worldview, God is constantly revealing God's purposes in the lives of persons and communities.

The New Testament abounds in divine-human encounters. The births of Jesus and John the Baptist are announced by angelic beings and through dreams (Matthew 1:18–25; Luke 1:18–23, 26–38). Jesus is guided in the desert by the Holy Spirit (Luke 4:1–13) and encounters the spirits of Moses and Elijah (Matthew 17:1–8). Indeed, Christian faith is grounded in the belief that Jesus of Nazareth is the supreme revelation of God and that an encounter with Jesus either in the flesh or through the companionship of prayer is an encounter with God in God's fullness. While the mechanics of the incarnation are vague and controversial, it is evident that the church came to see Jesus as "God with us," sharing our struggles and revealing God's loving will to humankind. To put it in the language of the new age, Jesus was believed to be the ultimate divine channel to humankind.

As I noted in Chapter Two, the early church lived in the expectation of "signs and wonders." On Pentecost, the disciples experienced the coming of the Holy Spirit. In the days that followed, the Comforter Jesus had promised, the Spirit who "teaches them all things" (John 15:26) and gives Jesus' followers the power to do "great works," became an everyday experience for the early Christians. The gospel was spread by dreams (Acts 10) as well as inspired preaching (Acts 17:16–34). The presence of God became the deepest reality of the personal and corporate lives of the earliest Christians.

The early Christians believed that they were inspired by the Holy Spirit in the same fashion as God had inspired the prophets of old. One recorded example of such inspiration is the revelation of John on the Isle of Patmos. John's encounter with God bears a strong resemblance to the guidance that many channels receive today insofar as it claims to speak of the cosmic destiny of all things from the perspective of the spiritual realm.

> The revelation of Jesus Christ, which God gave him to show to
> his servants what must soon take place; and he made it known
> by sending his angel to his servant John, who bore witness to the
> word of God and the testimony of Jesus Christ, even to all he saw.
> . . . Then I turned to see the voice that was speaking to me.
> (Revelation 1:1–2, 12)

The world of John's Revelation is populated by visions, auditory
revelations, spiritual dictation, and prophecies of the future. John recognizes that humankind is not alone in the universe, but is surrounded by a spiritual world of angels and demons, of God and Satan. In
light of the moral ambiguity of the spiritual world, the New Testament
counsels Christians to trust only those spirits that proclaim that Jesus
is the Christ. While other spirits may seem benevolent, they may also
be demonic messengers whose purpose is to turn us from our true
relationship with God. Accordingly, the messages of spirits must be
"tested" by the "good news" of God's grace as revealed in the life and
teachings of Jesus Christ.

Closing the Canon
The early Christians experienced liberating movements of divine
inspiration in terms of freedom from the sin and bondage of the past. The
Holy Spirit moved according to its own terms and could not be con-
strained by the boundaries of gender, ethnicity, or tradition. Soon, however, the freedom of the Spirit became a source of conflict in the early
church. In the second century, Montanus and his followers spoke of a
new outpouring of divine revelation. They felt that the church had lost
the vitality of the Pentecostal experience. God was as fully present in his
age, Montanus proclaimed, as God was in the age of the disciples.
Montanus felt that Christians of his time were channels of the Holy
Spirit, who participated in the ongoing dynamic encounter of God and
the world. Accordingly, Montanus and his followers believed that divine
revelation extended far beyond the apostles and the written words of
Scripture. Authority was not ultimately in the books of Scripture but in
the Holy Spirit as it continued to speak through human beings.

In the second century, the church was confronted with a new spirit
not unlike the new age movements for spiritual transformation within

and beyond Christianity in our own time. Orthodox Christians, troubled by the freedom of the Spirit to move in new ways and to reveal itself to women as well as men, wondered how the new revelations related to the original message of Jesus and his disciples.[21]

The orthodox church eventually labeled these unrestrained movements of the spirit as heretical. In so doing, it limited the realm of authoritative inspiration and defined the standards for inclusion of books into the Scriptures. As a bulwark against heresy and heterodoxy, the canon, or authoritative witness of Scripture, was closed. Only those books that could be directly traced to the apostles, or first witnesses to Jesus' ministry, were admitted as normative for the spiritual life of the church. No new authoritative revelations could be added. While Christians could recognize the insights of noncanonical or non-biblical writings and even mystical encounters with God, these writings and experiences had to be judged in accordance with their conformity to the original revelation.[22]

The results of closing the canon have been ambiguous, to say the least. On the one hand, the closing of the canon clearly defined the standards for orthodox Christianity and provided a foundation for the institutional stability and growth of the church. On the other hand, it stifled innovative, inclusive, and lively interpretations of the gospel and encouraged a patriarchal, backward-looking, rationalistic, and book-oriented faith. To many Christians, especially in the years following the Reformation, the revelation of God became virtually identified with the written and codified words of Scripture. The "paper infallibility" of the fundamentalist substituted a dead letter for the living word of God.

In the past century, liberal and mainline Christians have challenged the orthodox and fundamentalist interpretations of scriptural authority. They rightly recognized that in the course of history Christians have seldom restricted revelation and inspiration solely to the words of Scripture. Tradition, experience, and reason were also recognized as vehicles through which God encounters humankind. Further, mystical experiences as well as encounters with the Virgin Mary were accepted by some Christians as revelations of God, provided they conformed to the traditions of Scripture and the teachings of the church. However, the rationalistic and one-dimensional worldview of most mainstream and liberal theologians could provide no theological grounding for direct revelations of God to humankind. Human experience became the norm for revelatory experiences. The ecstatic, visionary, and emotional experiences of poets, mystics, and charismatics had no place in the liberal worldview.

The struggles of today's mainstream Christians to encounter the lively presence of God parallel an experience from my son's childhood. When our son was a toddler, he owned a small computer that spoke back to him the words he typed. One day, just as an experiment, we typed in the letters "g-o-d." The computer replied, "not found." Tragically, a similar limit has characterized the spiritual experiences of many fundamentalists, who restrict divine inspiration to the pages of a book, and of many liberals, who restrict the divine-human encounter to the norms of culture or to narrow and one-dimensional understandings of the historical Jesus.

But the very spirit that has been denied entry in liberal and fundamentalist churches has exploded in new forms of inspiration. As different as they seem at first glance, spiritualism, new thought, the pentecostal movement, and the new age movement reflect not only the thirst for spiritual experience but the gift of living waters that restores the human soul. Tongue speaking, prophetic utterances, voices from beyond the grave, and communication with spirit guides all attest to a need that has not been addressed within fundamentalist or mainstream churches. This is the need not only to hear about God but to experience God firsthand, and with it the further need for spiritual guidance in the interpretation of encounters with realities beyond ourselves.

While liberal Christians may chuckle at the ecstatic behavior of charismatics and the theatrical personae of some channels, many liberal Christians feel envious of these encounters with other dimensions of reality. They sadly recognize that liberal, mainstream, and even fundamentalist Christians have adopted a religion consisting primarily of words and thoughts rather than the whole range of human experience. There is a growing awareness within mainstream churches that intuition, emotion, and inspiration are as essential to a living and holistic faith as are rationality, ethical behavior, and intellectual soundness. Ironically, the tongue speakers, the channels, and the mystics have opened the doors of the spirit for the liberal churches. Perhaps the time has come for letting the spirit breathe life into the church once more.

Inspiration and Revelation for a New Age

Today, most mainstream Christians no longer limit divine revelation to the words of Scripture. Through their studies of Asian philosophy, Jungian psychology, new age thought, as well as the many diverging strands of church history, they have discovered that God's witness to humankind is dynamic, evolving, and universal in scope. Vatican II affirmed for Roman Catholics that it is possible for individuals outside the church to be saved. If there is salvation outside the church, then there must also be saving knowledge of God beyond the walls of Christendom and the words of Scripture. Many mainline Christians recognize that a dynamic understanding of God requires them to be open to the insights of non-biblical and even non-Christian literature and religious experiences. With or without the support of their pastors and churches, they are reading the scriptures of other faiths and studying Buddhist and Hindu meditation, yoga, and attitudinal healing techniques. Yet, few of them have found an adequate theology of revelation to help them integrate the diverse strands of divine inspiration.

In chapter two, I used the analogy of God as the soul of the world and the world as the body of Christ as a means of understanding God's presence in the universe and the possibility of spiritual experience. In the body of Christ, each cell or member is influenced by the divine mind directly in the depths of its own experience and indirectly through its interactions with every other cell. Accordingly, all creatures, including ourselves, reveal God to those who have eyes to see and ears to hear. Within the body of Christ, divine revelation, or inspiration, can be specifically defined as the conscious awareness of the ever-present, yet often veiled, divine wisdom coming to us through a multitude of "channels."

In contrast to those who limit revelation to a single channel or stream of truth, the image of the world as the body of Christ proclaims that all creatures experience and can serve as vehicles of divine revelation. There is a democracy of revelation, a global priesthood of believers that includes not only monks, priests, and gurus but common persons, agnostics, and even animals, birds, and trees. In the language of the new age, every person and, indeed, every living being is capable of becoming a channel of the divine, because God speaks from the inside as well as the outside of each being.

Although God is present everywhere, God's presence and wisdom are not uniformly or homogeneously present in all beings. As H. Richard Niebuhr and others have noted, revelation is always contextual and historical. While God's will is eternal in terms of its quest for love, justice, and abundant life, the revealing and recognition of God's will is always "personal," that is, unique to the particular time and place it is experienced. For example, the will of God, revealed in the challenges, ideals, and possibilities relevant to each person and community, differs markedly for a five-year-old child born in America, a ninety-year-old grandparent living in a nursing home, or a teenager living in a Bosnian village. The call of God takes a different form in a suburban Protestant church in America, a new age gathering in Scotland, or an Orthodox church in Russia. God appears to each person in terms of her or his present needs and unique personal and cultural characteristics. As the message of the Old Testament prophets makes plain, God's word to the wealthy oppressor differs radically from God's word to the oppressed and downtrodden. Although the divine call is always toward loving transformation, no absolute and uniform experience of that call is possible or even desirable.

Revelation always requires a receiver or channel. The personality, historical context, and spiritual commitment of the receiver determine what will be received. The spirit of God, the soul of the universe, is intensely personal. The "one to whom all hearts are open and all desires known" actively responds to each being in the way that is best for the individual and the body of Christ as a whole. Accordingly, all experiences of the divine, even those shared by disincarnate beings or angels, are conditioned and limited by perspective, life experiences, and personal concern. As much as divine guidance and channeled messages reflect God's deepest desires in the particular situation, they also reflect the deepest desires of those to whom they are addressed. This does not diminish their value, but rather accents the personal and relational nature of truth. While truth has an eternal pole, it is also dynamically and temporally embodied in terms of God's action and our creaturely response.

In the experience of the spiritual world, nonphysical existence does not imply omniscience. Even in the spiritual world, there are standpoints and concerns that shape what any disincarnate being is able to experience and share. Not even Jesus claimed to know the totality of the divine (Mark 13:32).

If disincarnate beings exist and are able to communicate to humankind, they must also encounter God from a particular standpoint and reveal God through a particular human vehicle. Readings and prophetic messages may reveal the spiritual world, but this revelation is always within the limits of both human and nonhuman experience and perspective. However helpful it may be, the guidance of channels and other finite spiritual beings must not blind us to our own insights, for we are also constantly receiving divine guidance, and we are also channels of God's truth. Embodied beings like ourselves also have a perspective on the truth. Indeed, disincarnate spirits may have a less insightful standpoint on certain human issues precisely because they are disembodied.

Though divine revelation is universal in scope, certain places and persons may become more powerful channels of divine revelation than others. Certain moments or places may, to use a new age term, become "vortices" or "energy points" of divine revelation. These are the moments theologians have described as the "special revelations" of God. Accordingly, Scripture can be described as "the word of God" not only because it reflects vivid divine-human encounters but also because people have historically sought God's guidance in reading Scripture. The "synchronicity," or meaningful coincidence, of finding a scriptural passage that speaks to one's condition reflects not only the Spirit of God present in Scripture but also one's own inner openness for the divine spirit to speak through the words of Scripture. Our openness to God in Scripture, sacrament, and silence enables God to act more decisively in our lives. Whether we speak of these moments in terms of healing, inspiration, insight, or social transformation, these moments of enhanced energy and consciousness surely reflect the deeper meaning of Jesus' words from Matthew 7:7: "Ask, and it will be given you; seek, and you will find; knock, and the door will be opened to you."

Yet what about new age channeling? Can this phenomenon fit into a Christian understanding of revelation? From a biblical perspective, persons can encounter spiritual beings. Visitations of angels and possession by demons dot the landscape of the New Testament. We are always surrounded by a "cloud of witnesses," members of the "communion of saints" in this world and the next. If the body of Christ is characterized by an intricate weaving of relationships, then, as near death experiences attest, there is no absolute boundary between the living and the dead, the incarnate and the disincarnate. Angels and other spirits, perhaps deceased friends and spiritual guides, may choose to cross the boundary of the living and dead in order to transmit information or personal reassurance, or may be contacted by persons seeking transrational experiences. Accordingly, Christians can affirm the existence of the channeling without accepting *all* channeled material as equally valuable or accurate in its description of the universe.

Christians are challenged to evaluate channeled material in terms of the dynamic revelation of God in history and in the life of Jesus Christ. In Christian experience, Jesus is seen as the supreme and normative channel, or ultimate revelation, of God's presence for humankind. As they encounter channeled material or disincarnate spirits, Christians are invited to look beyond the channeled beings or intermediaries to Christ for their guidance and evaluation. Paul's words "It is no longer I but Christ who lives in me" (Galatians 2:20) reflect the possibility that Christians may come to experience the "mind of Christ" in such a way that they themselves may gain a transcendent perspective and experience special revelations of the divine that go far beyond everyday experience.

Recent discussions of the nature of revelation note that biblical revelation is not so much the transmission of information or doctrine as it is the personal encounter with the living God who comforts and challenges. While our encounter with God is ultimately personal, it may also contain intuitive insights into the nature of reality or problems we or others are experiencing. New agers often speak of intuitively encountering the Akashic Record, or the library of cosmic history, as a means of gathering information on personal issues and problems. Many of Edgar Cayce's "readings" are attributed to his experience of this universal memory. In the same fashion, Christians can speak of prophetic insight, clairvoyance, or higher intuition in terms of encountering the "memory" or "mind" of God. If God embraces the totality of experience, then openness to God's presence may enable us to experience a deeper vision of the history we share in.

While most encounters with the mind of God are less dramatic than channeling, speaking in tongues, or biblical prophecy, we can contact the energy and knowledge of the divine mind as it penetrates our spirits, most especially in the context of prayer, meditation, Scripture, or worship. In such moments, we seek to listen to God's call in our lives. What we experience at such times is as much due to God's grace and freedom as it is to our own openness.

God cannot be invoked magically, and God, like any other person, may choose to withhold certain aspects of reality from our experience. While channeling often seems to focus on our ability to contact spiritual beings, inspiration and revelation in a Christian context are grounded in the divine quest for humankind. Our invocations of God always follow God's invoking of ourselves. God is not an impersonal being, but a lively and loving parent who seeks to communicate with us personally. As such, revelatory experiences are not merely about knowing God but being known by God. In this deeper knowledge, we may come to know others and ourselves as we are known by God.

A Christian theology of revelation and inspiration is grounded in our experience of the body of Christ as a social reality. Each person's spiritual journey and encounter with God is part of a larger process of planetary and cosmic transformation. Knowing God and one's deepest self is not merely a validation of one's spiritual quest, it is a constant process of conversion and transformation, both of oneself and one's community. Ultimately, the focus of experience is God and not the individual self. The aim of divine inspiration is social justice and global community as much as it is personal transformation.

In contrast to the moral relativism of many channeled messages, biblical revelation is grounded in the "ethical monotheism" of the Hebraic prophets and Jesus of Nazareth. God, from this standpoint, is not merely the all-accepting power of the universe, God also has a bias toward justice and holiness. Authentic revelation issues in acts of love. Those who neglect justice will eventually experience what the prophet Amos described as a "famine of hearing God's word" (Amos 8:11–12).

Even if channeled beings exist and communicate with some level of insight, Christians must still ask themselves how they should respond to the truth claims of channeled material when they differ from Christian revelation. While not rejecting differences as demonic or false or denying that differences exist, Christians must recognize the relativity and limitations inherent in channeled material as well as in biblical revelation. As theologians of world religions have noted, the metaphysical differences of religious traditions can be partly attributed to those aspects of reality each faith encounters and emphasizes. Whereas new age channelers emphasize the importance of personal growth, Christian faith has focused on the growth of the self in its social and political context. Christian inspiration arises from an encounter with a living, dynamic, and personal God, while new age visions focus on the divine as changeless and impersonal. While individuality and community both reveal the divine, Christians, however, must urge new agers to consider the importance of community and social responsibility in the formation of spiritual life. In inviting new agers to reflect on the social dimensions of life, Christians enable them to transcend the tendencies toward cosmic individualism, political quietism, and self-absorption that often characterize new age spirituality. New agers can urge Christians to focus on self-development as well as social concern. Still, the "mind of Christ" in its humility, suffering, and care for others must be the ultimate criterion by which Christians evaluate the revelations of the new age movement.

God's voice constantly echoes across the universe and in our hearts. For Christians, the power, energy, and authority of that voice come from our encounter with Christ. Christ's unity with the "Father" binds us to God as well. As Christians seek to experience the mind of Christ, they may encounter new insights and deeper intuitions; they may see new realities and encounter higher beings. These, too, must be tested, since, even in our insight, "we see into a mirror dimly" (1 Corinthians 13:12). Our most treasured insights into God's nature are still "treasures in earthen vessels" and not the divine itself.

Despite the metaphysical differences between biblical revelation and new age channeling, Christians must thank the new age movement for reminding us about the vast possibilities available in encountering the spiritual realm. As David Spangler suggests, the ultimate impact of today's channels may not be in what they reveal to us but in the inspiration to common people to draw close to the divine. In this critical era of human history, Spangler believes that "we are all asked to be channels for the spirit of the New Age, to use our bodies and minds to give flesh and blood to an holistic and harmonious future."[23] Then channeling would reach beyond the tendencies toward self-absorption and spiritual pulse-taking and find its place alongside Christian inspiration in bringing about a just and life-affirming global spirituality.

QUESTIONS FOR REFLECTION AND DISCUSSION

1. In what ways does God communicate with humankind? Does God still communicate with persons?

2. How do you respond to the channeling phenomenon? Can it be a source of truth and revelation? How do we discern the spiritual from the demonic in the channeling movement?

3. Where do you see the Holy Spirit in today's world? Is it possible to discern the Holy Spirit in today's channelers?

4. Why was the canon of Scripture closed? What problems were created by closing the canon? Does the church require an authority to determine what is orthodox and heretical?

5. How do you respond to the statement that "all creatures experience and can serve as vehicles of divine revelation"?

6. Do you think God reveals Godself to different people and cultures in different ways? Does a contextual understanding of revelation provide a sufficient basis for authority in the life of the church? How can we discern between truth and falsehood in the messages of biblical revelation and new age channeling?

7. Can new age channeling fit into a Christian understanding of revelation?

CHAPTER FOUR

"THE HEALING CONNECTION"

HEALING IN THE NEW AGE

One Saturday morning, I found myself sitting in front of the television captivated by the antics of a televangelist. As this preacher strutted up and down the stage, clad in white shoes, a white suit, and a poorly fitting toupee, he cried out to the heavens, "Heal, God, heal. Heal, God, heal! Heal, God, heal!" In the midst of his petitions, my young son entered the room and asked me innocently, "Is that man trying to train his dog?"

Sadly, when many Christians think of healing, their minds turn not to the compassionate Jesus but to the dramatic, manipulative, and often comical techniques of TV preachers. As a young child in the 1950s, I was raised listening to Oral Roberts's lively healing revivals and the soft purring of Kathryn Kuhlman as she whispered, "I believe in miracles." My mother often sent gifts to the TV preachers and advised me always "to expect a miracle." But even as a child I felt uncomfortable with the flamboyant style and the constant appeal for money characteristic of these preachers. I wondered if anyone was ever really healed at their meetings and why some were healed and others were passed by. To me, their message implied that if you just had enough faith or gave enough money, God would heal you. My grandparents, relatives, and Sunday school teachers were all faithful people who prayed for healing. Yet nothing could save them from death—not even God. Did God play favorites? If so, why didn't God heal the persons I loved? All I heard in response to my questions were the typical evangelical platitudes—"It was God's will" or "All things work together for good." As a child I wondered why God would suspend the laws of nature just to heal one person while millions were dying of cancer or starving in Asia and Africa.

I suspect that my childhood experience in many ways parallels the problems that many contemporary Christians have with the healings of Jesus and the many alleged healings of our own time. Many mainline Christians have taken a dim view of any healing apart from medical care. Revolted by the manipulative approaches of TV healers and their miracle-based theologies, many mainstream Christians have denied the possibility of healing altogether. They are convinced that if healing involves the violation of natural laws as we understand them, then we must reject it, even if we do not fully understand the principles behind these laws.

While mainstream theologians affirm that God works through medicine, their understanding of reality allows virtually no distinction between the work of the medical doctor and the activities of the Great Physician. If the doctor cannot bring healing, neither can God. To many theologians and ministers, the healing stories of Jesus are relics of a superstitious age that confused the spiritual with the physical worlds. In a world of polio vaccines, heart transplants, and CAT scans, there is little God can do that isn't already being done by our own medical deities. Unable to articulate an alternative understanding of healing, most mainstream Christians have placed their hope for well-being in the arms of the physician, nurse, and psychiatrist.

In spite of the church's attitude toward healing, people still seek healing, and unexpected healings still seem to occur at revival meetings, in answer to prayer, or at holy places such as Lourdes. Many persons are intrigued by the claims of alternative healers or the interplay of mind and body suggested by Bill Moyers's recent PBS series "Healing and the Mind" or alternative physician Larry Dossey's recent book *Healing Words*, which explores the scientific research on the power of prayer.[1]

Since health is one of the major preoccupations of our technological society, the church must pay attention to the health of its people. Over ten percent of the Gross National Product of the United States of America relates to health care. Persons are constantly being bombarded with products promising to take off weight, add hair, calm anxiety, or reduce pain. Although our life expectancy has increased since the beginning of the twentieth century, the death expectancy has remained at one hundred percent, and the diseases that kill persons today are often chronic, debilitating, and painful. In a world of technological wonders, it is ironic that we fear dying slowly and torturously at the hands of the physicians and machines that are meant to help us, more than we fear death itself. The ambiguities of medical technology have inspired a growing interest in alternative forms of health and healing. Whether it is called alternative medicine, holistic health, or spiritual healing, there is a growing recognition of a healing connection that goes beyond technical medicine—a connection among spirit, emotions, and physical well-being.

Mainstream Christianity has lagged far behind the alternative healing approaches in the quest for spiritual and physical healing. While mainstream Christians have emphasized the healing of society, the environment, and the emotions, they have left the healing of the body and spirit almost entirely to physicians, pentecostal faith healers, and new age healers. Within mainstream Christianity, only a few voices—including Olga and Ambrose Worrall, Agnes Sanford, and Morton Kelsey—have risen to proclaim a vision of healing congruent with modern science, the laws of nature, and the ministry of Jesus. Today, when people think of healing, they do not think of the church. Their minds turn to a metaphysical healer, a reiki practitioner, a massage therapist, or an acupuncturist. If they think of Christian healing at all, they imagine a "holy roller" or Oral Roberts and his vision of a nine-hundred-foot Jesus. As exotic and as unregulated as today's new age healers may be, their very existence is an indictment of a church that has forgotten the vital healing ministry of its founder.

Healing is a major preoccupation within the new age movement. While many new agers accept the value of modern medicine, they see it as incomplete and often unsuccessful in treating the wounds of body and soul. Authentic healing must be holistic. It must address the spirit as well as the body. It must be preventative as well as responsive, active as well as receptive. New agers often pick and choose between a variety of healing modalities ranging from herbal remedies and colonics to crystals and massage. In the eclectic and pragmatic spirit of the new age movement, people are counseled to choose the method or methods that seem to work among the smorgasbord of alternative approaches.

Although there is no uniform approach to healing in the new age movement, I will focus on three of its representative streams of healing: the scientific approach of Barbara Brennan, the mental approach of Louise Hay, and the spiritual approach of *A Course in Miracles*. After reviewing and critiquing these three healing movements, I will reflect on the problems and possibilities of healing within mainstream Christianity by considering: 1) the healing ministry of Jesus, 2) the eclipse of healing in Christianity, and 3) a revival of the healing ministry within the Christian church.

Barbara Brennan and Her Hands of Light

Of all the new age healers, Barbara Brennan is perhaps the most scientifically grounded. Her textbook on healing, *Hands of Light,* has sold nearly 300,000 copies, and her lectures and workshops are well attended. Over 300 students currently participate in the four-year program of the Barbara Brennan School of Healing, located on Long Island. An atmospheric physicist and expert in weather satellites, Brennan left Goddard Space Flight Center in the 1960s to explore the science of healing. She describes her own work as a marriage of science and mysticism. Her lectures are peppered with scientific explanations of energy fields, chakras, auras, and clairvoyance. Interspersed between comments on holograms and the new physics, Brennan speaks of spirit guides and past lives as if they were everyday, ordinary, and scientifically verifiable realities.

Brennan's work is practical and experiential in nature. Brennan asserts we can affirm that auras or energy fields exist because we can see them and feel them. She asks her listeners, as she asked the members of a workshop I attended, to feel the energy radiating between their hands and see the colors surrounding their neighbors. She even asks them to take a leap of faith and feel themselves exploring the contours of a ceiling by extending their own energy fields and conscious awareness. While her experiments aren't always successful—I, for one, could not feel the energy radiating from the ceiling—her listeners often feel an energy that they had not experienced before.

Brennan bases her understanding of healing on a spiritual interpretation of the new physics. Most persons, Brennan believes, adhere to the outmoded worldview described by Newtonian physics. We assume that reality is solid and that each entity is separated from every other entity. In contrast to the insentient and isolated world of Newton's physics, contemporary physics reveals a world of dynamically interconnected energy events. What we call matter is merely energy that moves at a lower vibrational frequency. Following David Bohm's theory of the implicate order—the theory that the physical world arises from an unmanifest and intelligent substratum—Brennan believes that the body arises from the more subtle energy surrounding it. According to Brennan, all things are composed of different frequencies of this same energy, which has been traditionally identified by words such as "light," "prana," and "chi" within the world's religious traditions.

There is no dualism of mind and matter, or body and spirit. "Mass is nothing but a form of energy. Matter is simply slowed down or crystallized energy. Our bodies are energy."[2] Accordingly, thoughts and emotions are also forms of energy that interact with the body for good or for ill.

Our bodies are part of the universal energy field. Our relatedness to this divine energy is the source of all healing. Brennan suggests that "since we are inseparable parts of that whole, we can enter into a holistic state of being, become the whole, and tap into the creative powers of the universe to instantaneously heal anyone anywhere."[3] Therefore, "becoming a healer means to move toward the universal creative power that we experience as love by reidentifying self with and becoming universal; becoming one with God."[4]

Brennan believes that healing and illness are spiritual as well as physical issues. As long as we are connected with the flow of universal divine energy, we will be healthy in body and spirit. Illness arises from a blocking or imbalance of this ever flowing universal energy. The major way we create bodily illness is through the emotional defensiveness that weakens the energy fields and lowers our resistance to disease.[5] Accordingly, illness is always meaningful: "It is a message from your body . . . that says 'Wait a minute, something is wrong. You are not listening to your whole self; you are ignoring something very important to you.'"[6]

Like many other new age thinkers, Brennan asserts that we create our own realities and that our thoughts and emotions eventually will be reflected in our physical well-being. Brennan asserts that "illness is the result of imbalance. Imbalance is a result of forgetting who you are. Forgetting who you are creates thoughts and actions that lead to an unhealthy lifestyle and eventually to illness."[7] But within each illness are the seeds of healing. Illness not only shows us what is wrong but also how to return to our true self and health.

Illness and health are, however, not limited to the physical body. Each person is surrounded by an aura or energy field that mediates the energy of the universe to the physical body. Each of the seven layers of the energy field is related to a *chakra*, or vortex, which channels energy from the universe to the body. Healing takes place not only within the physical body but also at the level of one's energetic field. When the *chakras* are closed through negativity and defensiveness, they receive less energy; this eventually leads to illness. The task of the healer is to heal the energy field and the *chakras* as well as the physical ailment. Brennan claims that "a torn chakra has occurred in every cancer patient I've seen."[8] Although most persons are unaware of these auric or energy fields, virtually anyone can be trained to see and evaluate a person's health according to the color and vitality of their auric field. Brennan believes that by learning "higher sense perception," persons can experience those dimensions of reality that lie beyond the five senses. By working with the auric fields, a disorder can be healed before it is physically manifested.

Brennan humorously notes that as a child she wanted to see through bodies just like the cartoon character, Wonder Woman. Today, she uses this higher sense perception and clairvoyance in her diagnosis and treatment of illness. She claims to be able to see into the very tissues of our bodies as well as scan the invisible energy fields that surround us.

Brennan asserts that the healer is never alone in her vocation. As a manifestation of universal energy, the body naturally moves toward health and balance. By nurturing inner and outer healing, the healer evokes the already present tendency toward wholeness within each person. Further, the healer is guided by spiritual beings, or guides, who provide information and assist in the healing process itself. As the healer practices laying on of hands and balancing and repairing the energy field, these spiritual guides also channel their energy for the well-being of the patient.

Brennan's work combines the metaphysical, the spiritual, and the scientific. Reality for her is a unified field of spiritual energy in which each one of us participates. From moment to moment and life to life, we choose whether we will accept or block the energy of life that flows through us. Love opens us to healing, while fear brings illness. By words, insight, the channeling of energy, and the laying on hands, the healer invites the patient also to become a healer and, thereby, to bring harmony to his or her own life and to the world. Brennan describes her own work and the work of all healers in terms of love.

> The work of a healer is a work of love. The healer reaches into these painful areas of the soul and gently reawakens hope. S/he gently reawakens the ancient memory of who the soul is. S/he touches the spark of God in each cell of the body and gently reminds it that it is already God and, already being God, it inexorably flows with the Universal Will towards health and wholeness.[9]

While mainstream Christians will struggle with Brennan's emphasis on the power of the mind to create reality, as well as with her bold claims to be clairvoyant, her identification of the individual soul with God, and her openness to spirit guides, there is much they can learn from her approach to healing. Brennan's work is a challenge to transcend the outmoded atomistic and materialistic worldview that has undergirded the contemporary understanding of health and illness. In her emphasis on healing as a balancing and channeling of universal energy, Brennan also provides an alternative model for healing not unlike that of traditional Chinese medicine. Healing is not a violation of the laws of nature, but the evocation of omnipresent forces within nature itself. Healing does not disrupt, but intensifies and focuses the universal movement toward harmony and order.

Still, Brennan's approach leaves little room for grace. Although healing energy always surrounds us, it is ultimately passive in nature. Sickness is contingent upon our failure to receive this energy. Health involves the application of the proper techniques and attitudes. While Christians have argued about the relationship of grace and human effort for centuries, it is clear that, for Brennan, human effort is the ultimate source of health and healing. The unexpected surprises of grace by which the helpless and unenlightened find solace, healing, and new life seem absent from Brennan's worldview.

Louise Hay and the Power of the Mind

"We are each 100 percent responsible for all of our experiences. . . . We create our experiences, our reality and everyone in it. . . . We create every so-called illness in our body."[10] So proclaims California healer Louise Hay. Cancer, AIDS, starvation, and even rape are choices we make either at the conscious or unconscious level. At first glance, Louise Hay's philosophy of life seems fatalistic or guilt-centered. Yet Hay believes that the recognition of the power of the mind and emotions is the source of our healing as well as of our illness. By her logic, if we create our illnesses through our negativity and fear, then positive thinking and affirmations can bring us healing and new life.

Louise Hay is another of the leading voices in the new age healing movement. Her self-published *You Can Heal Your Life* has been on the New York Times best-seller list and has sold over a million copies. Her tapes, videos, and recent publication *The AIDS Book* bring in millions of dollars each year. Hay's message is simple. She focuses on what has worked for her and avoids scientific explanations and philosophical concepts. She asserts, "I am not a healer. I do not heal anyone. I am a very simple lady who knows and teaches the power of love; that's all I do."[11] Hay's philosophy is straightforward: every thought and emotion has an impact on our lives. Loving thoughts heal; negative emotions and thoughts destroy our self-esteem and our bodies. We always reap what we sow. We can never escape the results of our actions. Our karma, or personal energy, follows us in this life and the next. "When we really love ourselves everything in our lives works."[12] Who we are today is a result of our choices. What we will be tomorrow is equally the result of the choices we make today. Accordingly, our salvation is found in our ability always to choose our future by right choices in this present moment.

Although Hay's philosophy might easily lead to feelings of guilt and punishment, her work has been embraced by countless persons with AIDS as well as other persons experiencing serious illnesses. Each Wednesday night, hundreds of persons with AIDS gather in Los Angeles for her "Hayride," an opportunity to share, sing, cry, and be healed through the power of love. Through her tapes and books she invites persons with AIDS to claim the power of choice and to learn to love themselves. AIDS exists, Hay asserts, "to show us we are making a mess of our lives and our planet. Our physical bodies and physical world are in a great need of healing. . . . the whole planet has a form of AIDS."[13] To Hay, AIDS is a disease of lovelessness, which initially affected the oppressed, marginalized, and unloved: Africans, Haitians, gays, hemophiliacs, drug users, and persons who receive blood transfusions.[14] Hay suggests that lack of self-love and fear of growing old may be the ultimate cause of AIDS within the gay community.

While Hay does not promise a cure for AIDS, she proclaims that persons with AIDS do not have to be victims and that they can choose to live spiritually healthy and joyful lives, whether or not their disease disappears. Through affirmations, visualization, and positive thinking, persons can change their lives.

Hay connects all illness to conscious or unconscious choices. Her list of causes and cures reads like a cookbook. Ear problems indicate that there is something we don't want to hear, while eye problems represent our desire to avoid seeing some aspect of our lives.[15] For those with ear problems, Hay suggests an affirmation, "I hear with love." For those with eye problems, a similar affirmation, "I see with love and joy," is suggested. Heart attacks are brought on by the inability to love oneself or others.[16] A healing affirmation Hay suggests for those with heart problems is, "My heart beats to the rhythm of love."[17] Bladder problems obviously have to do with anger, that is, with being "pissed off."[18] Although persons may seek medical care, they must realize that healing, like illness, is a result of their choices.

While Hay's philosophy empowers many persons to choose health rather than illness, the dark side of the need to explain everything in terms of a linear cause-effect relationship can lead to feelings of false omnipotence as well as debilitating guilt. Hay's philosophy of mental omnipotence is summed up in her belief that

> we are all on an endless journey through eternity. We come to this planet to learn particular lessons that are necessary for our spiritual evolution. We choose our sex, our color, our country; and then we look around for the perfect set of parents who will "mirror" our patterns. Our visits to this planet are like going to school.[19]

Our present lives not only are responses to our past choices but are the basis for our future lives. Rather than suggesting that our fate is "God's will," Hay and many other new age leaders proclaim that my fate is "my will."

Such absolutism can lead to feelings of guilt and personal failure. Physician Larry Dossey, himself active in the alternative healing movement, recalls the incident of a woman who nearly died from a ruptured appendix because she felt too embarrassed to seek help when the alternative approaches she tried did not alleviate her pain. When Dossey asked her why she didn't call, she exclaimed tearfully, "Because I was ashamed." Guided by her belief that all illness is connected with the mind, she felt guilty when the power of the mind did not heal her. As Dossey adds, "She did not want to come into my office and have to 'confess' her methods and reveal her failure."[20]

In this same vein, a well-meaning but spiritually insensitive friend might seek to help a person with cancer by asking, "Why did you choose to give yourself cancer? What lesson are you trying to learn?" At a recurrence of cancer, one might be counseled to discern what resentments he or she is still holding on to.

While the linear approach to health and illness suggested by Hay and others makes each person the sole cause of his or her good fortune and bad luck, it neglects the importance of social relatedness, genetic inheritance, and environment in health and illness. In so doing, it creates a new age version of rugged individualism in which the strong deserve their good fortune and the weak get exactly what they deserve. It also gives persons the illusion that they are totally in control of their lives. Such a vision of reality is a far cry from Paul's notion of the body of Christ in which each one shares in the pain and joy of all the others.

Hay's philosophy of life may, in fact, be too simple. Its focus on individual choice neglects the complexity of human life and its embeddedness in a universe in which everything relates to everything else. The existence of starving children may be the result of choices—the decisions of parents, landowners, multinational corporations, and governments—but weather conditions also enter the picture.

The difficulties of Hay's linear approach to health and illness are highlighted in an interview recorded in Michael D'Antonio's *Heaven on Earth*. When D'Antonio asked Hay why AIDS exists in spite of all the affirmations and self-help techniques, Hay responded, "There has to be an answer. It has to be curable. I know there has to be a good reason, on a cosmic level, to explain AIDS."[21] Hay noted the resemblance between persons with AIDS and Nazi concentration camp survivors. Perhaps, Hay averred, persons with AIDS may be the reincarnated souls of Nazi tormentors, who now must endure a fate similar to that of their victims. When D'Antonio asked if AIDS might involve some form of karmic justice, Hay responded, "I am not saying that for sure. . . . But I look for connections in things, to explain things."[22]

A passion for connections and a desire for control haunt both Louise Hay's version of karmic justice and the fundamentalist Christian's proclamation that all things are willed by God. But the world is not that simple, nor can our lives be understood merely as learning experiences or reflections of the Almighty's will. In either case, a person's life is devaluated and rendered only a means to an end—either of a soul whose needs and purposes one cannot fathom in this lifetime or a god before whom one must bow regardless of its intentions for us. In either case, despite the words of love and care, there is little to inspire compassion and sharing. After all, "You have your reality and I have mine. You've chosen yours, just as I've chosen mine."

In a world of chaos and uncertainty, persons often desire a sense of security and control, whether it comes from the working of an omnipotent god or an omnipotent self. The possibility that some events may be random or unfathomable shakes this sense of order. In

Louise Hay's case, her philosophy of life reflects her experiences of having been an impoverished and abandoned child, the recipient of sexual and physical abuse. Could a little child be responsible for being physically and sexually abused? Certainly many children mistakenly feel guilty when adults abuse them. Could the cancer Hay contracted in midlife be a result of her resentment and low self-esteem? Could her cure have been entirely the result of changed behavior and dietary patterns? For Hay, the answer to all these questions is "yes"; the rape, the abuse, and the cancer were not random; they were the working out of her own personal karma. Her healing was equally the result of her own efforts. In response to her own cure, Hay proclaims, "Disease can be healed, if we are willing to change the way we think and believe and act."[23]

There is much power but little grace in Hay's philosophy. It is clear to me that the mind can kill as well as cure. Equally true, however, is the reality affirmed by Christianity: in a world of relationships, our healing and illness are part of a larger whole in which persons are never sick or healed on their own. Within the body of Christ, there are always implicit and explicit forces of grace that work toward healing and appropriate responsibility. If I am not God, but one of God's children or a cell in the body of Christ, as Christian faith maintains, then I can neither boast of healing nor take full responsibility for illness. My thoughts and emotions are powerful, but they are not *all*-powerful. As I will suggest later in this chapter, the "healing connection" involves the interplay of personal faith and choice, the results of one's life-style and previous decisions, the impact of the environment, and the presence of God. Apart from its relationship to the others, none of these factors can explain either healing or illness. Seen as components of a dynamic interplay, however, they enable us to penetrate, at least partially, the mystery of healing and illness.

Does the Body Exist?: Reflections on A Course in Miracles

One way to deal with issues of illness and physical imperfection is to claim that the body does not exist or has no value in human self-realization. Historically, this is the path taken by philosophical idealists, Hindu monists, Christian Scientists, and the first-century Gnostics. From this perspective, either the body is an illusion, the result of confusing the spiritual with the physical, or a prison hindering the growth of the soul. Accordingly, salvation comes from knowing one's unchanging and disembodied self.

Many critics of the new age movement describe it as a twentieth-century version of such gnostic ideas. While most new agers, like their gnostic forebears, understand salvation in terms of right knowledge, not all new agers scorn the body. Interest in body work, natural foods, and alternative medicine is a multimillion-dollar enterprise within the movement. Barbara Brennan proclaims the spirituality of the body through her energy work. New age environmentalists and wiccans cherish the creation spirituality of Native American religion and the ancient feminine wisdom of the earth. Still, much of new age philosophy promotes the notion that the body is an illusion or a temporary vehicle for the eternal soul.

Among the streams of new age thought, *A Course in Miracles* articulates the most consistently radical denial of bodily existence. According to the *Course*, "Whatever is true is eternal, and cannot be changed or change."[24] The only true reality is the divine mind that embraces every center of experience. In contrast to the eternal, unchanging unity of the divine mind, the world of bodies is a dynamic and ever changing multiplicity. Yet, as real as the world of bodies seems to be, it is, in fact, an illusion, the dream of the unenlightened and illusory ego.

In contrast to the traditional Christian and Hebraic affirmation of the goodness of the created world, the *Course* proclaims that "the body was not made by love" and that "God cannot come into a body."[25] The world we see is not evil, it is just an illusion, like a shadow on the wall. "God did not create it for what he creates must be eternal as Himself."[26] Further, "God did not make the body, because it is destructible and therefore not of the kingdom."[27] The goal of human life is to awaken from the dream, to realize that the world of separation and embodiment is an illusion, and to claim our reality as a child of God.

Since the world of flesh and bone is an illusion, the *Course* suggests that there is ultimately no need for medicine or even alternative modalities of treatment such as acupuncture, reiki, or massage. In many ways, the *Course* resembles Christian Science in its denial of sickness, death, and embodiment. Sickness, like embodiment itself, is the result of illusory thinking. According to Kenneth Wapnick, one of the most insightful commentators on the *Course*, "Sickness is a conflict in the mind that is displaced onto the body."[28]

In the words of the *Course*, "Sickness is a decision. . . . It is a choice you make, a plan you lay, when for an instant truth arises in your own deluded mind and all your world appears to totter and prepares to fall."[29] The only escape from illness is the spiritual awakening that delivers each child of God from the false world of embodiment and separation. When we discover our divine identity, both the body and sickness will disappear.

While the *Course* does not forbid the use of medicine or body work, it sees them as "spells" and "magic" that work only because of our false faith in them. The use of technological medicine and alternative somatic therapies is a compromise with truth for those who are not awakened enough to see reality as it is. Even to speak of universal energy fields, as does Barbara Brennan, is to fall into the illusion of separation. All children of God are one and to speak of different frequencies of energy is already, from the point of view of the *Course*, to make distinctions that lead to fear and isolation.

In its stark spiritual monism, *A Course in Miracles* points out some of the most severe tensions in the new age movement. If mind is the ultimate or only reality, then issues of health, politics, and relationships have no meaning except at the spiritual level. The concern one feels for one's own illness or global issues such as starvation, cancer, and apartheid is ultimately illusory. The pain we feel from sickness or injustice is merely the product of our attachment to separation and individuality. To be sick or oppressed is to be a victim of one's own delusion. "Sickness and sin are seen as consequence and cause."[30]

The *Course*, like Christian Science and Louise Hay, ultimately lays the blame for illness and injustice on individuals themselves. Though it speaks of love, the love proclaimed by the *Course* is a distant and unfeeling love that dares not share the pain or illusion of another, since to do so would risk one's own spiritual equanimity. Ironically, a philosophy based on the unity of all things can lead to an isolated individualism where persons are afraid to share their weakness or embrace the pain of their neighbor.

Most mainstream Christians would agree that separation from the

body of Christ is a form of sin and that feelings of loneliness and isolation may lead to disease. Yet Christian faith affirms that feelings of
separation do not create the body but are misguided ways of looking
at the body God has created and blessed. To be a member of the body
of Christ does not imply homogeneity or uniformity. Indeed, the diversity of gifts and the uniqueness and variety of persons is an essential
characteristic of the body of Christ (1 Corinthians 12:14–26). It is only
when we see the body of Christ through the eyes of separation and
fear that we feel alone. To embrace the body-mind-spirit unity is to
find healing, wholeness, and companionship even in the midst of illness and death. In contrast to the *Course*, Christian faith maintains that
to treat the body as an illusion is to deny the incarnation of God in
Christ and in the everyday world.

HEALING FOR A TRANSFORMED CHURCH
The Healing Ministry of Jesus
For a number of years, every Wednesday evening, a small group of
men and women met for a Service of Meditation and Healing at the
Westmoreland Congregational United Church of Christ in Bethesda,
Maryland. The service was simple—a few Scriptures, a time of quiet
and chanting, the sharing of concerns, the celebration of communion,
and the laying on of hands for anyone who desired. Each week the
participants brought their burdens for prayer and healing. Seldom
were the concerns dramatic by the standards of the televangelists—
grief, marital struggles, spiritual questions, chronic illness were the
usual focus—and seldom did the participants expect a dramatic
unveiling of divine power. Yet, each participant, including myself,
came in need of healing and wholeness.

Whether it is cancer, arthritis, or merely mental confusion, all forms
of disease are seen as reminders of the universality of pain and brokenness. Within such small circles of prayer, Christians are reminded
that no need is too small or too great to share with God and our friends
in Christ. Although dramatic healings may not always be observed,
the simple rituals of touch and prayer consistently bring experiences
of hope, peace, and wholeness.

Although it has been discontinued recently, the Wednesday night
healing service at Westmoreland United Church of Christ was part of

a quiet revolution in mainstream Protestant and Catholic Christianity. There is deep desire among many Christians for a faith that brings peace and healing to our chaotic world. Persons are asking their spiritual leaders and pastors to teach them how to pray and meditate even as they continue to challenge social injustice. Previously rationalistic churches, traditionally unaccustomed to the mystic realms of meditation or spiritual healing, are exploring ways of holistically addressing body, mind, and spirit. While these same liberal and mainstream Christians remain revolted by the theology and style of faith healers, they are nevertheless discovering new images of spiritual and holistic healing. They are rediscovering the healing ministry of Jesus.

Recently, I participated in a discussion of healing ministries with a number of my clergy colleagues in the Potomac Association of the United Church of Christ. Each of us was struggling to find a healing ministry appropriate to our various congregations. We shared our own problems with prayer and healing even as we confessed our need to go beyond the dry rationalism and mind-body dualism that has so long characterized our church. The fact that many Protestant as well as Catholic churches are open to this new holistic spirit is reflected in a "Resolution on Healing" approved by the General Synod of the United Church of Christ in 1978, which challenged that church to "reclaim healing through prayer, touch, and the Sacraments as a valid ministry of the church." Today, the very same Christians who are combing the Scriptures for historical and theological insights on issues of political action, homosexuality, and the role of women in the early church are also reclaiming those often omitted stories of Jesus the healer.

The gospels clearly portray Jesus as a healer. Salvation, for Jesus, was multidimensional in nature. A saved person requires a saved society, a healed spirit, healthy relationships, and a sense of physical well-being. Jesus' inaugural sermon in the Gospel of Luke (4:18) presents a holistic understanding of the new age God is initiating:

> The Spirit of the Lord is upon me, because God has anointed me
> to preach good news to the poor. God has sent me to proclaim
> release to the captives and recovery of the sight to the blind, and
> to set at liberty those who are oppressed.

Morton Kelsey notes that nearly one-fifth of the gospel stories are devoted to Jesus' healing ministry and the discussions occasioned by it. Forty-one distinct instances of mental and physical healings are described in the gospels.[31]

The significance of Jesus' healing ministry is revealed in his response to John the Baptist's disciples when they asked if he were the Messiah. "Go back and tell John what you hear and see; the blind see again, and the lame walk, lepers are cleansed, and the deaf hear, and the dead are raised to life and the Good News is proclaimed to the poor" (Matthew 11:4–5). Herein, Jesus' understanding of sickness and health differed greatly from the Hebrews of yesterday and many new agers of today. The Hebrews identified sickness with sin or with divine punishment, and health with moral uprightness and divine favor. Persons who were sick and women in their monthly cycle were considered unclean. Lepers and persons suffering from skin diseases were banished from society. A sick person was assumed to have committed a sin or violated divine law. Even to touch or be in the company of a sick person was to become unclean oneself.

Jesus challenged this isolationist, linear, and graceless notion of health and illness. When Jesus was asked about the source of a man's blindness, "Who sinned, this man, or his parents," he responded by saying that, "It was not that this man sinned or his parents, but that the works of God might be manifest in him" (John 9:1–3). Jesus challenged those who identified the accidental deaths of eighteen persons with their sinfulness (Luke 13:1–5). God does not hate the sinner or the outcast, for "God makes the sun to rise on the evil and good, and sends the rain on the just and the unjust" (Matthew 5:45).

While sickness may result from sinful behavior, sinfulness is not, for Jesus, the only cause of illness. Jesus maintained that persons were often possessed by forces beyond themselves, whether these be demons, illnesses of spirit and flesh, or habitual guilt. Accordingly, Jesus recognized that healing required the "hands on" presence of a loving community or a person to activate the faith and healing power of the sick. Just as illness reflected the presence of "a power greater than oneself," trust in "a power greater than oneself" was necessary for healing.

Not only did Jesus' words and touch bring healing, his very presence as an object of faith brought new life to sick and broken persons. To a woman with a chronic flow of blood, Jesus simply proclaims, "Your faith has made you well" (Matthew 9:20–22).

Jesus' healing ministry was ultimately inspired by his vision of God as a parent who desired that all God's children be whole in body, spirit, and relationship. Whatever challenged God's aim at love and healing must also be challenged. Whether by the laying on of hands, by words of forgiveness and ritual gestures, or by activating a person's faith, Jesus sought to reveal and mediate God's love to wounded humanity, even when encountering outcasts, such as persons with leprosy, would cost him his own ritual cleanliness.[32]

Physician J.W. Provonsha has suggested that Jesus of Nazareth rather than Hippocrates of Cos deserves the title of the spiritual father of medicine.[33] Indeed, Jesus seldom asked what caused a particular illness before he "treated" it. Like today's emergency medical teams, Jesus treated the sick, regardless of the illness and cause, and left the issue of moral edification to follow the experience of healing. Although Jesus identified personal faith with healing (Matthew 9:20, Mark 5:34, Luke 8:48), faith, virtue, and spiritual awareness are not seen as prerequisites to healing. In our spiritually "high-tech" age, Jesus' healing ministry reminds us that love is the ultimate source of healing. Only God's love is able to transform a tragic past into a glorious future and overcome the seemingly inexorable laws of cause and effect and karmic destiny.

As the creator of humankind, body and soul, in the divine image, God seeks the healing of every aspect of the human and global condition. Whatever destroys any child of God—be it social injustice, religious elitism and persecution, or bodily or mental illness—is an attack felt by God, and God's response was made clear in Jesus. God will remedy these ills by any means necessary, including God's own suffering (Philippians 2:6–11; Romans 5:5–11).

In contrast to those who claim that the age of healing ended with the first century, the Scriptures make clear that Jesus intended all of his followers to be unique healers of body and soul. As ambassadors of God's coming new age, the disciples were sent out "to heal the sick, raise the dead, cleanse lepers, cast out demons" (Matthew 10:8). In his final messages to men and women then and now, Jesus proclaims (John 14:12–14):

Truly, truly, I say to you, whoever believes in me will also do the works that I do; and greater works than these will he do, because I go to the Father. Whatever that you ask in my name, I will do it, that the Father may be glorified in the Son: if you ask anything in my name, I will do it.

The same healing power revealed in Jesus was also available to his disciples and is available to us today. As the Acts of the Apostles demonstrates, the early church lived in the expectation of signs, wonders, and healings.[34] Healing, then and now, is not a matter of human work, but a revelation of the power and love of God, which is the foundation of all things. From this perspective, the ever-present healing power of God is not a violation of the laws of nature or a supernatural intervention, but a disclosure in action of the deeper laws of the universe. While the apostle Paul maintains that healing is but one of the many spiritual gifts found in the body of Christ, healing of body and spirit is, nevertheless, essential to the body of Christ and has as much a place in the life of the church today as it did in ancient Corinth (1 Corinthians 12:4–12).

The Eclipse of Healing in the Church
In many ways, the eclipse of a lively healing ministry within the Christian church parallels its loss of spiritual vitality. No one has chronicled the movement from the healing of the whole person to the healing of the soul alone more thoroughly and insightfully than Episcopalian priest and theologian Morton Kelsey.[35] Kelsey notes that whereas Jesus and his followers understood salvation holistically, inclusive of body, emotions, spirit, and relationships, over the centuries Christians, influenced by the chaos of society as well as the impact of Greek philosophy, turned their attention to the life of the soul and its escape from this world of pain. For them the age of healing had passed. While once miracles and acts of healing were necessary to establish Jesus' divinity, God no longer needed to intervene supernaturally in bodily existence. Christians should focus on their eternal souls rather than on their swiftly deteriorating bodies.

Further, the recognition of God's role in healing diminished as the intimate parent of Jesus was eclipsed by the vision of God as an omnipotent and transcendent judge. In contrast to Jesus' vision of divine lovingkindness, the church of the Middle Ages revived the earlier image of illness as the result of sin, divine punishment, or the will of God. If sickness was God's will, passive acceptance was the only appropriate response. On the other hand, if sickness was punishment for sin, then confession, penance, and suffering were mandated as the appropriate responses. Whether it be the sickness of body, spirit, or society, there was little inspiration to challenge the status quo as "ordained by God." When divine healing was sought, it was understood as a supernatural interruption of nature bestowed only on the chosen few.

In the modern era, a total eclipse of Christian healing occurred through the impact of the dualistic philosophy of René Descartes (1596–1650) and his followers. Descartes maintained that the body and soul were separate and unrelated substances. Apart from God's will, there is no mind-body interaction. Whereas God speaks directly to the soul, the body is of little concern to God. Medicine and science care for the body, while the church is given custody of the soul. This neat separation of body and soul, however, led to a spirituality unconcerned with the physical world, and a science and medicine for whom values, spirituality, emotions, and justice are of little consequence. Within this dualism, the body-machine can be treated like any other machine, without considering the environment or the emotional and spiritual needs of the patient, and spiritual direction can occur apart from any concern for social justice or physical well-being.

Western medicine and religion have followed the guidance of Descartes. Yet this soulless medicine has proven to be as deficient in meeting human needs as the disembodied faith characteristic of much modern Christianity. Today, as modern technological medicine has been revealed to be a "god that failed," countless persons are seeking the guidance of alternative healers and practitioners of traditional Chinese and Indian medicine. An equal number have abandoned a church that has no place for the power of God or a holistic understanding of human existence.

A Healing Revival in the Church?

In spite of the eclipse of the belief in divine healing within mainstream Christianity, there has always existed a quiet healing movement within the church. At the fringes of rationalistic Christianity, mystics and pentecostals have affirmed that God encounters persons directly in spirit, mind, and body and that such encounters reveal new dimensions of human experience. This quiet healing movement is now making an impact on mainstream Christianity, especially as it invites mainstream Christians to embrace both holistic health and spiritual healing. In the following paragraphs I will tell the stories of five Christians who opened the doors to a healing ministry within the church through their marriage of mysticism, science, and holistic health.

The experience of Mikao Usui reflects the profound adventure in spirituality and healing that lies ahead for mainstream Christianity.[36] Educated by Christian missionaries in the last half of the nineteenth century, Usui embraced the Christian faith and became a minister-philosopher. He rose to the position of minister and principal of a boys' school in Kyoto, Japan. His comfortable world of devout but rationalistic faith was shaken one morning during the chapel service when he was asked by his students whether or not he believed the Bible to be God's word. When Usui affirmed that he did, his students wanted him to demonstrate his belief by performing a healing in their midst. When he was unable to perform such a feat, his students complained that his faith was too weak to lead them in their own spiritual journeys.

Usui left his position to learn about healing at a seminary in a "Christian country," the United States. Yet, despite his desire to learn the secrets of Jesus' healing ministry, neither his seminary teachers at the University of Chicago nor his advanced study of Scripture could provide the answer to his quest. Usui returned to Japan, where he turned to Buddhism, the faith of his parents. Yet, to his disappointment, he found that Buddhism, like Christianity, focused only on spirituality and left physical healing to physicians. Usui continued to search until he discovered a number of ancient healing symbols from Tibetan Buddhism. Still unable to experience the power of divine healing, Usui retreated to a mountain outside the city limits of Kyoto, where he meditated and fasted for twenty-one days. On the morning of the last day of his retreat, a light emerged from the darkness and rushed toward him, striking him unconscious. Within the light were the symbols of healing he had previously discovered. Now Usui realized the universal meaning and the power of Jesus' healing ministry. Just hours later as he walked down the mountain, he encountered a young girl with a toothache. When he touched her, the pain disappeared.

Filled with the spirit of Buddhist compassion and Christian love, Usui went to the slums of Kyoto, where he offered healing to the beggars. Soon, however, he realized that physical healing alone could not bring happiness. Physical well-being must be balanced by spiritual health.

Usui brought to Japan the practice of reiki, or universal energy. Over the years, reiki has migrated from Japan to the United States, where it is taught and practiced by a wide variety of persons in search of healing: ministers, nuns, and laypersons. As the term indicates, reiki involves the channeling of universal or divine energy through the practitioner's hands to the person receiving treatment. According to the philosophy of reiki, we exist in a sea of divine energy. We thirst for healing because we do not know how to access this divine energy. Reiki, like the laying on of hands, is simply a technique of sharing love and, in so doing, accessing the healing power of divine energy. Though it involves modest technical training, reiki is, in fact, only a sophisticated means of channeling the same energy that an untrained parent gives to her or his infant, or that two friends give to one another through regular hugs and prayers.

Reiki is a powerful witness to the healing connection in our time because it integrates both East and West and Christianity and Buddhism. I first learned reiki in 1986 and since that time have shared it with friends and family. To me, it is merely one of many ways of laying on of hands. After spiritually preparing, the reiki practitioner lays his or hands in a prescribed pattern on different sections of the body in order to balance as well as give divine energy. The healer is not the source of the energy. Rather, it flows from the divine source of all energy to the recipient through the hands of the practitioner. In receiving a treatment, one feels the peaceful warmth and comfort of touch and a deep sense of well-being. In giving the treatment, one notices variations in warmth, density, and energy movement in different parts of the body, depending on the well-being of a particular part. While the results of reiki are seldom dramatic, I am convinced from my own experience that reiki promotes healing as well as prevents illness. My wife and I have found that when someone is hurt or feeling ill in our family or among friends, our natural reaction is to touch them, to calm them down, and to channel the divine energy to the points of pain. At times, the results have been surprising—bruises have disappeared, headaches, toothache, and backaches have vanished, and panic has been stilled. As I give a treatment, I focus on God's light flowing though me and embracing the recipient with love and well-being. Within the philosophy of its teachers, the touch and sharing of energy essential to reiki are not violations of personal space or the laws of nature, but are reflections of the ever-present and beneficent divine energy permeating all things and giving health of spirit and body to all who are open to it.

Today, gentle movements of healing are also emerging from within the institutional church. Among Protestants the ministries of Morton Kelsey, Ruth Carter Stapleton, and the Order of St. Luke have touched the lives of many persons. Within the Catholic tradition, the work of Dennis and Matthew Linn and Francis McNutt is becoming well-known. Many of today's mainstream Christian healers find their inspiration in the lives of Ambrose and Olga Worrall and Agnes Sanford, ordinary and undramatic persons whose ministries have quietly channeled God's healing energy.

Olga and Ambrose Worrall's ministry had its geographical focus in Baltimore, Maryland, where for nearly forty years Olga worked actively in local Methodist churches and Ambrose worked as an aerospace engineer for the Martin Marietta Company. In many ways, their ministry parallels the healing practice of Barbara Brennan and provides a link between new age and Christian techniques of healing. As an aerospace engineer, Ambrose Worrall examined the phenomena of healing with the same care that he would examine an aircraft design. He concluded that healing is not a violation of the laws of nature but a revelation of the deeper laws of the divine energy that surrounds us. The Worralls affirm that "we are surrounded by a healing power, just as we are surrounded by magnetic fields, electricity, air, ether, and all the other forces around us that we do not see but which we are able to measure and study in various ways."[37]

The faith of the Worralls is profoundly empirical in nature. From the beginnings of their lives, both were sensitive to forces beyond themselves and had inclinations toward healing. Even as a child, Olga was clairvoyant and able to see the energy fields, or auras, surrounding the body. She had a natural desire to heal those around her. Whenever anyone was sick, Olga affirmed, "I will make it well, I will touch it and make it well."[38] As a child, Ambrose startled his Methodist Sunday School teacher by asking why persons today could not perform the miracles of the New Testament. When his teacher responded that Jesus healed only because he was the Son of God, Ambrose was disappointed and asked himself, "Did not Jesus set an example to us—to do as he did? Why should God stop such healing after sending His Son to give us the example of His healing love?"[39] Until they met one another, Olga and Ambrose kept their gifts to themselves and their close friends.

Although their adult lives were spent in the Methodist church, the worldviews and experiences of the Worralls would astonish and shock most liberal and mainstream Christians. In his quest for a scientific understanding of healing, Ambrose discovered that "miracles" are the working out of the omnipresent and unchanging laws of God at a higher level of consciousness than we habitually experience. In their openness to higher levels of experience, the Worralls, like Barbara Brennan, also encountered spirit guides who gave them guidance in their healing ministry. Ambrose explains the encounter with spiritual helpers in the following way:

> When a person has a need, he is sending out signals into what has been referred to as the Universal Mind. The Universal Mind responds to the signals and if the response can find a channel through which it can pass, it will be transmitted to the one in need.[40]

During their lifetimes, the Worralls worked closely with physicians and saw medicine and spiritual healing as different, but complementary, ways God seeks to heal persons. Indeed, they believed that spiritual healing is at work in every recovery from illness. While healing reflects the natural movements of divine energy, illness and accidents may occur as a result of insulating ourselves from divine energy through wrong thinking, wrong living, and lack of balance in one's life. The task of the healer is to serve as a conductor between the divine energy and the patient.

In their own ministry, the Worralls used prayer, the laying on of hands, and touching, as well as visualization exercises. Meditation and contemplation are essential to their understanding of healing. In moments of quiet, the healer as well as the person in need are able to attune themselves to the spiritual power, or frequency, of divine healing. As Ambrose Worrall notes, "Silence is vital for our study of healing. . . . for out of silence comes the power that heals."[41] In that silence, there is contact between the spiritual bodies of healer and patient.

Dramatic healings are not anomalies but revelations of the psychosomatic nature of reality. Long before the word "holistic" became fashionable, the Worralls saw health and illness as holistic in their embrace of the whole person. In the words of Ambrose Worrall,

> I think the spiritual body is greatly affected by the way a person thinks; I think the orbits of all the electrons, protons, neutrons . . . respond to the condition of the spiritual body, which in itself is affected by the way people think and their emotions. This is the source of illness, and we can destroy ourselves by our way of thinking or limit ourselves. . . . Practically everything is probably psychosomatic.[42]

Visualizing a person being well or an organ reaching its well-being is essential to this process of psychosomatic healing. For example, when parents brought their son to the Worralls to treat a hole in his heart, Ambrose affirmed that "the heart is becoming perfect," even as he visualized the hole growing smaller. Eventually, the child recovered to the point that plastic surgery could be done on the heart. In the process of healing, the Worralls saw themselves as open channels to divine energy. They did not claim to be healers, but rather to be instruments through which God worked in order to bring about healing of body and spirit.

Episcopal priest Morton Kelsey and his guide and mentor Agnes Sanford have been significant influences in the revival of sacramental healing within the Episcopal Church. A layperson and wife of an

Episcopalian priest, Agnes Sanford's work could be summarized in her belief that "Jesus Christ is with us and heals today."[43] Like the Worralls, Sanford believed that the whole universe, including our bodies, is permeated with divine energy. In contrast to the insentient world of Newtonian physics, Sanford affirmed that the universe is composed of lively energy units, each of which lives by the presence of divine light and spirit. Through prayer, one experiences an intensification of energy that brings abundance and healing to one's life and those one encounters. Healing is simply "channeling the flow of energy from God's being through man's being."[44] The gift of healing joins mysticism with the deeper science, revealed in divine law. "The essence of all healing is to become so immersed in the being of God that one forgets oneself entirely."[45]

Although Sanford saw healing as a gift of God, she, like the Worralls, noted that certain techniques can open a person to God's healing energy either for oneself or another. She used four steps of prayer as a means of opening to divine energy: 1) relaxation, 2) meditation on the reality of God, 3) asking for the indwelling of God's life, 4) making a picture of yourself or another as well, or whole, and giving thanks for the increase of divine power within one's life.[46] Like the Worralls, Sanford used both visualizations and affirmations in her healing ministry. In responding to a child suffering from a leaky heart valve, Sanford told him to

> pretend you're a big guy going to high school on the football squad. Shut your eyes and see yourself holding the ball and running ahead of all the other fellows. "Look at that guy!" the other kids will say. "Just look at him run. Boy he's strong. I bet he's got a strong heart!" Then you say, "Thank you, God, because that's the way it's going to be."[47]

By wrestling against the powers of destruction by using his imagination as well as traditional medical care, this young boy—like the heart patient treated by the Worralls—was healed of his leaky heart valve.

Sanford believed that illness is often related to our thought patterns. We bombard ourselves with such thoughts as "I'm getting the flu" or "catching a cold," rather than living by God's promises of health. As Sanford asserted, "the love vibrations and faith vibrations of God enter through our thoughts of life and love. In the same way, the destructive thought vibrations of Satan enter through our thoughts of illness, hate, and death."[48] Rather than surrendering to negative thinking and illness, Sanford counseled persons to make spiritual affirmations such as: "My nose and throat and chest are filling with God's light and if there are any germs there, they are being destroyed immediately" or "God's light shines in me and God doesn't have any headaches."[49] By turning toward God, Sanford believed that our lives are placed in a wider perspective that not only lessens the importance of pain but also releases the energy of healing.

Sanford, however, did not limit healing to individuals. She recognized that our world is sick and in need of healing. Accordingly, she suggested that the same prayers, affirmations, and visualizations used for persons may be used for the whole Earth. In our unity in Christ, we are inextricably related to one another. Our prayers change the spiritual atmosphere of the world and open the nations to higher guidance and greater harmony. Sanford asserted that "When enough people in a nation have learned to pray for a nation's forgiveness and for the world's forgiveness, nations will build their policies on the rock of loving-kindness and wars will be no more."[50]

Following in Sanford's footsteps is Morton Kelsey. Each year, Kelsey leads workshops and seminars on healing, the most well-known of which is at Kirkridge Conference Center in Bangor, Pennsylvania. At Kirkridge, his goal is "to provide an understanding of healing," including "its physical, emotional, liturgical, and spiritual aspects."[51] Kelsey believes that Christians are called to reclaim the spiritual gifts of the early church, such as mystical experiences, interpreting dreams, speaking in tongues, and healing.

Kelsey asserts that healing is possible because humans are "a hybrid of flesh commingled with what can only be called spirit."[52] When persons are touched by the transcendent, healing and mystical experiences are possible. Like Usui, Sanford, and the Worralls, Kelsey sees the intersection of divine and human love as the ultimate source of healing. According to Kelsey, "The basic idea upon which the Christian healing ministry is founded is that the healer is the instrument and carrier of the healing love of God transmitted through the Holy Spirit."[53] Following the thought of the German psychologist Carl Jung, Kelsey sees healing as involving not only the conscious mind but the awareness and healing of unconscious forces and memories. Journaling and dance as well as psychotherapy, prayer, and dream work can bring wholeness to our lives.

Healing, however, cannot be manipulated. It rests ultimately on the love of God. As Kelsey contends:

> Healing of the body, mind, and soul is a living process and an inner mystery. In the end this process is known only to the body and to the psyche, the whole psyche—conscious and unconscious—and to the One who created both body and psyche, who dwells in the psyche and draws it to the Kingdom. . . . In the end healing is given by God, the creative center of all things who is not only loving, but who has given us many ways of facilitating healing.[54]

In the healing ministries of Usui, Sanford, Kelsey, and the Worralls, mainstream Christians are empowered to recover the healing ministry of Jesus for an age of science and technology. Using the images of divine energy, mind-body relatedness, and the body of Christ, Christian healers can address the needs of new agers as well as old line rationalist liberals. In the emphasis on the universality of divine energy, mainstream Christian healers can become partners and guides of physicians, new age healers, and pentecostals alike.

Christian Healing for a New Age

Healing is at the heart of Christianity. The ministry of Jesus, of the early church, and of contemporary Christian healers proclaims the loving presence of God that permeates and unites mind, body, emotions, and spirit. In contrast to the modern rationalistic worldview, Christianity affirms a holistic vision of human existence in which there is no ultimate boundary between body and mind. While many Christians may be skeptical of the spontaneous and dramatic healings claimed by certain healers, our faith leads us to affirm, at the very least, the gradual and undramatic healings characteristic of holistic medicine and spiritual healing in tandem with modern medical treatments. Christians are called to be partners in the creation of health care systems that address the whole person from cradle to grave and from mind to body and spirit.

While many Western physicians define healing solely in terms of curing an illness, Christian faith claims that even the dying can be healed and that spiritual healing is the ultimate goal of prayer, visualization, and touch. In recent years, it is significant that Christians such as Dr. Cicely Saunders of St. Christopher's Hospice in London have been at the forefront of the hospice movement in England and the United States.[55] When medicine can do nothing more, Christians recognize the power of loving touch, companionship, and autonomy for the terminally ill. Christians have long understood that even when a person cannot be cured of an illness, he or she can be healed and experience a wholeness that transcends suffering and imminent death.

A Christian vision of healing is grounded in the image of the "body of Christ" and the human body as "temple of the Holy Spirit." As members of the body of Christ, we are constantly bathed in the energetic life of the Spirit. The Spirit that energetically courses through each cell brings with it life and health. The divine energy in the universe and in our bodies flows in the direction of healing at every dimension of life. When we close ourselves off to this spiritual energy, we suffer the very concrete consequences of alienation and isolation: ill health of body and soul. Reawakening to the movement of divine energy brings a renewal of health in both body and spirit.

Within the body, health and illness are not merely an individual issue. Christian faith challenges the linear cause-effect thinking characteristic of modern medicine as well as some new age healers. While we must take responsibility for our choices and behavior, our choices are never isolated—they emerge from a complex matrix that includes our parents, church, society, our past decisions, countless spiritual forces, and, last but not least, God. Each of these factors has an impact, however small, on our well-being. Negative thinking, parental emotional or physical abuse, social injustice, and unhealthy religion, for example, may leave scars in body and spirit that emerge in later life in terms of physical, emotional, or spiritual disease. While we are not entirely victims of our surroundings and may surmount even the most

toxic environments, we cannot escape the impact of our social relationships, for good or for ill.

Within the body of Christ, the healing connection is also profoundly relational in nature. If sin is grounded in our personal separation
from God and our neighbor, then reconciliation and openness to God
and our neighbor can activate the healing powers of body and spirit.
As Jesus' own ministry reveals, healing is a communal effort involving
personal faith in God, the openness and love of the healer, the presence
of a larger praying community, as well as the healing movements of
God's own presence. Each member of this healing matrix is both a
healer and a receiver of God's ever-present love. As Sanford and the
Worralls note, openness to God activates new dimensions of power
and insight. As we conform ourselves prayerfully and meditatively to
the movements of the divine Spirit, the boundary between ourselves
and God disappears and the Christ within us becomes a determining
principle in our knowing and doing. We become conscious participants in the mind of Christ and can know and act with the same
authority as did Jesus. From this perspective, the spiritual guidance of
the Worralls and the "high sense perception" of Barbara Brennan represent an achievable discipline, or practice, of the deeper awareness of
God's presence unavailable to normal everyday experience.

These deeper experiences of God are rooted in personal commitment to spiritual discipline and participation in a healing community.
In this context, the healing power of the eucharist, or holy communion,
is evident. As a place where Christians have encountered God through
the centuries and as a place where God chooses to be explicitly present, holy communion may be seen as a vortex or field of energy—that
is, a visible means of an invisible grace—by which God's presence is
mediated to humankind. The joining of bread and wine with Christ's
body and blood points to the holistic nature of all healing—what transforms the body influences the spirit, and spiritual growth brings
greater well-being to the whole body. Those who come to communion
in search of healing are surrounded not only by the power of God and
the faith of the gathered community but the energy of the "cloud of
witnesses" who have experienced God in the breaking of the bread
and the sharing of the cup throughout the ages. When God's healing
is expected and sought in such moments of worship and prayer, the

presence of God's healing love is magnified in ways that open our lives to a greater experience of divine power.

The healing ministry of the church must reclaim the power of prayer. The old adage "prayer changes things" is a truth for Christian healing in this new age. Experiments in long distance praying by the Worralls revealed that plants that were prayed for grew eight times faster than normal over a period of several hours.[56] An experiment conducted by physician Randolph Byrd indicated that cardiac patients who were the recipients of prayer experienced fewer side effects, had a lower rate of mortality, regained their strength more quickly, and left the hospital sooner than those patients who were not objects of prayer.[57] While prayer may not always change everything, such experiments suggest that prayer is an important influence in bodily as well as spiritual well-being. Physician Larry Dossey suggests that the most effective prayers, from a scientific perspective, are those that simply seek to follow God's will rather than seek a particular outcome.[58] From the perspective of the body of Christ, such nondirected prayers enable a person to attune her or himself to the divine current, which seeks what is best for the person and community alike.

While the expected cure does not always happen, spiritual healing, at some level, *always* occurs. A Christian healing ministry for the new age does not assume that sickness is God's will or completely the choice of any individual. There are times when even great faith cannot effect a somatic cure. Even spiritual leaders have died of cancer. The example of the apostle Paul provides an important insight for Christian as well as new age healers. Though he sought healing from his mysterious "thorn in the flesh," Paul was not cured in the way he had expected. But he was healed when he received the message that "My grace is sufficient for you, for my power is made perfect in weakness" (2 Corinthians 12:9). Lack of faith, the progress of illness, or the condition of society may all limit the healing power of God we experience.

Ultimately, all healing has whole-person spiritual healing as its goal. If physical healing, in the narrow sense of the word, is the only goal, then eventually all of us will be failures. Spiritual healing, whether or not it is reflected in physical improvement, finds its inspiration in the experience of God's presence and the support of the community of faith, the body of Christ, with which we are always connected even when we are unaware of it. Peace and joy in living and dying arise from the recognition that we are not limited to the apparently isolated body but are connected with the whole universe, the ultimate "body of Christ," and the divine spirit that brings life to the body. In affirming our connectedness in the body of Christ, we can proclaim with the apostle Paul that whether we live or whether we die, we are with God.

Although Christians may critique the approaches of various new age healers, a faith for the new age may well embrace those new age insights that affirm the gracefulness of life as it is reflected in the interplay of mind and body. While Christians may need to disregard Louise Hay's notions of absolute responsibility for health and illness, they may still find her affirmations helpful or choose to employ equally powerful Christian affirmations such as "the light of the world permeates my being" or "God loves and forgives me" or "God's grace is sufficient for me." In the spirit of Usui, the Worralls, and Sanford, Christians may even learn from the energy work of Barbara Brennan and others. All these healing modalities are ours through Jesus Christ, who has given us the grace and freedom to exercise the spirit of discernment as we seek to nurture and experience the graceful presence of God in sickness and in health.

QUESTIONS FOR REFLECTION AND DISCUSSION

1. How do you understand the healing power of God? Is healing in the spirit of Jesus still possible today?

2. What role do persons play in their illness and healing? What is the role of faith in the healing of body and spirit?

3. What factors have contributed to the eclipse of healing in the church? Is the growing interest in healing ministries a positive trend in the life of the church?

4. Does Christian healing differ from new age healing? What contributions can they make to one another?

5. How can unsuccessful healing prayers be explained? Why aren't all those who are prayed for healed? What factors, if any, make a difference between successful and unsuccessful healings?

CHAPTER FIVE

CHRIST IN THE NEW AGE

THE CHRIST OF THE NEW AGE

Introduction

Jesus once asked his disciples, "Who do people say that I am?" Their response was hardly uniform. "They answered him, 'John the Baptist; and others, Elijah; and still others, one of the prophets'" (Mark 8:27–28). From the beginnings of his ministry, there was no consensus as to the identity and mission of Jesus. To some, he was a miracle worker, to others, a false prophet. In the eyes of the sick and sinful, he was the giver of grace and new life. To the Pharisees, however, his table fellowship with sinners and women was a perversion of their sacred religious tradition. Those whose aims were political saw him as a messiah in the spirit of David and the Maccabees, one who would overthrow the oppressor and restore Israel to prosperity and political freedom.

Then, as now, people saw Jesus in terms of their own needs and expectations, and they interpreted him in terms of their own philosophical systems. Even the nineteenth-century "quest for the historical Jesus" and the twentieth-century "new quest" and "Jesus Seminar" have failed to discover a uniform picture of Jesus. Each scholar's picture of Jesus reflects the peculiarities of their own understanding of culture, the human condition, and the essence of Christian faith.

From the very beginning, Jesus was known by many names and many characteristics. The early church wrestled with what it meant for Jesus of Nazareth to be called the "Christ," "the Messiah," "the Son of God," "the light of the world," "the word of God," and the "son of man." While today some of us may recite the traditional creeds of the church with a sense of comfort and security, these ancient creeds arose in the context of heated battles over the nature of Jesus and his relationship to God and humankind. The various warring parties knew that our understanding of Jesus is a matter of life and death, of salvation and damnation.

Like our parents in the faith, contemporary Christians seek to know who Jesus truly is. Is Jesus truly the "Son of God"? Is Jesus fully human and fully divine, or some synthesis of these two natures? Is Jesus Christ eternal and one with God, or is he a creation of God like ourselves? How can the infinite God be present in a mere mortal? Is Jesus the only way humans can find salvation? These questions were not settled in the fourth and fifth centuries. In fact, these are the very questions that still perplex Christians who seek to be faithful to Christ as they dialogue with the new age movement in our time.

Today's Christians are confronted not only by persons who claim with certainty and boldness the saving power of Krishna and Allah and the liberation found through yoga and Zen meditation, they also hear the voices of persons raised in the church who now invoke the name of Christ in ways that seem strange and unfamiliar. Christians today, like the first disciples, must ask themselves, "Who is Jesus Christ for us today?" The responses we give are not just philosophical or theological in nature, they are personal statements that define how we look at the world, how we address the pluralism of our time, and how we seek comfort in our living and dying. They also define how Christians will share the gospel with the surrounding culture. But ultimately the question is not "Who do persons say that I am?" or "How does twentieth-century culture understand Jesus?" but "Who do *you* say that I am?" (Mark 8:29), that is, what does Jesus Christ mean to us personally in our own living, learning, loving, and dying? When we answer with Peter, "You are the Messiah," or "Christ," we must struggle, as did those first-century disciples, with the meaning of Jesus for

our time and to what extent we can embrace the many diverse interpretations of Jesus Christ without surrendering Jesus' special meaning,
derived from our own experience and the witness of the Christian tradition.

The new age movement often invokes the name of Christ. Indeed,
many new agers claim that they represent the true teachings of
Christianity, which were lost or repressed by a misguided, patriarchal,
and power-hungry church. This view is at the heart of James Redfield's
new age best-seller, _The Celestine Prophecy_.

At first glance, one might believe that the Christ of the new age is of
one piece with the Christ of the creeds and historic Christianity. Yet a
closer look reveals that the Christ of the new age is typically not the
suffering servant or crucified one of the gospels but a teacher whose
relationship to the historical Jesus of Nazareth is often only incidental.
An even closer look reveals that there is no absolute uniformity even
within the new age visions of Christ. While most new age visions of
Christ agree that the exoteric, or public, presentation of Jesus' teachings hides the true Christ, they differ in emphasis on the exact nature
of the esoteric, or secret, teachings they claim for Christ.

In this chapter, I will focus on the meaning of Christ for our time. In
particular, I will consider three strands of new age Christology: the
apocalyptic Christ represented by Benjamin Creme, the hidden Christ
found in Edgar Cayce's writings and in the _Aquarian Gospel_ of Levi
Dowling, and the Gnostic Christ affirmed by _A Course in Miracles_. I will
then reflect on the meaning of these images of Christ for Christians
today and suggest—in dialogue with new age thinkers as well three
prominent Christian theologians: John Cobb, Thomas Berry, and
Matthew Fox—an inclusive and empowering vision of Christ that
mainstream Christians can affirm.

The Apocalyptic Christ of Benjamin Creme
The flyer read, "The World Teacher, Maitreya, is now here." Beneath
the headline, the pamphlet stated:

He has been expected for generations by all of the major religions. Christians know Him as the Christ, and expect His imminent return. The Jews await Him as the Messiah; the Hindus look

for the coming of Krishna; the Buddhists expect him as Maitreya
Buddha; the Muslims anticipate the Imam Mahdi. The names
may be different but they all designate the same one: THE
WORLD TEACHER, whose personal name is Maitreya. His followers believe that he has returned now at the beginning of the
Age of Aquarius, as the teacher and guide who will unite the
world's religions and usher in the age of peace.

Could the long-expected Messiah be in our midst? Has Christ come
again—quietly and unobtrusively—as he did two thousand years ago?
Christians and new agers alike have anticipated the coming of a new
world order, a "new heaven and new earth," in which justice and
peace will prevail and God will be revealed in every heart.
    New age hopes for global transformation find their historic basis in
the Jewish and Christian expectations of a messianic age. In Christian
faith, the historical hope for a new age has traditionally centered
around the return of Jesus to bring about God's age of shalom and justice. From the very beginning, many Christians expected Jesus to
return during their lifetimes. The author of the First Letter to the
Thessalonians (4:16–17) proclaims that the Lord

    will descend from heaven, and the dead in Christ will rise first.
    Then we who are alive, who are left, will be caught up in the
    clouds together with them to meet the Lord in the air, and we will
    be with the Lord forever.

Although the expectations of these early Christians were not realized, there has always been a small minority of apocalyptic thinkers
within Christianity who seek the Lord's coming and constantly con-
sult the "signs of the times" in hope that Christ will come during their
lifetimes. Discontented with this world of sin and death, they study
world events and await Christ's full revelation.
    While liberals and Bible scholars in our time have labeled such
apocalyptic expectations foolish and ungrounded, the twentieth century has seen a resurgence in interest in the second coming of Jesus
Christ. In the 1960s, Hal Lindsey's guidebook for the final days, *The
Late Great Planet Earth*, sold millions of copies. Pentecostal and evan-

gelical Christians have speculated on the identity of the Anti-Christ and have identified the evil one with such personages as Hitler, Khruschev, Henry Kissinger, and even Ronald Wilson Reagan (since the combination of the letters of his three names comes to 666). Ironically, President Reagan noted the importance of these apocalyptic prophecies as he reflected on the possibility of nuclear war, while coincidentally he and his wife also consulted astrologers.

Although Jesus maintained that "no one knows" when the Messiah will come again, Christians throughout the ages have left their jobs and homes to await his coming. Although the date of Christ's return must constantly be revised, a sizable minority of Christendom still waits in expectation.

As we approach the year 2000, we are confronted with the death of one age and the possible birth of another. Even those who scorn messianic and new age thinking recognize that our world must be transformed if we are to survive into the twenty-first century. Borrowing the words of new age prophet and theosophical teacher Alice Bailey, former President Bush proclaims that we are the eve of a "new world order." It is clear that the old order can no longer be sustained politically, economically, and environmentally. Something new must take its place.

While new age visions of the future lack the cataclysmic imagery of fundamentalist Christian thought, they nevertheless share in the vision of a hopeful future for the faithful: the old age, the "Age of Pisces," the age of war, environmental destruction, patriarchy, and individualism is being eclipsed by a new age, the "Age of Aquarius," the age of spirituality, community, and prosperity. Like the early Christians, they look hopefully toward the future and imagine the possibility of divine beings who will lead our world from darkness to light. Whether working for a "green agenda" in the political realm or meditating regularly in groups in preparation for the "harmonic convergence," many participants in the new age movement believe that humanity must be transformed if it is to survive and that this transformation must come from an outside spiritual source as well as human effort. In images reminiscent of the eighth chapter of the Letter to the Romans, many new agers realize that this transformation must be cosmic and planetary as well as human.

Esoteric philosophers and mystics of the past and present have believed that, over time, Earth moves into and out of alignment with each of the twelve constellations of the zodiac, with a complete cycle of all twelve taking approximately 26,000 years. As we move toward the twenty-first century, we have just completed a 2150-year sojourn in relation to Pisces and are now entering into a new relationship with Aquarius.

Whereas the age of Pisces emphasized individuality, doctrinal certainty, and external exploration, the age of Aquarius will bring a greater concern for spiritual exploration, direct religious experience, and global community. In the last days of the Piscean Age, the dangers of technology, individualism, and exploration without spiritual foundation have led to a planetary crisis that must be confronted if the planet is to survive. As one age ends and another begins, there is much upheaval and doomsaying, but there is also much promise and hope. Some new agers claim that, in this time of crisis, a Christ will enter our world just as Christ entered before as Jesus of Nazareth at another critical time, the beginning years of the Piscean Age.

Has Christ come again without our knowing it? The flyer I had picked up asserted that Maitreya the Christ has indeed already come but is in seclusion in London. Perplexed by this announcement, I accepted the flyer's invitation to listen to the man described by the pamphlet as Christ's primary public spokesperson, Benjamin Creme.

The ballroom at the Holiday Inn in Bethesda, Maryland, was buzzing with activity as I arrived on a brisk November evening. Two hundred persons, mostly well dressed and affluent, gathered to hear the news of Christ's return to earth. A few minutes after the appointed hour, a genteel and kind-looking Englishman of seventy was introduced. Rather than addressing us directly, Creme invited us to listen to a taped address from Maitreya himself, channeled through the voice of Benjamin Creme. As a result of his intense training and commitment to the work of Maitreya the Christ (Maitreya, being the name of the expected one in Buddhism), Creme says that he is in constant contact with the World Teacher, and that Maitreya often "overshadows," or speaks through, his personality. Creme asked the audience to listen and meditate upon the message of the Coming Christ. The voice was slow and peaceful, almost hypnotic in effect. As the voice from beyond droned on, I found myself noting how appropriate that a tape recording, rather than a person, would be the chosen vehicle for revelation in a technological age.

Creme's lecture to the curious and the faithful gathered that evening summarized the philosophy of his earlier published works.[1] In every age, Creme proclaims, a spiritual teacher comes forth. In the Aquarian Age, this world teacher will be Maitreya the Christ, the teacher foretold by Jesus when he commanded his disciples on the eve of the Passover to follow "a man carrying a jar of water [the sign of the Age of Aquarius]" (Mark 14:13–14).

The World Teacher has now come into our midst, though to date he has been recognized by only a handful of followers. Since 1977, Maitreya the Christ has been living in relative obscurity in the Asian district of London. He has come to respond to our current crisis and is waiting for the right time to announce his presence to all of humankind.

Who is Maitreya the Christ? Creme asserts that while he is the World Teacher for the Aquarian Age, he is not the one and only son of God. Everyone is equally a divine child of God, a reflection in time and space of God. Christ differs from us only in terms of his God-realization. While we are entangled in the world of separation and conflict, Christ, in whatever form he is manifest, experiences and demonstrates the divinity we have forgotten. In the words of theosophical teacher Alice Bailey, who first acknowledged the imminent coming of the new age Christ, "Jesus was the forerunner of the future, an embodiment of all that was possible for humanity to achieve."[2] Because "the germ of Christ is in every person," each of us can accomplish Christ's own journey.[3] According to Creme, Maitreya the Christ invites each of us to "take your stand at my side, and let us together prove that Man is God, and that there is nothing other than God."[4]

Creme asserts that Jesus of Nazareth is only one of the many Masters who have come to lead humanity from darkness to light. There have been many other teachers or avatars, including Hercules, Hermes, Appolonius, and Buddha, whose purpose has been the revelation of God to humankind. Jesus' own Christhood is a result of his openness to God's guidance in his own human life.

Creme claims that historical Christianity's focus on the uniqueness of Jesus is a distortion of Jesus' essential message. Instead of focusing of Jesus' basic teachings—the value of the individual, the invitation to new birth, and the message of love—historic Christianity has created a gulf between God and sinful humanity, and Jesus and ourselves. It has focused on doctrine rather than experience. Creme suggests that the failure of Christianity to proclaim the original message of Jesus is due to its emphasis on the doctrine of sin rather than on love, and the continuing association of Christianity with Judaism's notion of a wrathful God. The Aquarian Christ will correct these misunderstandings and call Christianity to a new spiritual reformation. Creme speculates that, because of their rigidity and attachment to the exclusive possession of truth, fundamentalist Christians will be the last to accept the Christ in our time. The Christ of the Aquarian Age will bring an end to the narrow-minded dogmatism that stands in the way of the birth of the one world religion and the new world order.

Following the theosophical teachings of H.P. Blavatsky, Annie Besant, and Alice Bailey, Creme sees Christ as the supreme member of the brotherhood of Masters who guide the spiritual evolution of humankind from their sanctuary hidden in the Himalayas. The primary task of the Masters is to stimulate and guide humanity so that it might achieve, individually and corporately, the perfection the Masters themselves have already realized.

In words that stretch the imagination, Creme claims that although Jesus died on the cross, his personality was reincarnated as Appolonius seven years later in India. What Christians call the resurrection was the life-giving entry of Maitreya into the body of the lifeless Jesus on the third day. Since his ascension, Maitreya the Christ has been living in the Himalayas in expectation of his next embodiment. Creme proclaims that the human Jesus is still alive and is preparing to purify Christian faith in the new age. "Jesus is a real living man, who never left the world; who descended not from heaven but from his ancient retreat in the Himalayas, to complete the task he began in Palestine as great Master, Adept and Yogi."[5]

Today Christ is alive and well on planet Earth, and is preparing to reveal himself to humankind. In 1945 Maitreya the Christ announced to the other Masters his intention to return to the world at a time when humankind had more fully opened itself to God and to the needs of others. True to his promise, Maitreya the Christ arrived at London in 1977 by airplane, fulfilling, according to Creme, the Thessalonian prophecy that Christ would "descend from the heavens." Since that time, he has anonymously guided Gorbachev and has appeared incognito as one of President Bush's bodyguards. Maitreya the Christ has been joined by fourteen other Masters, including the historical Jesus who assists Maitreya in his work of transformation. The new age Jesus, an incarnation of Jesus of Nazareth, has lived in Rome since 1988 and will eventually mediate the new age to persons in the Christian church. Following the death of Pope John Paul II, Jesus will assume the throne of St. Peter and become the spiritual head of Christians.

Although Creme's vision of Christ is confusing and mythical in presentation, it has captivated thousands of persons who have not been touched by the message and church of the historical Jesus of Nazareth.

Creme claims that Maitreya will make his presence known to humankind through the use of mass communications. Though the day of Christ's appearance to humankind has been anticipated by Creme and his followers for decades, the full disclosure of Christ has yet to come.

The teachings of the apocalyptic Christ of the new age are similar to those of many other new age groups: the immortality of the soul, spiritual evolution through reincarnation, the inner divinity of each person, and the possibility that planetary and spiritual evolution may be enhanced dramatically through the cooperation of humankind with the Masters.

Followers of Maitreya the Christ are called to become "world servers." Whereas Jesus' initial message was aimed at personal spirituality, today Christ focuses on planetary issues. In a world of massive starvation and nuclear threat, Christ is concerned about politics and economics as well as personal evolution. As Creme notes, "Christ's message is sharing, justice, cooperation, and good will—the keynotes of the new age."[6] As Maitreya himself is reported to say, "There is only one way to know God and that, my friends, you already know. The way to God is the way of Brotherhood, of Justice and Love."[7]

Followers of this new age Christ are to become the political, economic, and spiritual forerunners of the Aquarian Age. They are to work for the achievement of a peaceful and just world in which

humankind will realize its oneness with all created things. The new
world order reflects Christ's own aims for equality, sharing of the
earth's resources, disarmament, and caring for the earth.

Meditation is at the heart of global transformation. Creme states
that in 1945 Christ inaugurated the Great Invocation, the Lord's Prayer
for the Aquarian Age. When it is used in groups, the Great Invocation
is said to bring forth cosmic energies and invoke the divine presence
for the transformation of the world. Since avatars or teachers enter the
world as a result of the interplay of divine will and human demand,
the use of the Great Invocation is claimed to be an essential factor in
the return of the Christ and the Hierarchy of Masters. If enough persons commit themselves to the Great Invocation, Christ will visibly
come again.

The philosophical vision of the apocalyptic Christ is reflected in this
Great Invocation to the Masters.

> From the point of Light within the Mind of God
> Let light stream forth into the minds of men.
> Let light descend upon Earth.
>
> From the point of love within the Heart of God
> Let love stream forth into the hearts of men.
> May Christ return to earth.
>
> From the centre where the Will of God is known
> Let purpose guide the little wills of men—
> The purpose which the Masters know and serve.
>
> From the centre which we call the race of men
> Let the Plan of Love and Light work out.
> And may it seal the door where evil dwells.
>
> Let Light and Love and Power
> Restore the Plan on Earth.[8]

The purpose of the Invocation is to spiritualize the planet through
channeling the subtle energies of the Masters to the dense energies of

matter. Its essence is to be found in the phrase, "May Christ come to earth." As Creme counsels, persons who use the Great Invocation can "invoke the energies of the Christ and the Masters and, acting as instruments, alter these energies to pass through their chakras [energy centers] in a simple and scientific manner."[9] As Creme continues, "the Invocation forms a telepathic current which draws them [the Masters], under law, into the world."[10]

Although political transformation is important, Creme believes its basis must be spiritual. By regularly meeting with other "transmission meditators," followers of Maitreya the Christ fulfill their vocation to spiritualize matter and contribute to the evolution of the planet by attracting the energy and presence of the Masters.

While mainstream Christians will struggle with Creme's complicated Christology and its departure from historical Christianity's understanding of Jesus of Nazareth, I believe that mainstream Christians can appreciate the interplay of action and meditation in the spiritual counsels of the apocalyptic Christ of the Aquarian Age. Unlike many other new age groups, the followers of Maitreya the Christ are committed to social justice and the transformation of the world.

Nevertheless, mainstream Christians must note that the Aquarian Christ of Benjamin Creme differs greatly from the Christ proclaimed by the Scriptures and creeds of historical Christianity. First, the incarnate Christ of the new age apocalyptic is but one of many saviors, different from ourselves only in degree of self-realization. He can teach us, but he cannot save us, for he is one of us and we are, even in our ignorance, like him. This is a far cry from the traditional Christian claim that Jesus is God's "only begotten Son" (John 3:16).

Christians must recognize that Creme, Bailey, and others challenge the scriptural and historical bases of Christianity. Today's Christianity, they claim, presents a false and parochial Christ. The true Christ preaches the unity of all religions and the divinity of humankind. The false doctrines of historical Christianity must be replaced by the more illumined doctrines of esoteric and theosophical Christianity. From Creme's point of view, the Bible is a hindrance rather than an aid in understanding the true Christ.

As they reflect on the claims made for Maitreya the Christ of the new age, Christians must affirm that although the Christian faith proclaims that Jesus Christ is the fullest embodiment of God's presence in the world, the Christ of historic Christian faith is not restricted to the church but is present in the spiritual transformation of humankind in its entirety. The truth and saving power present in Jesus Christ may appear under many guises. In contrast to Creme's teaching, however, Christians must assert that although humans, by their openness to God and commitment to justice, may become cocreators in the realization of the kingdom, they cannot compel its arrival or coerce God through any particular invocation. The Great Invocation resembles the incantations of magicians and sorcerers of ancient times. Against all such magical formulae, the Christian church has claimed that the grace of God precedes, even when it cooperates with, human efforts, and that God is always free to move in unexpected and surprising ways.

Still, the ultimate and underlying question in all Christological conversations is the relationship between Maitreya the Christ, or any other claimant to the title of Christ, and Jesus of Nazareth as revealed in the Scriptures and traditions of Christianity. Is Maitreya truly the Christ we should expect in the age to come or is he merely another false prophet? Is there any continuity between the One we as Christians worship and the spiritual leader Creme and others believe has come? While we cannot, from our human standpoint, fully discern the false from the true, we must trust the presence of God in the deepest insights of Scripture and Christian experience. Accordingly, we must seek to judge all claims to Christhood from the vantage point of the biblical witness to Jesus Christ and our evolving understanding of his work of personal and global transformation.

The Hidden Christ of Cayce and Dowling

Jesus' life has always been shrouded in mystery. From the "messianic secret" of Mark's Gospel (Jesus' desire to veil his divinity) to the "lost years of Jesus" (the unrecorded years between ages 12 and 30), Jesus' full identity has always eluded exact description. Even the resurrection, the most important event of Jesus' earthly ministry, was witnessed only by the faithful, and the accounts of this decisive event are vague and conflicting.

As we read the gospels, we learn very little of Jesus' inner life and even less about his childhood and family life. Jesus' formative years seem unimportant and irrelevant to the early church. The exact nature of Jesus' divinity remains a mystery and a source of controversy and heresy. Though the recently discovered Gnostic gospels have contributed another facet of the first-century understanding of Jesus, these gospels—like the other "histories" of Christ—reveal more about the community that produced them than they do about Christ.

Many persons in the new age movement are interested in the life of Jesus. Like many mainstream Christians, they have been turned off by the dogmatic and parochial Jesus of fundamentalist Christianity and are searching for an image of Jesus that reflects their own universalistic worldview. Consequently, in recent years, the works of Levi Dowling and Edgar Cayce have attracted the interest of many new agers. Although neither Dowling nor Cayce sought to displace the Bible, their insights come from what they believe to be an entirely different locus of revelation, the direct encounter with the memory of God, or the Akashic Record, and they present a picture of Christ far different from the New Testament accounts of Jesus' life. According to the esoteric, or secret, tradition, the Akashic Record is the "book of memory" that records every event that has occurred in the universe. When one encounters this "book of memory," one gains information not only of past historical events and one's own past lives but also may discover the hidden life of Jesus. For those with sufficient spiritual insight, these records are said to provide a more detailed and accurate source of Jesus' history than do the Scriptures of the church. As one might expect, this new source of revelation unveils a new Christ, one who resembles a new age teacher rather than a messianic savior.

Levi Dowling's *The Aquarian Gospel of Jesus the Christ* has become one of the bibles of the new age movement. Levi Dowling (1844-1911) was an Ohio-born son of a Disciples of Christ minister. A minister and physician himself, Dowling was a crusader for Prohibition. During the early hours of the morning, usually between two and six, Dowling received revelations that he transcribed for his new age gospel.

Although the *Aquarian Gospel* parallels the New Testament in many ways, it also presents a picture of Jesus' life and mission greatly different from the image of Jesus treasured by historical Christianity. The spirit of the Aquarian Christ can be found in one of Levi Dowling's manuscripts:

Thus Christ made manifest Love's power to save; but men forget so soon, and so Christ must manifest again and again.

And ever since man took his place in the form of flesh the Christ has been manifest in the flesh at the first of every age.[11]

In the spirit of other new age writings, the *Aquarian Gospel* affirms a continuity between Jesus Christ and ourselves. "What I have done," Jesus states, "all men can do, and what I am all men shall be."[12]

What is most remarkable about the *Aquarian Gospel* is its picture of the "lost years" of Jesus. According to Dowling, Joseph, Jesus' father, was a devoted member of the Essenes, a secret monastic order living near the Dead Sea, whose members sought to purify themselves in preparation for the coming of the Messiah. As a child, Jesus read the Hindu Vedic hymns as well as the Psalms and desired to "go from Jewry and meet my kin in other countries of my Fatherland."[13] At age twelve, following his encounter with the priests in the Temple, Jesus set off on a journey that would take him to India, Tibet, Persia, Assyria, and Greece. In India, Jesus learned the arts of healing and challenged the caste system. Among the Hindus, Jesus proclaimed his universalist message: "The God I speak about is everywhere; he cannot be compassed with walls, nor hedged about with bounds of any kind."[14] Though called by many names in many lands, God is everywhere "the causeless Cause, the rootless Root from which all things have grown."[15]

In Egypt, Jesus took his final initiation and, after strenuous efforts and the overcoming of temptation, was "Christed" by the spiritual leader of the Egyptian mystery religions. Jesus is a human like ourselves who earned God's blessing by his moral and spiritual achievements.

While the *Aquarian Gospel* often merely repeats selected New Testament stories, its greatest departure from the New Testament picture of Jesus is found in its affirmation of the doctrines of karma and reincarnation. Whereas the gospel accounts imply that sickness and ill fortune are not the result of one's previous sins, the *Aquarian Gospel* takes an opposite course: illness is the result of one's bondage to the past, that is, one's karma. While Luke's account of deaths due to

Pilate's irrationality and the fall of the tower of Siloam are challenges to repentance for those who smugly maintain their righteousness (Luke 13:1–5), the *Aquarian Gospel* identifies these events with the working out of one's karma.

> Did God bring on this slaughter [by Pilate] because these men were doubly vile? . . . Were these men vile [who died as a result of the fall of the tower of Siloam]? and were they slain as a punishment for some great crime?

> And Jesus said, we cannot look upon a single span of life and be judge of anything. There is a law that men must recognize: Result depends upon cause. Men are not motes to float about within the air of one short life, and then be lost into nothingness. They are undying parts of an eternal whole that come and go . . . just to unfold the God-like self. A cause may be a part of one brief life; results may not be noted till another life. . . . Now we look; the men who now are slaves, were tyrants once; the men who now are tyrants have been slaves. . . . And men are sick, and halt, and lame, and blind because they once transgressed the laws of perfect life, and every law of God must be fulfilled.[16]

In the *Aquarian Gospel*, there are no innocent victims, nor is there the unmerited grace of the Cross. The *Aquarian Gospel* follows certain trends in the Hebraic understanding of health and illness. Although this view is challenged by the author of the Book of Job and by the biblical Jesus, it was common for the Jews to identify poverty and illness with sin and disobedience. Dowling's account of the causes of illness shares the same spirit as Louise Hay's descriptions of the metaphysical causes of AIDS, that is, illness and injustice are ultimately the sufferer's own fault. In a world of strictly determined rewards and punishments, Jesus does not need to suffer on our behalf. Rather, he manifests the Christ to humankind and reveals by the cross and resurrection, "the power of man to conquer death; for every man is God made flesh."[17] Because we are divine, we do not need a savior; we need a teacher. As Jesus reflects on his own mission, he states that his life is a "pattern . . . which shows the possibilities of man. What I have done all men can do, and what I am all men shall be."[18] Like the lion who thinks himself a goat, we are Christs who have forgotten who we truly are.

The *Aquarian Gospel* concludes by revealing the "lost days" following the resurrection. In Jesus' final earthly days, he travels to India, Persia, and Greece as well as Palestine. His Great Commission to his followers is: "You shall go to all the world and preach the gospel of the omnipotence of man, the power of truth, the resurrection of the dead; He who believes in this gospel of the son of man shall never die; the dead shall live again."[19]

Edgar Cayce (1877-1945), like Levi Dowling, came from a conservative Christian background. A lifelong Sunday School teacher, Cayce read the Bible from cover to cover every year and proclaimed that, "I am determined that as long as I live, I will know nothing among men save Jesus Christ and him crucified."[20] Even though his psychic "readings" of the Akashic Record sharply contrasted with his fundamentalist roots, Cayce still maintained that the Bible was "the greatest of all vessels of psychic experiences."[21] In meditative and sleeping states, Cayce was able to "lay aside" his own personality in order to contact the universal memory. In his dreams, Cayce discovered a new Christ and a new understanding of human existence, one that would radically challenge the Christ of his waking Christian faith.

In many ways, Cayce and Dowling relate a similar version of the "lost years" of Jesus Christ. Cayce's Jesus also came from Essene roots, was tutored by the Essenes, and studied in Persia, India, and Egypt as well as Palestine. John the Baptist also studied in India with Jesus. By his presence in these foreign lands, Jesus influenced the development of Islam, Buddhism, and Hinduism. In contrast to Dowling, however, Cayce's Christ did not study in Greece.

Cayce's most innovative contribution to the "lost years" theory of Jesus is his concept of Christ's "many lives." Christ has had as many as thirty incarnations, including Adam, Joshua, the father of Zoroaster, Melchizedek, and Enoch. Indeed, in his incarnation as Adam, Jesus committed the "original sin." As a result of his sin, Jesus' incarnational task was to redeem fallen humanity.

Jesus of Nazareth is but one of the many incarnations of Christ. As Cayce puts it, "Jesus is the man, Christ is the message which incarnates in all ages—Jesus in one, Joshua in another, Melchizedek in another."[22] While the presence of Christ in Jesus is important, it is not unique or all-important.

The Christs of Cayce and Dowling are radical departures from the Christ of historic Christianity. Indeed, like the Christ of Benjamin Creme, these Christs are not rooted in the evidence of Scripture or history. The "lost years" of Cayce and Dowling and the "Himalayan retreat" of Creme and Bailey find their basis in an encounter with timeless knowledge rather than anything that can be historically verified. From the point of view of the biblical historian, there is little reason to believe that Jesus directly encountered the Essenes, even though both Jesus and the Essenes looked forward to the Kingdom of Heaven. Further, despite the claims of theosophists and new agers, there is no biblical evidence for the doctrines of karma or reincarnation. Followers of Creme, Cayce, and Dowling would suggest that passages relating to such esoteric concepts—the insights of the Gnostics, for example— have been eliminated from the texts for theological and political reasons. But there is little historical evidence that this occurred in the case of reincarnation.

Most important, the concept of grace seems to be virtually absent in the "hidden Christs" of Dowling and Cayce. The sinner must accept the results of his or her actions in this life and the next. No external force is present to save us. For Cayce and Dowling, forgiveness and pardon do alter one's karma or future, but only as they allow sinners to see who they really are—a part of God, a potential Christ. Salvation comes from self-knowledge and acts of love, rather than the active presence of God.

While Christians cannot absolutely deny the possibility that Jesus spent his "lost years" in India, Persia, Egypt, and Greece, there is no textual reason to affirm these revisions of Christ's biography. The Jesus of the Bible clearly did not criticize his fellow religious from the perspective of Hinduism but from his understanding of the essential message of Judaism. Jesus was crucified as a messianic figure and not a teacher of meditation or past lives. Creme, Cayce, and Dowling compel open-minded Christians to make a choice as to what is most definitive about Jesus and his message. Is Christianity a religion of the few or the many? Is Christ an esoteric teacher in the spirit of the Hindu

sages or a prophet of God and friend of sinners incarnating the highest values of the Hebraic tradition? Is the Bible the authoritative witness to the life and message of Jesus Christ? Without succumbing to
relativism or fundamentalism, Christians must assert that one horn of
the dilemma is closer to the truth than the other. The choice we make
will determine the Christ we follow.

The Gnostic Christ of A Course in Miracles

From the very beginnings of Christianity, the incarnation and death
of Christ were problematic to many Christians. Whereas some
Christians emphasized Jesus' humanity and continuity with
humankind, other Christians saw the incarnation and suffering of
Jesus as a scandal. Then and now, the idea that God participates in
earthly existence and shares in the pain and tragedy of the world has
been incomprehensible to a segment of Christendom. In the decades
following the departure of Jesus Christ, a sizable minority of
Christians were influenced by the Platonic notion that the body is an
unfit dwelling place for divinity. Historically, these Christians and
their non-Christian counterparts have been described as Gnostics.[23]
The term "gnostic" comes from the Greek word "to know" and
implies, on the one hand, the possession of a "special knowledge" of
reality and, on the other hand, the importance of knowledge of the
truth as the ultimate means of salvation.

In contrast to orthodox Christianity's emphasis on the incarnation
or embodiment of Jesus as revealed in his birth, childhood, cross, and
resurrection, Gnostic Christians claimed that the incarnation was an
illusion. Although Jesus' body may have suffered, the "real" Jesus was
beyond joy and sorrow. At the cross, Jesus laughed at the ignorance of
those who thought they were crucifying him.[24] The crucifixion of Jesus
did not redeem humanity from guilt, as Paul and other early
Christians felt, but was "the occasion for discovering the divine self
within."[25]

Whereas orthodox Christianity wrestled with the polarity of Jesus'
continuity and discontinuity with humankind and the scandal of "the
word made flesh" (John 1:14), the Gnostics held that Jesus and
humankind share the same spiritual essence. Whereas we are lost in
our ignorance, Jesus is a "divine spark" that has come to self-aware-

ness. Beneath the illusion of his body, Jesus is a divine teacher whose enlightenment enables him to be "a guide who opens access to spiritual understanding."[26] As a spiritual teacher, Jesus is ultimately expendable. "When the disciple attains enlightenment, Jesus no longer serves as his spiritual master: the two have become equal—even identical."[27] As the Jesus of the Gnostic *Gospel of Thomas* proclaims, "I am not your master. . . . He who will drink from my mouth will become as I am; I myself shall become he, and the things that are hidden will be revealed to him."[28]

In the spirit of today's new age Christologies, the Gnostics saw orthodox Christianity as the true heresy. The Gnostics felt that orthodox Christians, in their attachment to the physical world and the significance of the cross and resurrection, were ignorant of the true mysteries of Christ's life and teachings. The Gnostics denied the historicity of the cross and resurrection. They claimed to be the secret source of the apostolic tradition.

Today, in an age of quantum physics, evolution, and technological expansion, the voice of a new Gnostic Christ echoes within the new age movement. This Christ speaks through *A Course in Miracles*, a "channeled text" given to Helen Schucman (see chapters three and four).

Like his Gnostic predecessors, the Christ of the *Course* claims that historical Christianity has misunderstood the world and his mission. Whereas Judaism and Christianity have proclaimed that the physical world is the "good" creation of God, the *Course* contends that the physical world is an illusion resulting from our unenlightened perceptions. Only the eternal is real. Since the body is ever changing and physical, it must be an illusion. "God did not make the body, because it is destructible and not of the kingdom."[29] According to *A Course in Miracles*, salvation cannot be achieved by means of an illusion. Accordingly, the incarnation, crucifixion, and resurrection, taken as physical events, have no place in spiritual attainment.

Historical Christianity has misunderstood the meaning of the crucifixion, says the *Course*. Blinded by ignorance and guilt, Jesus' followers saw the crucifixion as an act of atonement and forgiveness of sin, rather than as an opportunity to discover that death and individual existence are illusions.

In the spirit of Gnostic as well as new age thought, the *Course* stress-
es the continuity between Christ and ourselves. We are all Christs.
Jesus' uniqueness was his own God-realization. Jesus "recognized
himself as God created him; and in so doing recognized all living
things as part of him" and one with God.[30] Jesus "became what all of
you must be—the perfect son of God. . . . He leads you back to God."[31]

From the point of view of the *Course*, Jesus is not a savior, but an
older brother and guide who shows us who we are and enables us to
become what he is. According to the *Course*, Jesus' mission was to
show that separation from God never really happened and that we
have always been one with God. As the Christ of the *Course* maintains,
"There is nothing about me that you cannot attain."[32] In Jesus' message, there is no cross or suffering. These concepts, so central to historic Christianity, are myths that must be understood spiritually rather
than physically or historically.

The Christ of the *Course* has no interest in physical healing or in the
transformation of society, themes so central to the mission of the biblical Jesus. Since the body does not exist, sickness and healing are equally illusions. The only captives to be released are those who think the
physical world is real, and the only blind to be cured are those who do
not know their true spiritual nature. Social justice is a matter of indif-
ference, since the body and unjust social structures are illusory. "Our
function in the world is not to feed the hungry, free the oppressed or
serve any other social cause. . . . How can we serve a world that is not
there?" asks Kenneth Wapnick, the primary philosophical commentator on the *Course*.[33] Spirituality is centered on the transformation of
perception rather than behavior. As we learn to see differently, we discover that all things are God and that our everyday judgments of
wealth and poverty, oppression and liberation, and war and peace are
illusions. There is nothing to liberate and no one to feed, since the only
reality is the one God. Even the doctrine of reincarnation, so important
to some new agers, is of no consequence, since there is no body to be
ensouled. Only the Divine Mind exists. The illusion of embodiment
and reincarnation arises from our attachment to a world of separate
and changing things.

While mainstream Christians can appreciate the spiritual discipline
and the use of affirmations characteristic of the *Course*, it is clear that

they must differentiate between the metaphysics, Christology, and ethics of traditional Christianity and those of the *Course*. While Christians proclaim that the sense of separation is an illusion, since we are all joined as members of the body of Christ, they also affirm that communion with Christ does not negate personal uniqueness or embodiment. Individuality and diversity are divine gifts meant for sharing and not the basis for competition or separation. In the body of Christ, "there is neither Jew nor Greek, there is neither slave nor free, there is neither male nor female; for you are all one in Christ Jesus" (Galatians 3:28).

Traditional Christianity affirms that the physical body is not the result of sin and need not be a vehicle of separation. From a holistic point of view, the spiritual unity we seek is specifically made manifest in physical terms through our sexuality, our friendship, and our empathy with those experiencing injustice, pain, and suffering. In light of the biblical proclamation that "the heavens declare the glory of God" and the "body is the temple of the Holy Spirit," embodiment is a means of understanding God and not an illusion to be overcome.

In contrast to the *Course*, mainstream Christians affirm the centrality and nonnegotiability of the incarnation of Jesus Christ. To proclaim that "the word was made flesh" is to recognize that salvation relates to every aspect of our lives and that there is no ultimate distinction between politics and spirituality. Because Jesus took flesh, we are able to worship God in the operating room, the soup kitchen, the gymnasium, and the picket line.

It is worth noting that in its doctrine that physical existence is an illusion, the *Course* presents a vision of Christ that stands apart from other new age conceptions of Christ. Although the Christs of the new age movement commonly preach a gospel of inner divinity and continuity between Christ and ourselves, the Christ expected by Benjamin Creme and the Christ of Cayce and Dowling take on the flesh and have at least some concern for the morality of persons and nations. Thus, while Christians may appreciate the insights of the *Course* as a means of psychological transformation, they must be willing to challenge its Gnostic metaphysical teachings. If it is to be any value to Christians, the *Course* must be "demythologized," that is, understood metaphorically and personally rather than as a description of reality as it is.

A CHRIST FOR THE NEW AGE

Christology in an Age of Pluralism:
John Cobb, Thomas Berry, and Matthew Fox

Each era has its own challenges and puts forth its own distinctive vision of Christ and his work. Christians at one time claimed a monopoly on truth and salvation, but such imperialistic claims seem anachronistic today. At the predominantly Catholic and Christian university where I minister and teach, Christ is no longer the only spiritual option for students and staff. Flyers proclaim enlightenment through Buddhist meditation, transcendental meditation, and the teachings of Baha'i. The university supports ministries to Islamic as well as Christian and Jewish students and occasionally sponsors lectures by Buddhists and Hindus.

In this age of pluralism, many Christians have abandoned the task of articulating a faith for our time. On the one hand, some Christians have denied the possibility of truth and salvation apart from an explicit doctrinal relationship to Jesus Christ. On the other hand, many mainstream and liberal Christians see faith in Christ as little more than a personal preference or the result of one's cultural upbringing. But if Christianity is to make any claim for truth, it must avoid the extremes of theological absolutism and cultural relativism. Christians must affirm that while Jesus Christ is universal in his relationship to all things, Jesus Christ is also particular and personal in his role as savior and teacher first among the Jewish people and then, through his disciples, across the whole earth. These polarities must be held in creative tension if Christians are to affirm the centrality of Christ as they dialogue with persons in the new age movement and the other religious traditions. Further, Christians must remember that there have been many visions of Jesus Christ in Scripture and church tradition and that Jesus Christ's universality is revealed in the ability of each age and culture to experience Christ in healing and liberating ways.

Among today's theological visionaries, no persons have explored the proclamation of Christ for our pluralistic, ecological, and ecumenical age more fully than Thomas Berry, Matthew Fox, and John Cobb. While the controversial former Catholic and now Episcopalian priest Matthew Fox is well known among mainstream Christians and is seen as the primary representative of "healthy" Christianity among many new agers, the scholarly John Cobb, Professor Emeritus at the Claremont Graduate School and the School of Theology at Claremont in California, is known primarily among college professors, ministers, priests, and lay Christians with a strong background or interest in theology. Thomas Berry, priest-ecologist, has been a major influence in the movements of ecological reflection and creation spirituality among Roman Catholic religious leaders.

Although he has not written explicitly on Christology, Thomas Berry's "new story" of the universe has profound Christological implications. In light of findings in physics, astronomy, and biology, says Berry, Christology and all Christian teaching must be transformed. Whereas the "old story" saw humankind and the work of salvation as unrelated to the natural world, the "new story" compels us to see Christ's presence in terms of God's creativity within all things and not just the redemption of human beings. Neither Christ nor salvation can be limited to the church or human existence. Rather, since the universe is the primary revelation of God, Christ must be seen at every stage of the evolutionary movement and the cosmos in which we live, move, and have our being. The creation-salvation story cannot be confined to human time frames but stretches into billions of years. Christ has been at work not only in Christianity but in Buddhism and Hinduism. The spirit of God has been revealed in all human cultures, each in its own form, as well as in the entire evolutionary and cosmic process. The cosmos, both in its parts and in its entirety, is the body in which God is incarnate.

While Berry does not explicitly mention the new age movement, it is clear that his understanding of Christ makes room for the divine revelation in the many-faceted new age movement. However, Berry's work would be critical of those aspects of the new age movement that deny the importance of embodiment, history, or our responsibility to seek justice for all beings.[34]

According to Matthew Fox, Christianity is in need of a living cosmology and a cosmic Christ. Doctrines such as original sin and salvation only through Jesus Christ fail to respond to today's most critical needs—world hunger, political injustice, and the destruction of Earth. If Christianity is to respond to contemporary persons, it must undergo a Christological reformation. While Christians need not abandon Jesus

Christ, they must balance the particularity of the historical Jesus with the universality of Christ, "the true light which enlightens everyone" (John 1:9) and "the pattern which connects all the atoms and the galaxies in the universe, a pattern of divine love and justice which all creatures and all humans bear within them."[35]

Through his examination of the Christological hymns of the New Testament, Fox contends that his vision of the cosmic Christ reflects the scriptural witness: Christ is the one "who reconciles to himself all things, whether on earth or in heaven" (Colossians 1:20); who "unites all things" (Ephesians 1:10); and from whom "all things came to be" (John 1:3). Jesus of Nazareth as a mystic, mystical teacher, and liberator of the oppressed awakens our own experience of the cosmic Christ residing in all things.

As a living reality in our world, Christ suffers with and cries out in the experiences of the poor and the oppressed and in the destruction of the earth. As "the word made flesh" (John 1:14), Jesus Christ is one with us as well as unique in human history. But, Christ's presence goes beyond the historical Jesus and the human race. Christ is not just the Lord of the church or humanity but the guiding presence of the universe.[36]

Fox's affirmation of the presence of God in the physical universe is the basis of his critiques of the new age movement. Fox maintains that certain trends in the new age movement are

> all space and no time; all consciousness and no conscience; all past life experiences, angelic encounters, untold bliss, and no critique of injustice or acknowledgement of the suffering and death that the toll of time takes. In short, no body.[37]

To those trends in new age thought that deny the body or the importance of history and social concern, the Cosmic Christ of Matthew Fox says, "Enter time. Behold my wounds. Love your neighbor. Set the captives free."[38] For Fox, divine immanence does not lead to apathy and amorality, but to the full realization of Christ's presence in the body as well as the spirit.

John Cobb sees Christ as the principle of "creative transformation." In contrast to the emphasis on the unchanging divine self characteristic of most new age thinking, Cobb envisages God, Christ, and the self in terms of dynamic movement and process. Christ is not a static and unchanging reality, but a dynamic and relational force that moves through all things. The work and meaning of Christ changes from age to age, moment to moment, and person to person.

As the principle of creative transformation, Christ is the source of novelty and adventure. Cobb maintains that while Christ is present in all things, Christ is most definitively present in Jesus of Nazareth. "What is present or incarnate in Jesus is present or incarnate in all things and is the light of understanding in all people."[39] Jesus Christ is unique not because he is the *only* place where truth or salvation are found, but because he most fully embodies the principle of creative transformation. "Whereas Christ is present in everyone, Jesus is the Christ because the incarnation [the principle of creative transformation] constitutes his very selfhood."[40] The incarnation of God in Jesus is not only a result of divine activity, it is also the result of Jesus' own receptivity to God's aim for him. Jesus' openness to God allowed him to reveal God fully in human existence. As such, he is not only different in degree of God-consciousness, he is also different in kind and, unlike ourselves, may appropriately be called divine as well as human.

The dynamic God revealed in Cobb's process theology is radically different from the unchanging God of the new age movement. In Christ, the status quo—whether it be political, ecological, interpersonal, or spiritual—is challenged. Far from being amoral, Jesus Christ's spirituality compels his followers to challenge every form of evil, whether it is manifest in sickness, political injustice, or religious intolerance. Divine perfection embraces, rather than represses, suffering and change. Indeed, God's perfection is found precisely in God's transformation of suffering and pain into something most holy and beautiful. God in Christ is not aloof from the world but is the "fellow sufferer who understands."[41]

Cobb and Fox present a vision of a transformed Christianity that opens its heart to otherness and is willing to grow by its relationship to non-Christian movements. Christ is the source and goal of this openness, for Christ is creatively present even beyond the walls of the church—even in theosophists, Buddhists, and new agers. Faithfulness to Christ calls us to internalize the pluralism of our time, even when it challenges traditional and cherished understandings of our faith.

A Christ for the New Age

Can mainstream Christians proclaim that Christ is "the way, the truth, and the life" in an age of pluralism and alternative religious movements? The answer is an emphatic "yes!" While Christians cannot claim to have the whole truth or even fully understand who Christ is, they can with vitality and humility proclaim that "God was in Christ reconciling the world" and that Christ has a relationship with all things as well as with each thing. Our understanding of Christ must be grounded in the surprising and unexpected good news that in Christ the lost are found, the sick are healed, and the oppressed are freed. Christ must be proclaimed today so that our faith is truly good news for all persons. Though intensely personal, the gospel must be inclusive of time, place, and perspective. As the early church fathers proclaimed, wherever truth, beauty, and love are found, surely Christ is present. Christ brings good news to every aspect of our lives—our relationships, our physical existence and sexuality, our emotions and intellect, our spiritual life and social responsibilities. There is no room for world-denial in a holistic Christology. In the life, death, and resurrection of Jesus Christ, we discover that every aspect of life is important and that God in Christ is truly with us.

As Christians, we can never limit the grace of God. While Christians must affirm that wherever there is truth, Christ is present, even when the name of Christ is not known, they must also assert that in Jesus Christ God has acted in a unique and decisive way for the salvation of all beings. Jesus Christ is not merely one of many incarnations of the divine; rather, he is the fullest revelation of the divine aim at wholeness present at the depth of all things.

Although we cannot fully explain the mystery of Jesus Christ's divine-humanity, we can assert that Christ's uniqueness involves both God's initiative and Jesus of Nazareth's creative response to his Parent. As the spirit of the universe, God is personally related to all things. God's presence in each creature is related to that creature's particular needs and its willingness to be open to God's presence. Just as some events of our lives reveal clearly our identity and intentions, some moments of God's activity reveal more fully who God is and what God intends for the universe. In contrast to the impersonal divinity of Asian religions and the new age movement, the God of the Hebrews and

Christians is lively, personal, dynamic, and active. God also is free, creative, and passionate. Christian faith affirms that the divine passion was revealed most fully in a unique human being, Jesus of Nazareth. While Jesus of Nazareth chose to follow his Parent, this choice—like all responses to grace—had been initiated by God's choice of Jesus to be God's channel for salvation to humankind. When we turn our hearts toward Jesus, we come to share more fully in that divine passion that flows through our own lives, and we share in Christ's own wisdom and truth. To say with the creeds that Jesus is fully human and fully divine is to affirm that although Jesus is unique, there is also a point of contact between Jesus and ourselves.

The Christ we encounter is above all a personal being. Christ's universality is grounded in flesh and blood moments of experience, most especially in four "moments" of Jesus' life—the incarnation, the cross, the resurrection, and the second coming.

The first moment, the incarnation, proclaims that "the Word was made flesh and lived among us" (John 1:14). From Bethlehem to Calvary, the life of Jesus reveals God's solidarity with humankind. In contrast to *A Course in Miracles*, the incarnation affirms the goodness and significance of bodily existence in all its aspects. God is revealed in every aspect of experience and not merely the spiritual realm. The story of the incarnation involves pregnancy and parenting, political power and economic instability, dirty swaddling clothes and political refugees. Jesus was "tempted and tried" and "grew in wisdom and stature" through the challenges of embodiment as well as experiences of spiritual ecstasy. As a carpenter, Jesus learned to bring order from chaos and see beauty in hidden places. Jesus cared for bodies as well as spirits, for he realized that spiritual liberation must take place at every dimension of life—physical, emotional, vocational, intellectual, spiritual, and relational.

Jesus Christ—the incarnate one—shows us "the way, the truth, and the life" in the midst of our own embodied lives. Although spiritual transformation can take place anywhere and anytime, each moment uniquely matters to God. To proclaim the incarnation is to deny both an equality and a homogeneity of divine revelations. Jesus Christ is unique as a revelation of God and not merely one of many divine incarnations. Christ's own uniqueness calls us to see each moment as an unrepeatable opportunity to share God's grace in word and deed.

The second moment of God's presence in Christ is the cross. Few new age Christologies have a place for the cross except as a metaphor for spiritual death and rebirth. The cross, however, is more than a metaphor; it is an affirmation that suffering and pain are real and that God shares in our deepest sorrows and tragedies. In contrast to the "amorality" of the *Course*, the cross of Christ starkly reveals the power of political institutions to do evil as well as good. Just as the incarnation brings holiness to every stage of human life, the cross brings new life to each moment of pain and suffering. Suffering is neither an illusion nor something to be repressed. Healing and transformation come through facing the pain and injustice and discovering God in the midst of it.

In its emphasis on spiritual affirmations and prosperity consciousness, the new age has little comfort to give to persons in physical, mental, spiritual, and political anguish. In the cross, we find good news for those who won't get well and who can't think positively. To those who suffer, the good news is that God in Christ truly experiences our pain and is present in the midst of our own personal hells to guide and comfort us.

At the cross, Jesus is "God with us," sharing our suffering. While many mainstream Christians struggle with traditional and exclusivist understandings of the "atonement," a holistic Christology sees the cross as the primary revelation of God's personal relationship to each one of us. God embraces the whole of life, even its darkness and pain. God appears to us even when we feel forsaken, and God bears our burdens so that we may be transformed. Sin and brokenness, especially as they are the results of human choices, must be addressed if they are to be transformed. Eventually someone must suffer for justice and peace to be restored. At the edges of life, the "suffering servant" becomes our savior and companion, the one who bears and works within our pain, to bring transformation to persons and political structures.

The third moment of Jesus' life, the resurrection, proclaims God's ultimate victory over the forces of evil, habit, fear, and political injustice. In contrast to those Christians and new agers who see the resurrection as a metaphor for the human spiritual journey, a holistic Christology must proclaim that salvation and transformation embrace body as well as spirit, the decaying as well as the eternal. While we need not accept a literal bodily resurrection, we must affirm with Paul the resurrection of a "spiritual body" that embraces the totality of our experiences, aspirations, and relationships (1 Corinthians 15:42–44). In an age of quantum physics, the resurrection can be understood in terms of a divine spiritual transformation that raised the vibrational frequency of Jesus' body in such a way that his flesh became a mirror of his spirit. Still, we must also remember that the glory of Easter cannot be fully experienced apart from the tragedy of the cross.

God's ultimate goal is the redemption of all things in earth and heaven. The resurrection of this one person, Jesus Christ—unique and not merely a member of a stream of incarnations for whom death was merely an inconvenience or illusion—announces God's willingness to reclaim and transform all things, physical and spiritual. Mainstream Christians must seriously challenge any metaphysical or ethical system—Christian, new age, or Eastern, which denies or minimizes the importance of individual, historical, and embodied existence. This life really mattered to Jesus of Nazareth, and it also matters to God.

The fourth movement of Jesus' life is the second coming. While few contemporary mainstream Christians expect a literal second coming of Jesus Christ, they share with Benjamin Creme, environmental activists, green politicians, and many other persons in the new age movement, a hope for global as well as personal transformation. But, from a Christian standpoint, transformation is not merely the result of human labors—be they political or spiritual. While Christians may appreciate Creme's "great invocation" and "transmission meditation," we must—even as we pray for peace and work for justice—remember that the future lies ultimately in God's hands and not just in our own efforts. As we await the "new heaven and new earth," we must, as the saying goes, "work as if everything depends on us and pray as if everything depends on God." Just as God acted decisively in the incarnation, God will also act decisively, yet in cooperation with human prayer and effort, to bring about the coming of a new age that will embrace all things. When we look forward to the day when "at the name of Jesus every knee shall bend, in heaven and on earth and under the earth, and every tongue should confess that Jesus Christ is Lord, to the glory of the Father" (Philippians 2:10–11), we are not proclaiming Christian imperialism but our hopes for a new age in which God will be revealed in every human heart, in the natural world, and in the affairs of nations.

As Christians reflect on the Christologies of the new age, we are called to recognize critically the insights of the Christologies, even if they may seem unsubstantiated or contrary to traditional Christian doctrine. While Christians cannot accept the gnosticism explicit in *A Course in Miracles*, we can learn something from its method of spiritual discipline and its concern for unity in a world of divisiveness. In our affirmation of the particular and unique history of Jesus, we must seriously question the theories of Jesus' "lost years" and Jesus' many incarnations. Still, the "lost years" remind us that we can never fully encompass Jesus Christ and that Jesus' teaching is relevant to all times and cultures. Our reflections about his life and relationship to God will always remain partial and tentative. Our doctrines will always be "treasures kept in earthen vessels." While we may judge these "lost years" as poetic and fictional, we must always remember the final words of John's Gospel: "But there are many other things that Jesus did; if everyone of them were written down, I suppose that the world itself could not contain the books that would be written" (John 21:25).

Today, we must answer for ourselves and in our time, Jesus' question: "Who do you say I am?" Our answers must be bold and transformative, but they must also be grounded in the insights of our mothers and fathers in the faith. We must affirm the insights of the new age movement, even when it speaks of Christ, but our dialogue must find its basis in our own personal relationship and commitment to Jesus of Nazareth, the Christ of every new age and every process of creative transformation.

QUESTIONS FOR REFLECTION AND DISCUSSION

1. How do you respond to the various new age pictures of Jesus Christ? Where are they in continuity with the Christian tradition? Where do they differ?

2. How do you respond to the global and ecological images of Christ found in the works of Berry, Cobb, and Fox? Do they adequately address the issues of new age spirituality?

3. Can salvation and truth be found outside of a personal or sacramental relationship with Jesus Christ? If so, how does this shape our understanding of Christ and Christianity?

CHAPTER SIX

DEATH AND HUMAN HOPE

HOPE BEYOND THE GRAVE

The night my mother died, she appeared to my son in a dream. In the dream, my family was walking along the beach in Santa Cruz, California. Only my father was missing. My mother asked my son to tell his grandfather, "Grandma says, tell grandpa not to give up." What was surprising about my son's dream was that although my mother was to have surgery, no one expected that she would die that night from its side effects. A few nights later, my wife felt a presence in the house—it was the image of my mother reaching out to her and telling my wife that my wife had never given her a reiki healing treatment and that she would like one now. As I reflect on these events, I wonder if these experiences—and countless experiences like them—were merely dreams inspired by wishful thinking, or the workings of the unconscious, or if they truly represent authentic contacts from beyond this life?

Today, there is a great interest in life after death. Inspired by the pioneering work in thanatology by Elisabeth Kübler-Ross and the exploration of "near death experiences" by Raymond Moody and others, many persons are now claiming to have had deathbed experiences or encounters with deceased loved ones that convince them that death is not final.[1] As a sign of the interest in life after death, Betty Eadie's account of her near death experience was one of the best-sellers of 1993.[2] Some of television's most popular programs deal with paranormal experiences that once would have been termed superstitious and occult. Recent movies such as "Defending Your Life," "Field of Dreams," "Always," "Flatliners," and "Ghost" portray life beyond the grave and communication with the dead.

According to sociologist and theologian Andrew Greeley, belief in survival after death and contact with the deceased is no longer considered eccentric: 70 percent of Americans believe in some form of life after death and 25 percent of Americans report having contact with the dead.[3] While some explore "near death experiences," a new focus of study, "the past life experience" has emerged and, with it, the possibility that our current lives and relationships reflect our need to address issues from previous incarnations.[4]

The increased interest in past and future lives is puzzling to many mainstream Christian laypersons and ministers. Although their worship services include the historic creeds of the church, such as the Apostles' Creed, whose conclusion affirms the reality of "the communion of saints, the forgiveness of sins, the resurrection of the body, and the life everlasting," many mainstream Christians are agnostic about life after death. Many seem to feel that giving too much attention to the concerns of eternal life might blind us to the needs of persons today. The task of Christians, they assert, is to "preach good news to the poor . . . release to the captives . . . and set at liberty the oppressed" in this lifetime. They have witnessed many Christians who have been so concerned about heaven that they are of "no earthly good," and they have seen the afterlife used as a tool to encourage acceptance of unjust economic, relational, and political conditions in this lifetime.

Still other mainstream Christians find the traditional Christian images of life after death morally repugnant and theologically distasteful. Literally understood, the images of heaven, hell, and purgatory deny the reality of God's grace and imply that salvation is a bargain made with God. Only those who bring the right currency, that is, the correct doctrinal beliefs, sacramental acts, or moral behaviors, are saved. Those who have not encountered Christ are damned, regardless of their spiritual maturity or their moral goodness.

Mainstream ministers and priests trained in the postwar era have been caught off guard by the current interest in survival after death among their congregants. Many attended the seminary at a time when concern for the afterlife found little place in theology. Even pastoral care, whose purpose was to help persons deal with spiritual crises, seldom addressed preparation for death and beyond.

This lack of imagination has been costly to mainstream Christianity. While fundamentalists have preached the glories of heaven and the flames of hell, mainstream ministers have been silent in the pulpit and largely impotent in responding to their parishioners' needs for a wider vision of reality. By failing to address the literal images proclaimed by the fundamentalists, mainstream pastors have inadvertently suggested to the public that the literal versions of heaven and hell are the only theological options available for Christians. Over the years, I have counseled scores of college students and adults from mainstream and liberal churches who have no other concept of immortality than the one they can no longer believe in—the vision of immortality that asserts the absolute division of the saved and the damned, based solely on a person's explicit relationship to Jesus. In this theological vacuum, many mainstream Christians have found the Asian and new age teachings of reincarnation far more attractive than the Christian messages they can no longer accept.

The failure to present positive images of life after death has been an important factor in the exodus of well educated and morally sensitive people from the church. Today's mainstream Christians would do well to remember the words of Martin Luther King: "You must make your plans big enough to include God and large enough to include eternity."[5] The current interest in "near death experiences" and new age interpretations of reincarnation is a challenge for the church to rethink its images of the afterlife and rediscover a positive vision of life after death.

Reincarnation and Human Hope

While mainstream Christians have been humble and reticent in expressing their beliefs in the afterlife, new agers have been bold in their proclamation that death is not the end of human existence, but merely a passage into a new life and further spiritual adventures.

Reincarnation, the belief that we have lived before and will live again, is one of the primary tenets of the new age movement. While reincarnation is often seen in terms of punishment and pain in Hinduism and Buddhism, the optimistic worldview of the new age movement transforms reincarnation into a spiritual adventure and learning process in which spiritual growth and personal experience rather than punishment are the primary focus. For new agers, reincarnation is the ultimate answer to our fear of death.

One of the most significant mysteries in human existence is the nature of birth. Every reflective person has wondered why they were born at this time, this place, and under these particular conditions. Seen in the midst of life, the varied conditions of our births seem random. None of us can claim to be responsible for our genetic code, gender, ethnic background, parents, or economic situation. From the perspective of this lifetime, we seem to be, as certain existentialist philosophers proclaim, "thrown" into existence by arbitrary chance.

In contrast to secular understandings of matters of life and death, the religious mind has always sought a wider perspective and a deeper understanding of the human journey. Christian theologians have often attributed our conception, the specifics of our birth, and the pivotal events of our lives to divine providence. Traditional Christian theology has held that God has chosen each person for a particular mission in life. Even the apparent setbacks and tragedies are part of this larger, spiritual mission.

In its most extreme form, articulated by the sixteenth-century reformer John Calvin, the belief in divine providence has been interpreted in terms of predestination and foreordination. From the very beginning, God has determined every event and the course of each person's life. Nothing, according to Calvin, occurs without the will of God. Even salvation is entirely a divine work. Accordingly, no person can boast of their own goodness, since before the creation of the world, God ordained not only who would be saved but also who would suffer eternal damnation. While this doctrine of "double predestination" is morally unacceptable to many Christians today, most Christians still hold some version of the belief that good and evil ultimately come from the hand of God and that everything occurs for a reason.

Popular Christian theology points to this belief through such sayings as: "God doesn't close one door without opening another," "God never gives you a burden you can't bear," or, at a death, "It was his time to go." We must have a reason why "bad things happen to good people" or "good things happen to bad people," and the ultimate answer to our quest for a rational universe leads us to God. Although many Christians no longer believe in the doctrine of divine omnipotence, *still* they seek to make sense of the interplay of God and freedom in the events of human life and *still* they struggle with the tension between divine love and the inequalities of birth and talent.

The doctrine of reincarnation suggests another answer to the quest for knowledge of our births and deaths. To those who seek to discern the presence of order within the apparent randomness of birth and death, the new age reinterpretation of the doctrine of reincarnation provides an answer. In this belief system, the apparent arbitrariness and inequality of birth and death find their source in human decision making rather than in the conscious purposes of God or the unconscious purposes of evolution. We are responsible for our births, deaths, and everything that happens in between. As Louise Hay maintains, "We are each 100 percent responsible for all of our experiences. . . . We create our experiences, our reality, and everything in it."[6] This is not only true in terms of the events of this life, it is also the source of our particular birth, gender, intelligence, ethnic background, and opportunities. In this way, new age thought blends the traditional Hindu concepts of karma (the belief that the results of one's actions and thoughts will shape the future destiny of their author) and reincarnation (the rebirth of the soul in one body after another from life to life) with the Western spirit of evolutionary optimism.

According to new age thinkers, each birth is a result of the soul's choice to learn certain lessons or respond to certain issues raised in previous lifetimes. Channeled entity "Seth" proclaims that "problems not faced in this life will be faced in another. . . . We choose the circumstances into which we would be born and the challenges that could bring about our development."[7]

New age philosopher Gary Zukav affirms that each person has "the freedom to become a king or a pauper, lover or loved, slave or freed man—whatever illusion will provide you the understanding your soul is needing for fulfillment."[8] Under hypnosis, one of past-life therapist

Helen Walmbach's patients stated that "I chose to be born and was helped to choose [by spiritual guides] because I need to continue and correct the work of my past life."[9]

The purpose of reincarnation is spiritual evolution and personal healing. Each soul, by its various births, seeks to enhance its evolutionary progress toward unity with God. As Zukav continues:

> Each personality contributes, in its own special way, with its special aptitudes and lessons to learn, consciously or unconsciously, to the evolution of its soul. . . . Each physical, emotional, or psychological characteristic that comprises a personality and its body—strong or weak arms, dense or penetrating intellect, happy or despairing disposition, yellow or black skin, even hair and eye color—is perfectly suited for the soul's purpose.[10]

From the perspective of the law of karma, each person reaps what they sow, or studies what they need to learn, in this lifetime and in the next. As theosophical writer Geoffrey Hodson notes:

> . . . conditions of human life, whether of health, happiness, capacity, or opportunity, or of disease, sorrow, weakness, and limitation, are the results of the operations of exact law, reapings from past sowings.[11]

As random as they may seem from the point of view of this lifetime, the circumstances and events of our lives are the means by which we spiritually evolve from ignorance to self-knowledge. In contrast to the apostle Paul's assertion that "the wages of sin is death," new age thinkers maintain that "the wages of ignorance and separation is rebirth and further adventure."

In the spirit of the Hindu doctrine of reincarnation, new age thinkers explain the inequalities of life in terms of the lessons we need to learn and the experiences we need to acquire. Every birth is intended by the soul. As "Lazaris," the voice who speaks through Jach Pursel, states, "Those who are suffering tragically did create their reality, but so did the one who witnesses—directly or indirectly—the human injustice."[12] Even the death of a child at birth or shortly thereafter from sudden infant death syndrome is no accident, but arises from a prenatal agreement between the parents and child. Perhaps the dying infant's task in its short incarnation is to teach its parents the meaning of grief and compassion.

To new age proponents of reincarnation, the argument that "starving and suffering children did not choose to lead this kind of life" fails to see the wider dimensions of the human journey. There is no unfairness in this lifetime. AIDS, starvation, homelessness, retardation, and even sexual abuse are all stages in the soul's educational process. As Gary Zukav maintains, "When we see a person sleeping in the gutter in winter, we do not know what is being completed for that soul."[13] While it is appropriate for us to feel compassion, we must remember that "it is not appropriate that we perceive it as unfair, because it is not."[14]

To the morally sensitive reader, such descriptions of the inequality of human conditions appear to be the musings of an elite, economically well-to-do, and healthy minority. To a certain extent, such critiques are valid, for the new age movement, like the ancient Hindu Brahmanical movement that produced the doctrines of karma and reincarnation in India, is an upper middle class, socially insulated, and well-educated movement.

Some new age thinkers, however, seek to soften the pain of inequality by proclaiming that the soul, which incarnates in the physical body, never truly suffers, but merely observes painful and joyful conditions as we would observe a movie or television program. Channeled entity "Samuel" likens the mind to an instrument used by the soul to interpret the world. While the mind sees only the finite experience and, thus, makes judgments of good and evil, right and wrong, the soul sees every event as part of its own spiritual evolution. "Ramtha," another channeled entity, concurs when he suggests that "everything you have ever done, however vile or wretched it has been, has enhanced life by the wisdom you have obtained by doing it."[15] Zukav holds that despite the appearances of pain, the soul feels no pain. "Everyone is infinitely happy however they are experiencing."[16]

The new age doctrine of reincarnation asserts a dualism not only between the soul and the body, but also between experience and reality, and good and evil. The pain felt by persons is not truly real. Metaphysically, the relationship of the soul and its experiences can be compared to the relationship of the author and the novel he or she is writing. While the author may become involved in the lives of the characters, eventually he or she will put down the novel and realize that the characters are fabrications and not *real* persons.

New age optimism sees pain, evil, and immorality as ultimately illusions because they have no eternal value. They are only lessons to be learned and mistakes, which eventually will be corrected, in the "tests" of life. The *essence* of a starving child or of a young woman dying of AIDS never feels any pain. Only the temporary self suffers. In reflecting on human fallibility, Gary Zukav notes, "You have never done anything wrong. . . . all your wrongs, your failings, your errors, are what is called, appropriately, 'steps to God.'"[17] As new age prophet Shirley MacLaine asserts, evil "doesn't exist. . . . Everything in life is the result of illumination or ignorance. These are the two polarities. Not good and evil."[18]

From the perspective of reincarnation, eventually all persons will be saved and all souls will discover their true nature as divine. In a "spacious" universe, there is no need to hurry, nor is any act or situation ultimately detrimental to the soul's salvation. While the doctrine of karma may seem harsh from the limited perspective, it is the essential means to salvation. Thanatologist Stephen Levine notes that

> [k]arma is not punishment. It is an aspect of the merciful nature of the universe to offer teachings that we somehow have misunderstood in the past, to allow us to learn from experience what we have not paid close enough attention to previously.[19]

There is no personal grace in the world of death and rebirth. While the forces of evolution and spiritual wisdom push one from life to life, ultimately salvation is a matter of personal effort. While most new agers might question the strenuous spirit of St. Paul's maxim to "work out your salvation with fear and trembling," they would assert that one is called to seek enlightenment through experience, insight, and self-awareness. By our acts and attitudes, we progress from life to life.

We are also liberated by our own efforts. As "Ramtha" counsels, "Be your own teacher, your own savior, your own Master, your own God."[20] There is no need for an external god or a freely given grace when each soul has all the resources it needs to be saved. Helena Blavatsky, founder of the theosophical movement and a spiritual fore-runner of the new age movement, proclaims that "reincarnation is the destiny of every ego, which thus becomes its own Savior in each world and each incarnation."[21] In the spirit of new age Christology, we are all Christs who have forgotten who we are, and we are all Christs who save the world by saving ourselves.

At the descending edges of life, we ask, "what comes next?" While the materialist sees oblivion and the fundamentalist expects salvation or damnation, new agers comfort the dying with the hope of a new birth and new opportunity to continue their journey to God. As Quincy Howe states, "The very center and core of our being, that ever-lasting essence which transmigrates from one life to another, is noth-ing less than a particle of God himself."[22] While our spiritual evolution may lead through times of joy and sorrow, of abundance and scarcity, eventually we will learn all the lessons that this world can offer us and discover who we are—birthless and deathless aspects of the divine. We will discover that we have always been enlightened, that our higher self has always been in touch with reality, regardless of how mired the everyday self seems to be in the struggles of life after life.

As optimistic as the new age vision of reincarnation may be, its opti-mism is purchased through the devaluation of historical and physical existence as well as the concern for social justice. While Christian faith has always seen history as relative and fragmentary, it has also claimed that human wholeness is achieved by the transformation of persons and institutions in light of the reign of God. Good and evil are not merely matters of perception or object lessons, but are realities that call us to commitment and social concern. To the Christian, this life truly matters not just as a lesson to be learned, but as the place where God calls us to seek justice and nurture beauty.

Christianity and Reincarnation

In recent years, a small group of Christians has sought to synthesize Christian faith with the doctrine of reincarnation. Leslie Weatherhead, Methodist minister and former pastor of the City Temple in London, has suggested that reincarnation more adequately expresses the Christian doctrines of justice and grace than do the traditional doctrines of heaven, hell, and divine omnipotence. At death, Weatherhead asserts, no person has fully exhausted their possibilities or even started to use their highest powers.[23] Persons need a larger horizon to become fit for unmediated companionship with God.

According to Weatherhead, the doctrine of reincarnation supports the Christian affirmation that God is just. The inequalities of this lifetime cannot be attributed to God, as Calvin and others have suggested, but must find their origin in the influence of one's previous lifetimes. By providing the opportunity for a new life, God insures that all persons will eventually be saved.

Weatherhead and Geddes MacGregor, another Christian proponent of reincarnation, maintain that, although the Bible does not explicitly teach reincarnation, they see no conflict between reincarnation and Christian faith. According to these theologians, passages such as the identification of John the Baptist with Elijah (Luke 1:17) and the questions regarding the origin of a man's blindness (John 9:1–3) suggest the existence of the belief in reincarnation during the time of the early church. MacGregor cites the early church father Origen (185–254) as a proponent of the preexistence of the soul and the long journey of spiritual evolution. What Roman Catholics have traditionally described as purgatory, the place of spiritual refinement and cleansing for souls destined for heaven, points to the need for spiritual growth as a prerequisite for fully encountering God. From the Christian perspective, karma integrates both grace and law. In an orderly universe, our behavior must have consequences. Yet, in an evolutionary universe, reflecting the purposes of God, each life must be a stepping-stone to greater awareness of God and oneself. Grace does not nullify human freedom. As MacGregor maintains, "God does not promise me to grow without my growing. He only promises the conditions for my success."[24] God seeks our spiritual growth in each incarnation by providing guidance as we face the particular lessons we need to learn.

In contrast to those Christians who feel that one life is sufficient to determine one's orientation toward God, Christian reincarnationists feel that the love and justice of God demand multiple lifetimes. The path may be arduous and may involve many births, but eventually all persons will come to know God fully.

Critiques of the Doctrine of Reincarnation

Unlike their fundamentalist companions, mainstream Christians cannot dismiss the doctrine of reincarnation in its many forms without serious conversation. Mainstream Christians realize that we live in a pluralistic age and that persons of different cultures may hold different visions of God, the nature of reality, and human destiny. Further, we recognize the relativity of our own doctrines and the harm that may occur when doctrines such as the immortality of the soul or survival after death are understood in a literal and dogmatic fashion. Accordingly, as mainstream Christians point out the shortcomings of the new age doctrine of reincarnation, we must also be aware of the problems that have plagued the Christian understanding of life after death.

My own critique of new age images of reincarnation will focus on the writings of actress, dancer, and new age popularizer Shirley MacLaine in the context of other more orthodox and philosphical notions of reincarnation. While MacLaine's views are not necessarily the most subtle or articulate expression of the new age movement and would not be accepted by all new age thinkers, her writings and films have touched millions of persons within the church and in society at large and express many of the popular new age understandings of reincarnation. MacLaine's best-selling books, along with the television mini-series *Out on a Limb,* have been the first contacts with the new age movement for millions of persons.

At the heart of the Christian critique of the doctrine of reincarnation is the apparent dualism, suggested by new age thinkers, between the true self and the everyday self. New age thought maintains that there is a "witness self" or "true self," whose existence is unsullied by the actions of the mind, body, and emotions. This self observes our everyday activities in the same way that we observe children playing in the park or widespread starvation in many parts of the world. The divine self is untouched by pain, sorrow, or empathy. It travels from life to life to learn the lessons of embodiment and face problems that have been created by the everyday and superficial self. When the superficial self feels love or pain, the divine self merely observes and guides; it does not feel the varied emotions. From this perspective Gary Zukav can assert that, beneath the various forms of suffering and struggle, everyone is "infinitely happy."

This dualism between the true and ideal self—the divine within—and the everyday self, leads to certain moral and theological problems within new age thought. First of all, there is an implicit denial of suffering and pain in oneself and others. The illusory nature of suffering is proclaimed in the classic of Hindu theology, the *Bhagavad Gita*. When the great warrior Arjuna ponders the countless deaths that will occur in the battle he is about to begin, he is pained by the death and grief that will follow. Yet, rather than giving him consolation, the god Krishna charges him to go into battle:

> The wise grieve not for those who live; and they grieve not for those who die—for life and death shall pass away. . . . If any man thinks he slays, and if another thinks he is slain, neither knows the ways of truth. The Eternal in man cannot kill; the Eternal in man cannot die.[25]

In this spirit, a Hindu guru Maharajji proclaimed, as he looked upon the chaos following the floods in Bangladesh, "Don't you see that it's all perfect."[26] From the point of view of the soul, the drowning in the flood and the starvation that followed are merely illusions, even though these things are all-consuming to the everyday mind and to those who are suffering.

In her first encounter with the doctrine of reincarnation, Shirley MacLaine expresses her own distaste for this apparently simplistic explanation of pain and suffering. When a friend explains that all suffering is a reflection of cosmic justice, MacLaine exclaims:

> You mean we should just be patient with the Hitlers of this world.
>
> I mean [her friend responds] that six million Jews didn't die. Only their bodies died.
>
> Beautiful! Tell the families of these six million hurting people that only their bodies died.[27]

Later MacLaine reversed her position as she came to believe that from a cosmic perspective, "the soul's existence was all that mattered and one's physical existence was literally irrelevant."[28] Taken literally, MacLaine's position asserts that the Holocaust victims experienced no more *real* pain from their persecution than I experienced as I watched the film "Schindler's List." The essential core of their being remained untouched and possibly unmoved.

In contrast to this dualism, Christianity proclaims the reality of the cross as testimony not only to the reality of life's pain but to the healing of those who suffer. While God is not fully consumed by our pain, the witness of the cross asserts that pain and sin are real and make a difference not only to ourselves but to God. Accordingly, the Christian is called to respond to pain and suffering in the spirit of Jesus the healer.

While the doctrine of reincarnation is often affirmed as a means of solving the problem of evil and the unfairness of birth, the dualism between the divine and the everyday self, and the everyday self's ignorance of its own karmic history, suggests another type of injustice and unfairness. The everyday self that has sought excellence or plunged into iniquity will not experience the results of its acts in a future lifetime. A new phenomenal self, unaware of its predecessor, will reap the benefits or the pain. In the spirit of the hedonism of the 1980s, "Ramtha," one of MacLaine's "spirit" teachers, proclaims that "there is no karma—only the ongoingness of experience. . . . You never have to pay for anything that you have ever thought or done in this or any life, as long as you forgive yourself for it."[29] While this is an extreme interpretation of the doctrine of karma and reincarnation, it points out another fundamental problem in the theory: the past incarnate self is dead and the future self is ignorant of its past history. There is little that abused children or babies with Down's Syndrome or persons with a mental illness can learn from the burdens of their past lives. Even persons with all the advantages of health, family life, and riches seldom discern why they have been so blessed. The fleeting phenomenal self usually learns very little that will aid in its spiritual evolution in any given lifetime, since each one of us suffers unknowingly for the sins of our past lives. Only the eternally detached soul can observe any continuity from life to life.

We as Christians must also challenge the apparent gracelessness of the doctrine of karma in which everything depends on the self, which has created our reality and will eventually fix it. While karma may be the source of novel experiences, it may also bring pain and disease. In contrast to many theosophists and new age thinkers who see karma solely as a tool of learning and experience, Helena Blavatsky presents the dark side of the doctrine of karma:

> Our philosophy [theosophy] has a doctrine of punishment as stern as the most rigid Calvinist, only far more consistent, and philosophical, with absolute justice. No deed, not even a single thought, will go unpunished; the latter more severely than the former, as a thought has more potential for creating evil than even a deed.[30]

While Blavatsky points out the inexorableness of karma, MacLaine points to the omnipotence of the self. "If I acknowledge that I had created my reality at every level, then I had to be totally responsible for everything that had gone on."[31] For MacLaine, the world is entirely the projection of the soul's thoughts.

> I realized I created my own reality in everything. I must therefore admit that, in essence, *I was the only person in my universe.* . . . I went on to express my feeling of total responsibility *and power* for all events that happen in the world for the world is happening only in my reality. *And* human beings feeling pain, terror, depression, panic, and so forth, were really only aspects of pain, terror, depression, and so on in *me!*[32]

MacLaine asserts that even those persons who object to her views are little more than actors in her universe, whose objections occur only to show her things she hasn't resolved in her own life.

While such omnipotence and cosmic narcissism may comfort MacLaine, such responsibility can overwhelm the mere mortal or lead to psychological trauma for those who have been abused and come to realize that they are completely responsible for the abusive acts of others. In these cases, like so many, the victims see themselves as the guilty party and as deserving of the abuse and injustice that have been inflicted upon them.

In contrast to MacLaine's optimism, everyday experience reveals the impotence of the self to create its reality or liberate itself from the bondage of past memories, thoughts, or behaviors apart from the interplay of grace, receptivity, and effort. The apostle Paul captures the hopelessness of one caught in the wheel of karma: "I do not do the very thing I want, but I do the very thing I hate. . . . For I do not do the good I want, but the evil I do not want is what I do. . . . Who will deliver me from this body of death?" (Romans 7:15, 17, 21). While we are not impotent, we are also not omnipotent. As the gospel proclaims and the twelve step recovery movements affirm, we require a community and a higher power in order to be healed. The combination of the denial of the actuality of evil and the affirmation of the omnipotence of the self make it very difficult for persons in new age groups to explore conflict issues and admit their fallibility and pain. To admit one's needs or explore conflicts would be to admit that one is neither in control nor able to live up to the image of a perfect self.

Implicit in the new age version of reincarnation is a certain amorality that counters the attempts of new agers to be socially responsible. While many persons in the new age movement are working to save the planet and bring justice and peace to war-torn nations, the underlying philosophy of the new age is that such injustice is ultimately either illusory or the result of the victim's own previous behavior.

In the new age movement's most extreme form, "Ramtha" proclaims that "God allows you to create your life any way you desire. . . . God sees no wrong . . . or failure."[33] This same tension is found in Ram Dass and Marabai Bush's book on social concern. While they encourage persons to become socially active in the healing of the planet and are themselves active in addressing the needs of the sick and broken, the authors note the paradox of compassion in action: "It accepts that everything is happening as it should, and it works with a full-hearted commitment" to change the present world.[34] To the Christian, however, much that happens in our world is _not_ happening as it should. There are forces of evil that must be countered whether they dwell in ourselves or in others. Even if pain and suffering are not the ultimate realities of life, they are _real_ to those who experience them.

Jesus is the ultimate example of God's bias toward health, healing, and justice. Jesus healed the sick and freed the oppressed; he did not give metaphysical or karmic advice to those who suffer. Rather, God in Christ challenged poverty, oppression, and sickness precisely because *they should not exist* and are counter to God's will for the world.

In the calculus of karma, every event is perfect and everyone is getting what they deserve. In a statement reminiscent of the political adage that "the poor are lazy," Quincy Howe states that "the man who is born in abject poverty may have made ill use of his wealth in an earlier life; the wealthy man is reaping the fruits of earlier generosity."[35] While we may help suffering people, our motive is not necessarily compassion but the desire to avoid a similar fate in this lifetime or the next. The assumption that the sexually abused, politically oppressed, and mentally ill somehow deserve their fate diminishes our desire to help them. Our compassion might even prevent them from facing the lessons that they must learn for their own evolution. Indeed, their suffering on the psychophysical plane is of little importance. The soul's learning journey is the only value. Such new age images are a far cry from Jesus' tears over Jerusalem or Amos' denunciation of economic injustice in Judah.

In the Christian tradition, God is profoundly moral and deeply interested in the affairs of the transitory, everyday world. While we are counseled to "consider the lilies" and remember that God will take care of us, we are also reminded of the biblical doctrines that "as you have done unto the least of these, you have done unto me" and that our call is to "let justice roll down like waters and righteousness like an everflowing stream." The God of biblical revelation takes this world and its affairs seriously. Creation is not an illusion, and embodiment is not the result of ignorance of our true self. Creation emerges from God's loving care and is intended to be a place of wholeness and peace.

While many new agers are interested in "green politics," ecology, feminism, sustainable technology and economics, and equality, their social concerns are implicitly challenged by the amorality and spiritual dualism characteristic of the new age worldview. Only their metaphysical naivete allows the worlds to merge without "collision." Their interest in ecology, for example, is supported by a "creation spirituality" that affirms the goodness of Earth, the interrelatedness of all things, and the beauty and divinity inherent in embodied existence.

These beliefs are grounded, however, in Native American religion or, more often, in the Jewish and Christian theology of creation they often disparage, rather than in the Hinduism, Buddhism, or theosophical metaphysics more often affirmed by new agers.

In addition, it is ironic that while most new age thought maintains that separation, or the loss of cosmic unity, is the primary form of disease, the doctrine of reincarnation is often articulated in a purely individualistic form. While souls interact and choose their journeys in cooperation from a cosmic perspective, the soul's karmic journey is often described as if it were solitary and individualistic. Rather than asserting the social nature of reality and the interrelatedness of our spiritual journeys, the typical new age understanding of spiritual evolution speaks of "creating your own reality," "being your own guide and savior," or of "separate universes of experience." As Christian reincarnationist Geddes MacGregor asserts:

> My karma is peculiar to _me_. It is _my_ problem and _my_ triumph over it is _my_ triumph. I may need the help of teachers; I may even profit from my belongingness; but in the last resort I am responsible for what I am; as I am responsible for what I shall be.[36]

Christian faith at its best affirms that, in the web of relationships, there is no ultimate separation. While individuality is real, interrelatedness is primary. Separation, even in terms of the concepts of reincarnation or heaven and hell, is an illusion. In the ecology of the spirit characteristic of the body of Christ, all of our destinies are interrelated in this life and the next: we all rejoice and suffer together. We have our origins in the body of Christ, and we shape, by our lives, the ongoing history of this same body of Christ.

In a world of relationships, we are all saved by grace and we are all called to become actors in the vast cosmic movement of God's graceful spirit. From this perspective, we are relieved of the burden and the pride of being fully responsible for our worlds. We are not gods, and we are not the sole creators of our own reality. Our creativity and responsibility are social and cooperative as well as personal in this life and the next.

A CHRISTIAN VISION OF SURVIVAL AFTER DEATH

Martin Luther once asserted that "in the midst of life, we are surrounded by death." From its beginnings, Christianity has taken death
seriously. The birth of the Christ child is followed by the slaughter of
innocents. Jesus' first proclaimer, John the Baptist, is beheaded for
challenging the political and moral status quo. The primary symbol of
Christian faith is the cross. In our churches or around our necks, the
cross is an ever-present reminder that death is an inevitable as well as
transforming part of life. While a primary tenet of the theory of reincarnation is the illusory nature of death, Christianity affirms that the
painful reality of death applies even to the Son of God and that the triumphant resurrection can only emerge from the darkness of the tomb.

Our everyday lives are filled with death. We see countless deaths on
television—starving children and atrocities in various parts of the
world, the casualties of war, the anguish of parents grieving the brutal
drive-by murder of their school-age children, and the agony of persons
with AIDS. While few persons die at a university such as Georgetown,
where I minister, the intercessory prayer requests at the university
church include concerns for cancer striking a teenager, auto crashes,
and the deaths of aging relatives. Even as I write today, I am preparing
to attend a memorial service for a student who died suddenly of heart
failure at the age of 23. While death is not the whole picture, it is an
ever-present reality we must face. Following the death of a loved one,
our grief and sense of loss are real. We do not need to have our grief
and sorrow minimized by easy answers such as "it's God's will," "the
soul never dies," or "it was the soul's choice." At the painful edges of
life, we need assurance that our grief matters not only to us but to God
and that, somehow, our relationships and affections in this world are
not transitory illusions but are as important to God as they are to ourselves.

The earliest proclamations of the gospel message weave together
death and resurrection, grief and victory. To the Christians in Corinth,
the apostle Paul proclaimed that "Death has been swallowed up in victory. Where, O death, is your victory? Where, O death, is your sting?"
(1 Corinthians 15:54–55). For Paul and his listeners, the faithfulness of
God was the foundation of Christian hope. Immortality and resurrection are not natural occurrences but depend upon the surprising grace

of God. As he pondered the future, Paul was filled with gratitude to the God who makes the afterlife both possible and hopeful: "Thanks be to God, who gives us the victory, through our Lord Jesus Christ" (1 Corinthians 15:56).

While the theory of reincarnation depends on the impersonal workings of cause and effect, the Christian doctrine of survival after death depends on God's personal relationship to each human being. We can face death because God has already embraced the terror of death and the alienation of sin. As Paul wrote, "God proves his love for us in that while we were yet sinners, Christ died for us" (Romans 5:8). In light of God's unexpected grace, Christians can also affirm with Martin Luther that "in the midst of death, we are surrounded by life."

Our image of death reflects our vision of the ultimate reality. In most sectors of the new age movement, the ultimate reality is envisaged as impersonal and unchanging. It cannot experience our pain and struggle. Our own deepest reality, the spirit, is also envisaged as being immune from suffering. In contrast, ultimate reality for Christians is intensely personal. God—who can never be addressed as an it, but always as a "thou," "he," or "she"—has a passion and love for this world. Nothing is either too small or too large to escape God's care. God does not avoid death, but transforms it by God's own love, tenderness, and judgment. Created in God's image, the human spirit is also intensely personal; what happens in the flesh is not incidental to the well-being of the human spirit, which acts as well as suffers.

The Christian understanding of the afterlife is profoundly Christological. The Christ who is worshiped and imitated is also intensely personal and historical in nature. Each of the moments of Christ's life, discussed in the last chapter, shape how Christians are called to understand not only their dying but also their life beyond the grave.

Christian reflections on the afterlife, first of all, must be profoundly incarnational. To say that "God was in Christ" is to proclaim that embodiment and relationships are real and significant to God and to the human spirit. Everlasting life must not negate the value of this present life, but must transform and build upon it. Each person we encounter is a child of God and a person for whom Christ died. Their political, relational, physical, and spiritual lives are of everlasting consequence. They matter not only in terms of the spiritual quality of this lifetime but also in terms of their participation in everlasting life. The reality of the cross points to God's presence in our suffering and God's willingness to embrace the chaos and sin of our world.

The resurrection of Jesus Christ proclaims in act and symbol the good news that suffering and death are overcome by God and that the totality of our lives, including our deaths, will eventually be redeemed by God. In light of the resurrection, salvation must include the social order and one's personality and embodiment as well as the spiritual life. God makes "all things new" and that includes everything related to our embodiment: the lives of social groups, families, and the planet itself. Christians hope for a life that is *more* and not less than our current embodied and relational existence.

Today's images of survival after death must be grounded in our awareness of the world as "the body of Christ." Too often, Christians have succumbed to the same individualism and linear thinking that have plagued the new age understanding of reincarnation. Christians have asserted a sharp dichotomy between soul and body, saved and damned, heaven and hell, and God and the world. A holistic, relational understanding of reality suggests, in contrast, that our vision of the afterlife must stress the interrelatedness of all things. No one's birth or destiny is a solitary issue; no one's salvation is an individual and isolated decision. Salvation, or wholeness, arises from the creative interplay of God's grace, human responsiveness, and the impact of social institutions such as churches, families, and governments. In a world of relationships, we are never isolated from God or one another. God's love is stronger than death and will protect and challenge us even beyond the grave.

While traditional Christian theology has often affirmed a strict separation of the saved and the damned as well as of this world and the next, theology in our new age must affirm the ultimate relatedness and salvation of all things. Against fundamentalist Christianity, we must affirm that God's love never ends. The parables of the lost sheep, lost coin, and lost son proclaim the radical nature of God's grace. God seeks the lost *until* it is found. While the creature may turn from God, God will not turn away from any creature. Freedom is real, and sin, whether social or personal, is not an illusion. But to every creaturely "no," God responds with a loving "yes" time after time. In his triumphant account of the resurrection, the apostle Paul proclaimed God's ultimate redemption of our world: "So as all died in Adam, all will be made alive in Christ" (1 Corinthians 15:22). Through God's victory over sin and death, God will eventually be "all in all" (1 Corinthians 15:28).

From this perspective, evil is neither solely the result of God's will nor of one's own personal choice. Good and evil arise from a matrix of influences, including: cosmic and planetary history; genetic influences; parental attitudes and decisions; social, political, and economic decisions; and the presence of God's grace as the underlying factor in all things. We are cocreators rather than creators of our own reality in the context of this complexity of social, planetary, and cosmic relationships.

In the spirit of a relational vision of the afterlife, Christians must affirm that "the body of Christ" embraces every dimension of existence in this world and in any other post-mortem world. Traditionally, this insight has been described as the "communion of saints," which binds the living and the dead prayerfully and lovingly. Death does not obliterate personality or identity. A heaven in which our lives are forgotten is as detrimental to social concern and personal spirituality as a theory of reincarnation that asserts that only the enlightened are able to recall their previous lifetimes.

Christian faith affirms that we are always, both in life and death, in God's presence. Although our world is broken and sinful, it is still God's world and a revelation of the divine to those who have eyes to see and ears to hear. Accordingly, we prepare best for the afterlife by seeking to encounter God in this lifetime through spiritual growth, social responsibility, and concern for the oppressed and neglected. If God truly loves the world enough to share in its suffering and joy, then we are challenged to contribute to our world by bringing healing and restoration to the divine body "in whom we live, move, and have our being."

What we can hope for beyond the grave is the continuing adventure of growing in grace and expanding in love. Christians do not long for the loss of self but the transformation and expansion of the self. When Paul proclaims that he has "been crucified with Christ; and it is no longer I who live but Christ who lives within me" (Galatians 2:19–20), he is expressing the Christian hope for self-transcendence and personal transformation. Peace is not the result of clinging to the isolated, perpetually perishing self. Peace emerges when we realize that we are part of the body of Christ and that our self, at its deepest level, pulses with the divine rhythm that echoes through all things. Awakened to the movements of God's presence, we can affirm "that to live is Christ, and to die is gain" (Philippians 1:21), for even in our deaths we are being invited to deeper and richer experiences of God.

Salvation, from this point of view, is not a bargain between oneself and God. While I appreciate the concerns of a recently born again student who confessed that he had become a Christian initially to escape hell, I must challenge the view that would hold that salvation is a matter of escaping punishment or finding personal safety. Salvation is global and universal in scope. It is already here, but we do not see it. God will not rest until all creation is transformed and awakened to the grace within which we stand.

The process of transformation in this life and in the afterlife is ongoing. In God's kingdom, there are "many mansions." Accordingly, the afterlife is not a static rest or a dreamless sleep but a continuing adventure.[37] In this regard, the afterlife can be seen as a process of learning and growing in grace that integrates the insights of reincarnation as well as the traditional doctrines of purgatory and heaven. Beyond the grave, we can only assume that we will continue to discover insights about God and our lives. Many of these insights will parallel the issues and concerns we've encountered during our earthly journeys. Eventually, we will learn the lessons of healing, forgiveness, and love. While we will meet new persons within "the communion of saints," we can also anticipate continuing relationships that began in this lifetime. As the near death accounts of "welcoming committees" suggest, we will be guided and encouraged in our growth and transition by friends and family who have gone before us. I believe that we will also encounter "the being of light," the Christ, who will appear to us in the way we need to see him and who will enable us to see the significance of our lives as they relate to the past as well as the future. We will begin to glimpse reality from God's point of view and begin to structure our lives accordingly. While these images of survival beyond the grave go far beyond the biblical evidence, I believe that they are grounded in the communal understanding of the "body of Christ" (1 Corinthians 12) and the vision of the "New Jerusalem" presented in Revelation 21.

Spiritual growth continues beyond the grave. The journey to God-awareness is infinite. While a relational and graceful vision of the afterlife challenges the traditional understanding of hell as unending and purposeless torture, it must affirm that our decisions in this life shape our afterlife and determine the nature of our spiritual therapy, or healing, beyond the grave. Divine judgment is never final or puni-tive, but it is real insofar as it compels us to confront ourselves in our totality. Some persons may continue temporarily in self-destructive behavior beyond the grave. They may be so alienated from the divine in this lifetime that they fail to realize that they have always been and will always be in God's presence. Like persons coming from a cave into a brightly lit hall, they may find that the light of God is so painful they must initially recoil from its brightness. But, as they adjust to the light and as God continues to invite them to a personal relationship, they will come to see that they have been in God's hands throughout their journey and that in accepting God's love they will find what they truly desire.

Eventually, those who grieve in this life will be comforted. Parents and children will be reunited in a healing environment. The hungry will find "the bread of life" and "living waters." The alienated will be embraced in loving communities. Even the oppressor will find for-giveness as he or she is reconciled with those who have been oppressed.

Within the great body of Christ, the "communion of saints" breaks down the absolute division between this life and the next. Death is real and the grave is dark and cold for Jesus and ourselves. Yet by the mys-tery of God's grace the grave is not final. We are "born again" within the everlasting and all-encompassing "body of Christ."

As we reflect on the nature of survival after death, we must not sti-fle our imaginations. While we cannot fathom the divine mystery and must proclaim that "eye hath not seen or ear heard" what God intends for us, we are challenged to accept that God's plan is always larger than our imagination and that the dimensions of God's love are always greater than we can fathom.

For those whose vision includes eternity, this world is also of infinite worth and will be eternally treasured by God. When we pray "thy kingdom come, thy will be done on earth as it is in heaven," we recognize the unity of all things in God and realize that from the perspective of God's healing love there is no ultimate difference between heaven and earth. The immortality of the soul does not call us to political apathy, but to a morality and social responsibility that treats every person as if he or she is immortal. Politics and spirituality, feeding the hungry and healing the spirit, are all elements in the graceful movement of God's Spirit in our world and the next.

As we grieve the loss of a loved one or our own impending deaths, a Christian faith for the new age invites us to embrace the pain, fear, and anguish even as it beckons us hopefully and imaginatively to become citizens of God's new age in which "God will dwell with them; and they will be God's people. . . . God will wipe every tear from their eyes, and death shall be no more, neither shall there be mourning nor crying nor pain anymore, for the former things have passed away" (Revelation 21:3–4).

QUESTIONS FOR REFLECTION AND DISCUSSION

1. What is your reaction to the contemporary interest in near death experiences? Do they prove the existence of an afterlife?

2. What is your image of the afterlife? How do the traditional Christian images differ from the new age images of the afterlife? Do you find any aspect of the new age images problematic or insightful?

3. Are our births accidental, determined by fate, or do we choose our own births?

4. Do growth and adventure occur beyond the grave? Can the afterlife be seen as a time of spiritual evolution?

CHAPTER SEVEN

THE CRYSTAL AND THE CROSS

PRIMARY SYMBOLS

A primary symbol of the new age is the crystal. In its various shapes and colors, the crystal symbolizes for many new agers the intensified energy of spiritual transformation being released in our time.

For Christians, the cross has also been the symbol of the new age—the age of salvation initiated by the life, death, and resurrection of Jesus Christ. To Christians, the cross has been the primary symbol of God's transforming power in the midst of human sin and brokenness. By sharing in the power of the cross, we become citizens of a new world in which the alienation of humans with each other, the nonhuman world, and God has been overcome.

As I look across my own university congregation as well as the wider Christian community, I find many persons joining the crystal and the cross in their jewelry as well as in their personal spirituality. But, for the most part, the marriage of the cross and the crystal has been superficial and problematic. Few Christians have been able to integrate the insights of their faith with the new energies they have found through their participation in the new age movement. They have received little help from their pastors, who often evidence a

shocking ignorance, if not antipathy, toward one of the most significant spiritual revolutions of our time. Their new age teachers have
revealed an equally naive understanding of Christianity or have
implied, in contrast to biblical spirituality, that authentic Christianity
is more akin to Hindu mysticism than Hebraic world affirmation.

Thoughtful Christians and new agers alike ask, "Must we choose
between the crystal and the cross, between the insights of the new age
movement and good news of Christian faith?" Throughout this book,
I have contended that mainstream Christianity and the new age movement will both benefit from creative and honest dialogue. In contrast
to fundamentalists who see the new age movement as a diabolical
threat to orthodox Christianity, I believe that the new age movement is
a reminder—like the influx of Asian religions in the 1960s and 1970s—
that Christians must reclaim and revive their own spiritual and metaphysical roots. Beneath its varied forms, the new age movement points
to the hope of a new world of spiritual transformation and personal
healing in contrast to our current world of polarization, ecological
destruction, and spiritual disease.

Christianity also claims to be an alternative to our world of sin and
injustice. As I read the optimistic visions of human possibility characteristic of many new age texts, I am reminded of the messianic kingdom envisaged by the author of Revelation (21:1, 3–4):

> Then I saw a new heaven and a new earth . . . and I heard a great
> voice saying, "Behold the dwelling of God is with humankind.
> God will dwell with them, and they shall be God's people. . . .
> God will wipe every tear from their eyes and death shall be no
> more, neither shall there be mourning nor crying nor pain any-
> more, for the former things have passed away."

In many ways, the new age movement is a younger sibling to
Christianity. Many of its founders saw themselves as restoring
Christianity to its ancient and esoteric spiritual center. The new age
movement may be one of many current reforming movements, including feminist spirituality, liberation theology, and ecological spirituality, all of which are currently bringing new life to mainstream
Christianity. Accordingly, as Christians reflect on the new age move-

ment, they must evaluate it in terms of its highest manifestations as well as its fringe aspects. In the spirit of the Jewish teacher Gamaliel who chose not to condemn the emerging Christian movement of the first century, Christians of the late twentieth century must remember that "if this plan or undertaking is of humanity, it will fail; but if it is of God, you will not be able to overthrow them. You might even be found opposing God" (Acts 5:38–39).

In the meantime, mainstream Christians must recognize that the new age movement, like the long-standing charismatic movement and the more recent movements of liberation, is a judgment on its own inability to address many of humankind's deepest spiritual needs. In particular, the new age movement challenges mainstream Christianity's failure to provide creative visions of spirituality, healing, revelation, and survival after death.

Ultimately, the Christian response to the new age movement is grounded in our understanding of Christ and salvation. On the one hand, Christians must not limit God's grace and revelation solely to the historical Jesus and the sacraments of the church. The light of the world enlightens and inspires every person and is present, in its many disguises, in every quest for truth. While Christians must affirm that Christ is of universal significance and is responsive to each person's need, we must equally remember that Christianity as a religious tradition is only one of many religious options within our global village. God may have sheep in other pastures (John 10:16).

On the other hand, Christians must not succumb to a relativism that suggests that Christ is only meaningful to those persons born within the sphere of the Christian tradition or Western culture. Further, Christians must avoid creating a Christian ghetto from which we as "resident aliens" view a world of unbelief.[1] Today, as in every century in Christian history, we must avoid the pitfalls of absolutism and relativism in order to be faithful to Christ and sensitive to the needs of God's children. While our "treasure" is in "earthen vessels" and is imperfect and relative, the reality behind this treasure is universal and ultimate. The Christ, incarnate in Jesus of Nazareth, is the animating principle of all things and the source of all truths, even when the name of Jesus is unspoken or unknown. While Christians must proclaim that Jesus of Nazareth is the ultimate embodiment of God in the world,

Christians must equally affirm that Christ is present in every quest for salvation and healing, including the authentic streams of spirituality of the new age movement.

Faithfulness to Christ involves embracing new and unexpected experiences of God as well as fidelity to the ancient expressions of faith. As the followers of Martin Luther and Ignatius of Loyola discovered, obedience to God involves the willingness to be transformed and go beyond the insights of the reformers themselves; the reformation must always continue even when it challenges old certainties. Just as Christianity was transformed by its encounters with Greek thought, the renaissance, modern science, biblical criticism, and, more recently, feminism, multiculturalism, and religious pluralism, so it now must allow itself to grow and be renewed by its encounter with the new age movement. Its openness to growth is not a witness to compromise or doubt but to the depth of its faith in the Christ who "makes all things new." When Christians critically and prayerfully embrace the insights of the new age movement, it is out of faithfulness to Christ and our commitment to the Christian vision of reality and human existence.

As Christians encounter the new age movement, they must be willing to explore their faith experientially as well as doctrinally. The truths of the faith must become living words rather than dead letters. Through the use of guided imaging, body prayer, meditation, and Ignatian spirituality, mainstream Christians are challenged to rediscover the Bible as a living word, addressed to the contemporary spiritual, political, and social situation in which they live. The inner journey of spiritual illumination must accompany the outer journey of liberating action. In so doing, they will experience the meaning of divine revelation and insight in every aspect of life: in worship, prayer, political action, and Scripture study as well as in family life, employment, and recreation. Christians must be willing to allow the gospel to become their own personal story and not a tired witness to a faith long dead.

As mainstream Christians seek to understand their faith in the context of pluralistic culture and the global village, they are challenged to retrace the steps of the first Christians. In the spirit of the Acts of the Apostles, the church is called upon to be a beacon of light, a place where healing, spirituality, justice, and personal transformation are sought, expected, and experienced. Today's church will reveal its unique mission not by isolating itself in a spiritual ghetto or con-demning all who differ from it, but by its willingness to see the move-ments of the one Spirit within the diversity of human experience. Today's new age movement is a breath of the Spirit calling a fatigued and fearful church to remember its vital past, imagine its glorious future, and launch out into the strong winds of the Spirit.

However, in this age of pluralism, mainstream Christians must not shrink from sharing their faith with persons within the new age move-ment even as they listen to new age accounts of spiritual transforma-tion. Mainstream Christianity has much to offer the new age move-ment. Most important, mainstream Christianity offers the positive and life-affirming vision of the Christian faith. From my participation in many new age groups and conversation with many persons in the new age movement, I have discovered that most new agers are exiles and refugees from some form of rigid, lifeless, or doctrinally exclusive Christianity. Many complain of Sunday School and catechism classes that emphasized guilt rather than grace, and obedience rather than experience. Others found no room for their questions and struggles within the cramped confines of fundamentalist churches. Still others found the mainstream church unable to deal with issues of healing, death, and spirituality.

Tragically, the only god many persons have found in Christianity is a god they can neither love nor believe in. Yet, they still seek after God. Today, Christians must clearly proclaim that the tribal god of vengeance is not our God, but a perversion of deeper truths of divine love and justice. We must invite persons to look at Christian faith as if for the first time.

In our technological age, there is also a growing search for commu-nity. The new age movement has still not addressed this need on an ongoing basis. Trust and honesty, healing and acceptance, cannot be sustained solely by a diet of workshops and retreats. They require a community of love, challenge, and commitment. They require a church. Our churches must become havens for spiritual seekers even when their search takes them far beyond the boundaries of traditional Christianity. Our willingness to provide hospitality to the spiritual seeker will transform our churches into the "body of Christ" they are meant to be.

In conversations with persons in the new age movement, Christians must be willing to listen as well as to share. They must be thankful for the vital energies the new age movement is bringing to contemporary spirituality and healing. They must risk the possibility that traditional visions of Christianity and divine revelation will be transformed by the encounter with the new age movement. But Christians must also remember that they have a "treasure" to share—the vision and experience of God's grace revealed in Jesus Christ and in a loving community—that will transform new age spirituality. When new agers find themselves caught in the burden of their own personal omnipotence and the chaos of the realities they have created, Christians can remind them that they are not fully responsible for their sickness or their success. In the divine body, each person's life arises and is shaped by many forces. Though each person is responsible for how they shape their experiences, they are not the sole creators of that experience and, in the midst of even the darkest experience, they are not alone—there is a community and a God to share their burdens.

While Christians can learn much about healing and spirituality from new agers, they can also share the holistic message of the gospel with their new age companions. Healing in the Christian tradition is not just a spiritual issue, but involves the body, personal relationships, and the social order. Healing and sickness are not merely individual issues, the results of our thoughts and our karma, as many new agers would suggest. Even the spiritually advanced may become ill, and even negative thinkers may find comfort and transformation apart from their own efforts. The body of Christ is a reminder that well-being is a relational issue. Within a loving community, asking and receiving help are not signs of weakness but revelations of spiritual growth and openness to healing. In such a community, even the experiences of sin, sickness, and guilt can be vehicles of healing for persons and for the community as a whole.

Finally, Christians are called to challenge new agers to greater social responsibility and sensitivity to the needs of the poor and oppressed. While Christians must confess their own role in the creation of unjust and patriarchal social structures, they must challenge any doctrine, such as the new age version of karma and reincarnation, that lessens our sensitivity to suffering by defining those who suffer as deserving of their pain. Rape, starvation, racism, sexism, genocide, and AIDS are matters of spiritual and ethical importance and not merely experiences planned for the soul's education. Suffering is real, even when it is not the final word. Indeed, Christianity claims that God is so involved in this world that God suffers in and with our own suffering. Christian faith provides the basis for a transformed new age movement, one that will be ethically sensitive and socially responsible.

In the final decade of the twentieth century, many persons long for a new age. Fundamentalists read the newspaper in light of the book of Revelation and their hope of the Second Coming. New agers prayerfully gather for the "harmonic convergence" that will bring healing to our planet or for meditations that will bring forth hidden masters who will guide us toward a peaceful future. In the final days of this century, we are experiencing new and unsettling energies. Nations and political systems are rising and falling; the balance of political and economic power is in flux; the relationship of East and West and North and South is shifting. We can no longer live by the old ways—be they religious, economic, political, or ecological. We must be born again spiritually, institutionally, and personally.

The church, along with the political and economic institutions of the northern hemisphere and western world, has midwifed destruction as well as creation, and now it must be transformed. Like General Motors, IBM, and other industrial giants, the church has often failed to respond to the novel movements and vital energies emerging in our time. It, like many established institutions, has forgotten the ultimate source of its spiritual energy and lost the vision of its true mission. The energies of transformation are moving—through crystal, computer chip, quality circle, and the human spirit. But they are also moving through the way of the cross. The church of today and tomorrow must be reborn—and its rebirth will come from its embrace and transformation of these new and challenging energies.

Today's church has the opportunity of becoming both the womb and the midwife for the great spiritual changes of our time. Apart from the guidance, structure, and historical tradition of the church, these ungrounded creative energies may collapse into chaos. Just as the new age is a breath of the Spirit, the church is also a revelation of the Spirit of God in our time. Today, the church cannot travel alone. It must open its doors to the winds of the spirit in all its varied forms and open its arms, heart, and mind to all those who seek to travel by the spirit embodied in Christ.

During a recent visit to Southern California, I had the opportunity to tour the Crystal Cathedral in Garden Grove. As I jogged at sunrise through the grounds of this monument to "possibility thinking," I was fascinated by a crystal cross that stands in the shadow of the Cathedral. Although its pastor, Robert Schuller, is hardly an adherent of new age theology and probably is unaware of the purported power of crystals, the image of a cathedral and a cross in crystal form represents the challenge Christians face today. It represents my own quest for a vital Christianity for this new age. We must embrace and affirm the vital energies of the new age as we discover the beauty of the crystal in all its many facets. But, as we embrace these energies, we must also transform them and mold them into the shape of a cross. In faithfulness to the one who promises a "new heaven and a new earth," we must lift high the cross and treasure the crystal as we journey together toward God's new age.

QUESTIONS FOR REFLECTION AND DISCUSSION

1. What contributions can the new age movement make to Christianity? What contributions can Christianity make to the new age movement?

2. What sort of religion do you envisage for the twenty-first century? Do you see Christianity as a dynamic and evolving religious movement? Will tomorrow's Christianity differ markedly from today's version of Christianity?

Notes

CHAPTER 1—CHRISTIANITY AND THE NEW AGE

1. Eileen Caddy and Liza Hollingshead, *Flight into Freedom* (Shaftsbury, England: Element Books), p. 216.

2. The Findhorn Foundation, *Guest Programme: January-September 1991* (Forres, Scotland: The Findhorn Foundation, 1991), p. 2.

3. Caddy and Hollingshead, p. 222.

4. Caddy and Hollingshead, p. 222.

5. Marilyn Ferguson, *The Aquarian Conspiracy* (Los Angeles: Jeremy Tarcher, 1980), pp. 18-19.

6. Karla Harby, "Both Advocates and Critics Agree: 'New Age' Meets Spiritual Needs." *United Church News*, Vol. 8:4 (May 1992), p. 6.

7. Harby, p. 6.

8. Maurice Smith, "Understanding and Responding to New Age Movements" (Interfaith Witness Department, Home Mission Board, Southern Baptist Convention, 1983), p. 6.

9. David Spangler, *Revelation: The Birth of a New Age* (The Findhorn Foundation, 1976), p. 10.

10. David Spangler, *The New Age* (Issaquah, WA: Morningtown Press, 1988), p. 4.

11. Spangler, *The New Age*, p. 2.

12. Spangler, *The New Age*, p. 7.

13. Spangler, *The New Age*, p. 7.

14. Spangler, *The New Age*, p. 8.

15. Spangler, *The New Age*, pp. 12-13.

16. Spangler, *The New Age*, pp. 13-14.

17. Spangler, *The New Age*, p. 22.

18. Spangler, *The New Age*, p. 30.

19. Ferguson, p. 18.

20. Ferguson, p. 29.

21. George A. Maloney, S.J., *Mysticism and the New Age* (Staten Island, NY: Alba House, 1991), p. 5.

22. Maloney, p. 7.

23. Maloney, p. 6.

24. "Our Mission and Culture," *Documents of the Thirty-fourth General Congregation of the Society of Jesus*, 21, 27.

25. "Our Mission and Culture," 8.

26. "Our Mission and Inter-religious Dialogue," *Documents of the Thirty-fourth General Congregation of the Society of Jesus*, 3.

27. Ted Peters, *The Cosmic Self* (San Francisco: Harper, 1991), p. 5.

28. Peters, p. 5.

29. Peters, p. 170.

30. Peters, p. 196.

31. Peters, p. 197.

32. Constance Cumbey, *The Hidden Dangers of the Rainbow* (Shreveport, LA: Huntington House, 1983), p. 16.

33. Cumbey, p. 73.

34. Ron Rhodes, *The Counterfeit Christ of the New Age Movement* (Grand Rapids: Baker Books, 1990), p. 24.

35. Rhodes, p. 210.

36. Among the most scholarly and insightful evangelical and fundamentalist critiques of the new age are: David Clark and Norman Geisler, *Apologetics in the New Age: A Christian Critique of Pantheism* (Grand Rapids: Baker Books, 1990); Douglas Groothuis, *Confronting the New Age* (Downers Grove, IL: Inter Varsity Press, 1988) and *Unmasking the New Age* (Downers Grove, IL: Inter Varsity Press, 1986); Karen Hoyt and J. Isamu Yamamoto, editors, *The New Age Rage* (Old Tappan, NJ: Fleming Revell, 1987); Paul Reisser, Teri Reisser, John Weldon, *New Age Medicine: A Christian Perspective on Holistic Health* (Downers Grove, IL: Inter Varsity Press, 1990); Ron Rhodes, *The Counterfeit Christ of the New Age* (Grand Rapids: Baker Books, 1990); James Sire, *The Universe Next Door* (Downers Grove, IL: Inter Varsity Press, 1988).

37. Hoyt and Yamamoto, *The New Age Rage*, p. 19.

38. Groothuis, *Confronting the New Age*, p. 17.

39. Groothuis, *Confronting the New Age*, p. 44.

CHAPTER 2—FIND GOD IN A TECHNOLOGICAL AGE

1. Harby, p. 6.

2. John Naisbitt and Patricia Aburdene, *Megatrends 2000* (New York: William Mason, 1990), p. 275.

3. Dean R. Hoge, Benton Johnson, and Donald Luidens, *Vanishing Boundaries: The Religion of Mainline Protestant Baby Boomers* (Louisville: Westminster/John Knox Press, 1994), pp. 175-212.

4. Robert Bellah, et al, *Habits of the Heart* (Berkeley: University of California Press, 1985), p. 237.

5. John Cobb, *Can Christ Become Good News Again?* (St. Louis: Chalice Press, 1991), p. ix.

6. Cobb, p. viii.

7. Cobb, p. vii.

8. Bellah, p. 221.

9. Jerry Jampolsky, *Love is Letting Go of Fear* (Milbrae, CA: Celestial Arts, 1971), p. 65.

10. Susan Trout, *To See Differently* (Washington, DC: Three Roses Press, 1990), p. 32.

11. Trout, p. 33.

12. Charlene Spretnak, *The Spiritual Dimensions of Green Politics* (Santa Fe: Bear and Co., 1986), p. 41.

13. Spretnak, p. 42.

14. David Spangler, *The New Age*, p. 8.

15. Larry Dossey, *Recovering the Soul: A Scientific and Spiritual Search* (New York: Bantam Books, 1989), p. 161.

16. Dossey, p. 171.

17. *A Course in Miracles: Workbook* (Tiburon, CA: Foundation for Inner Peace, 1975), p. 403.

18. Kenneth Wapnick, *Love Does Not Condemn* (Roscoe, NY: Foundation for A Course in Miracles, 1989), p. 481.

19. Jampolsky, p. 62.

20. Trout, pp. 32, 73.

21. Jampolsky, p. 85.

22. Shirley MacLaine, *Going Within* (New York: Bantam Books, 1989), p. 76.

23. Ralph Waldo Emerson, "The Harvard Divinity School Address," in *Three Prophets of Religious Liberalism* (Boston: Beacon Press, 1964), p. 103.

24. Emerson, p. 108.

25. Dossey, p. 286.

26. Dossey, p. 286.

27. Dossey, pp. 290-291.

28. Richard Bach, *Jonathan Livingston Seagull* (New York: Macmillan, 1970), p. 27.

29. Bach, p. 59.

30. Bach, p. 77.

31. Ernest Holmes, *How to Change Your Life* (Los Angeles: Science of Mind Publications, 1987), pp. 25-26.

32. Spangler, *The New Age*, p. 13.

33. Spangler, *The New Age*, p. 13.

34. Jampolsky, p. 85.

35. MacLaine, p. 27.

36. Louise Hay, *You Can Heal Your Life* (Santa Monica, CA: Hay House, 1984), p. 5.

37. Hay, p. 56.

38. MacLaine, p. 182.

39. Robin Weston, *Channelers: A New Age Directory* (New York: Perigee Press, 1988), p. 83.

40. Holmes, pp. 249-251.

41. Holmes, p. 251.

42. Shakti Gawain, *Creative Visualization* (Mill Valley, CA: Whatever Press, 1978), p. 13.

43. Gawain, p. 22.

44. Stephen Covey, *The Seven Habits of Highly Effective People* (New York: Fireside, 1989), p. 23.

45. Thomas Keating, *The Heart of the World* (New York: Crossroad, 1981), p. 22.

46. For further reading on the nature of God in this new age, I suggest: Bruce Epperly, *At the Edges of Life: A Holistic Vision of the Human Adventure* (St. Louis: Chalice Press, 1992); John Cobb, *God and the World* (Philadelphia: Westminster Press, 1969), *Christ in a Pluralistic Age* (Philadelphia: Westminster Press, 1975), *Can Christ Become Good News Again?* (St. Louis: Chalice Press, 1991); Sallie McFague, *Models of God* (Philadelphia: Fortress Press, 1987).

47. Alfred North Whitehead, *Process and Reality* (New York: Free Press, 1978), p. 351.

48. Julian of Norwich, *Showings* (New York: Paulist Press, 1978), p. 177.

49. Quoted in Morton Kelsey, *The Christian and the Supernatural* (Minneapolis: Augsburg, 1976), p. 83.

50. Among the many texts available, there are a number of contemporary classics for laity as well as clergy: Maxie Dunnam, *The Workbook of Living Prayer* (Nashville: Upper Room, 1974); Tilden Edwards, *Living Simply Through the Day* (New York: Paulist Press, 1977), *Sabbath Time* (New York: Seabury Press, 1982); Marilyn Morgan Helleberg, *Beyond TM: A Practical Guide to the Lost Traditions of Christian Meditation* (New York: Paulist Press, 1980); Thomas Keating, *The Heart of the World* (New York: Crossroad, 1981); Morton Kelsey, *The Other Side of Silence* (Mahwah, NJ: Paulist Press, 1978); Thomas Merton, *What Is Contemplation?* (Springfield, IL: Templegate Press, 1978), *Contemplation in a World of Action* (Garden City, NY: Doubleday, 1971); M. Basil Pennington, *Centering Prayer* (Garden City, NY: Doubleday, 1980).

51. Thomas Merton, *Contemplative Prayer*, p. 139.

52. M. Basil Pennington, *The Way Back Home* (New York: Paulist Press, 1989), p. 19.

53. Anonymous, *The Way of the Pilgrim* (New York: Seabury Press, 1965).

CHAPTER 3—REVELATION AND CHANNELING

1. Jon Klimo, *Channeling* (Los Angeles: Jeremy Tarcher, 1987), p. 2.

2. David Spangler, *Channeling in the New Age* (Issaquah, WA: Morningtown Press, 1988), p. 7.

3. Klimo, p. 1.

4. Klimo, p. 4.

5. Klimo, p. 95.

6. Klimo, pp. 5-6.

7. Robert Skutch, *Journey Without Distance* (Berkeley: Celestial Arts, 1984), p. 61.

8. For further reading on *A Course in Miracles,* see *A Course in Miracles: Text, Workbook for Students, Manual for Teachers* (Tiburon, CA: Foundation for Inner Peace, 1975); Robert Skutch, *Journey Without Distance* (Berkeley: Celestial Arts, 1984); Robert Perry, *Introduction to A Course in Miracles* (Fullerton, CA: Miracle Distribution Center, 1989).

9. Ron Scolastico, *The Earth Adventure* (Pacific Palisades, CA: Universal Guidance Press, 1988), p. 3.

10. Scolastico, p. 24.

11. Scolastico, p. 25.

12. Klimo, p. 147.

13. Steven Lee Weinberg, *Ramtha* (Eastsound, WA: Sovereignty, 1980), p. 31.

14. Weinberg, p. 132.

15. Quoted in Klimo, p. 12.

16. Elliot Miller, *Crash Course on the New Age Movement* (Grand Rapids: Baker Books, 1989), p. 143.

17. David Spangler, *Channeling in the New Age,* pp. 12-13.

18. Roberto Assagioli, *Psychosynthesis* (New York: Viking Press, 1965).

19. Public lecture, Arlington Metaphysical Church, July 24, 1992.

20. David Spangler, *Channeling in the New Age,* pp. 43-44.

21. For an outline of the Gnostic impact on the closing of the canon and the role of women in alternative Christian movements, see Elaine Pagels, *The Gnostic Gospels* (New York: Random House, 1979).

22. An excellent discussion of the formation of the canon is found in Hans van Campenhausen, *The Formation of the Christian Canon* (Philadelphia: Fortress Press, 1972).

23. Spangler, *Channeling in the New Age,* p. 54.

CHAPTER 4—"THE HEALING CONNECTION"

1. Larry Dossey, *Healing Words: The Power of Prayer and the Practice of Medicine* (San Francisco: Harper, 1993).

2. Barbara Brennan, *Hands of Light* (New York: Pleiades, 1987), p. 24.

3. Brennan, p. 28.

4. Brennan, p. 28.

5. Barbara Brennan, Public Lecture, July 30, 1992, Arlington, Virginia.

6. Brennan, *Hands of Light*, p. 7.

7. Brennan, p. 131.

8. Brennan, p. 147.

9. Brennan, p. 132.

10. Hay, pp. 5, 7, 128.

11. Louise Hay, *The AIDS Book* (Santa Monica: Hay House, 1988), p. 7.

12. Hay, *You Can Heal Your Life*, p. 5.

13. Hay, *The AIDS Book*, p. 29.

14. Hay, *The AIDS Book*, p. 33.

15. Hay, *You Can Heal Your Life*, pp. 128, 129.

16. Hay, *You Can Heal Your Life*, p. 133.

17. Hay, *You Can Heal Your Life*, p. 168.

18. Hay, *You Can Heal Your Life*, p. 136.

19. Hay, *You Can Heal Your Life*, p. 36.

20. Larry Dossey, *Meaning and Medicine* (New York: Bantam Books, 1991), pp. 29-30.

21. Michael D'Antonio, *Heaven on Earth* (New York: Crown Publishers, 1992), p. 96.

22. D'Antonio, pp. 96-97.

23. Hay, *You Can Heal Your Life*, p. 201.

24. *A Course in Miracles: Text* (Tiburon, CA: Foundation for Inner Peace, 1975), p. 10.

25. *A Course in Miracles: Text*, pp. 359, 364.

26. *A Course in Miracles: Manual for Teachers* (Tiburon, CA: Foundation for Inner Peace, 1975), p. 81.

27. *A Course in Miracles: Manual for Teachers*, p. 97.

28. Kenneth Wapnick, *Forgiveness and Jesus* (Roscoe, NY: Foundation for A Course in Miracles, 1983), p. 84.

29. *A Course in Miracles: Workbook* (Tiburon, CA: Foundation for Inner Peace, 1975), p. 251.

30. *A Course in Miracles: Text*, p. 553.

31. Morton Kelsey, *Psychology, Medicine, and Christian Healing* (San Francisco: Harper, 1988), pp. 42-43.

32. For the most insightful discussion of Jesus' healing ministry, see Morton Kelsey's *Psychology, Medicine, and Christian Healing*, pp. 40-82.

33. Kelsey, *Psychology, Medicine, and Christian Healing*, p. 40.

34. For a more detailed description of healing in the early church, see Morton Kelsey's *Psychology, Medicine, and Christian Healing*, pp. 81-156.

35. Kelsey, *Psychology, Medicine, and Christian Healing*, pp. 1-25, 156-185.

36. My account of Mikao Usui's life comes from Helen J. Haberly, *Reiki: Hawayo Takata's Story* (Garrett Park, MD: Archedigm, 1990).

37. Ambrose and Olga Worrall, *The Gift of Healing* (Columbus, OH: Ariel Press, 1985), p. 173.

38. Ambrose and Olga Worrall, *The Gift of Healing*, p. 91.

39. Ambrose and Olga Worrall, *The Gift of Healing*, p. 33.

40. Ambrose and Olga Worrall, *Explore Your Psychic World* (Columbus, OH: Ariel Press, 1989), p. 29.

41. Ambrose and Olga Worrall, *Explore Your Psychic World*, p. 83.

42. Ambrose and Olga Worrall, *Explore Your Psychic World*, p. 66.

43. Agnes Sanford, *The Healing Light* (St. Paul: Macalester Park Publishing, 1947), p. 13.

44. Sanford, p. 87.

45. Sanford, p. 166.

46. Sanford, pp. 36, 61.

47. Sanford, p. 29.

48. Sanford, p. 43.

49. Sanford, pp. 44-45.

50. Sanford, p. 165.

51. Kelsey, *Psychology, Medicine, and Christian Healing*, p. 198.

52. Kelsey, *Psychology, Medicine, and Christian Healing*, p. 284.

53. Kelsey, *Psychology, Medicine, and Christian Healing*, p. 299.

54. Kelsey, *Psychology, Medicine, and Christian Healing*, pp. 325-326.

55. For further study on the religious dimensions of the hospice movement, see Michael Hamilton and Helen Reid, *A Hospice Handbook* (Grand Rapids: Eerdmans, 1980).

56. Ambrose and Olga Worrall, *Explore Your Psychic Power*, p. 52.

57. Larry Dossey, *Rediscovering the Soul* (New York: Bantam Books, 1989) pp. 45-47.

58. Dossey, *Healing Words*, p. xviii.

CHAPTER 5—CHRIST IN THE NEW AGE

1. Benjamin Creme, *Messages from Maitreya the Christ* (London: Tara Press, 1980), *The Reappearance of Christ and the Masters of Wisdom* (London: Tara Press, 1980), *Transmission: Meditation for the New Age* (London: Tara Press, 1983).

2. Alice Bailey, *From Bethlehem to Calvary* (New York: Lucis Publishing, 1968), p. 34.

3. Bailey, pp. 43, 44.

4. Creme, *Messages from Maitreya the Christ*, vol. 1, p. 59.

5. Creme, *Messages from Maitreya the Christ*, vol. 1, p. 7.

6. Creme, *The Reappearance of Christ*, p. 66.

7. Creme, *Messages from Maitreya the Christ*, vol. 1, p. 39.

8. Creme, *Transmission*, p. 17.

9. Creme, *Transmission*, p. 12.

10. Creme, *Transmission*, p. 22.

11. Levi Dowling, *The Aquarian Gospel of Jesus the Christ* (Eagle Rock, CA: DeVorss and Co., 1964), p. 13.

12. Dowling, p. 265.

13. Dowling, p. 52.

14. Dowling, p. 65.

15. Dowling, p. 65.

16. Dowling, pp. 164-165.

17. Dowling, p. 251.

18. Dowling, p. 265.

19. Dowling, p. 261.

20. Jeffrey Furst, *Edgar Cayce's Story of Jesus* (New York: Coward McCann, 1976), p. 17.

21. Furst, p. 390.

22. Furst, p. 195.

23. For further reading, see Hans Jonas, *The Gnostic Religion* (Boston: Beacon Press, 1967) and Elaine Pagels, *The Gnostic Gospels* (New York: Random House, 1979).

24. Pagels, *The Gnostic Gospels*, p. 87.

25. Pagels, *The Gnostic Gospels*, p. 114.

26. Pagels, *The Gnostic Gospels*, p. xx.

27. Pagels, *The Gnostic Gospels*, p. xx.

28. Pagels, *The Gnostic Gospels*, p. xx.

29. *A Course in Miracles: Text*, p. 97.

30. *A Course in Miracles: Manual for Teachers*, p. 53.

31. *A Course in Miracles: Manual for Teachers*, p. 83.

32. *A Course in Miracles: Manual for Teachers*, p. 5.

33. Kenneth Wapnick, *Love Does Not Condemn* (Roscoe, NY: Foundation for A Course in Miracles, 1989), p. 511.

34. Thomas Berry, "The New Story," *Teilhard Studies* 1 (Winter 1978); Thomas Berry and Brian Swimme, *The Universe Story* (San Francisco: Harper, 1992).

35. Matthew Fox, *The Coming of the Cosmic Christ* (San Francisco: Harper, 1988), p. 7.

36. Fox, p. 88.

37. Fox, p. 141.

38. Fox, p. 141.

39. John Cobb, *Can Christ Be Good News Again?* (St. Louis: Chalice Press, 1991), p. 36.

40. John Cobb and David Griffin, *Process Theology: An Introductory Exposition* (Philadelphia: Westminster Press, 1976), p. 105.

41 Alfred North Whitehead, *Process and Reality* (New York: Free Press, 1978), p. 351.

CHAPTER 6—DEATH AND HUMAN HOPE

1. Raymond Moody, *Life After Life* (New York: Bantam Books, 1975).

2. Betty J. Eadie, *Embraced by the Light* (Placerville, CA: Goldleaf Press, 1992).

3. Andrew Greeley, *Death and Beyond* (Chicago: Thomas More Press, 1976), p. 61.

4. Raymond Moody, *Coming Back: A Psychiatrist Explores Past-Life Journeys* (New York: Bantam Books, 1991) and Helen Walmbach, *Life Before Life* (New York: Bantam Books, 1981).

5. Martin Luther King, *Strength to Love* (New York: Harper & Row, 1963), p. 76.

6. Louise Hay, *You Can Heal Your Life*, pp. 5, 8.

7. Jane Roberts, *The Seth Material* (Englewood Cliffs, NJ: Prentice-Hall, 1970), p. 4.

8. Gary Zukav, *The Seat of the Soul* (New York: Simon & Schuster, 1989), p. 154.

9. Helen Walmbach, *Life Before Birth* (New York: Bantam Books, 1979), p. 42.

10. Walmbach, *Life Before Birth*, p. 34.

11. Geoffrey Hodson, *Reincarnation: Fact or Fallacy* (Wheaton, IL: Theosophical Publishing House, 1967), p. 58.

12. Ruth Weston, *Channelers: A New Age Directory* (New York: Perigee Press, 1988), p. 97.

13. Gary Zukav, *The Seat of the Soul*, p. 43.

14. Zukav, *The Seat of the Soul*, p. 43.

15. Weinberg, *Ramtha*, p. 36.

16. Zukav, *The Seat of the Soul*, p. 163.

17. Zukav, *The Seat of the Soul*, p. 205.

18. Shirley MacLaine, *Dancing in the Light* (New York: Bantam Books, 1985), p. 237.

19. Stephen Levine, *Who Dies* (Garden City, NY: Doubleday, 1984), p. 103.

20. Weinberg, *Ramtha*, p. 115.

21. Helena Blavatsky, *The Key to Theosophy* (Pasadena: Theosphical University Press, 1972), p. 27.

22. Quincy Howe, *Reincarnation for the Christian* (Philadelphia: Westminster Press, 1974), p. 49.

23. Leslie Weatherhead, *Life Begins at Death* (Nashville: Abingdon, 1967), p. 23.

24. Geddes MacGregor, *Reincarnation in Christianity* (Wheaton, IL: Theosophical Publishing House, 1978), p. 116.

25. Juan Mascaro, translator, *The Bhagavad Gita* (Baltimore: Penguin Books, 1969), pp. 49-50.

26. Ram Dass and Marabai Bush, *Compassion in Action* (New York: Bell Tower, 1992), p. 41.

27. Shirley MacLaine, *Out on a Limb* (New York: Bantam Books, 1983), p. 99.

28. MacLaine, *Out on a Limb*, p. 214.

29. Weinberg, *Ramtha*, p. 132.

30. Helena Blavatsky, *The Key to Theosophy*, p. 135.

31. Shirley MacLaine, *It's All in the Playing* (New York: Bantam Books, 1987), p. 5.

32. MacLaine, *It's All in the Playing*, pp. 173-174.

33. Weinberg, *Ramtha*, p. 31.

34. Ram Dass and Bush, *Compassion in Action*, p. 3.

35. Howe, p. 31.

36. MacGregor, p. 4.

37. I have discussed this issue in greater detail in *At the Edges of Life*, pp. 159-172.

CHAPTER 7—THE CRYSTAL AND THE CROSS

1. Stanley Hauerwas and William Willimon, *Resident Aliens* (Nashville: Abingdon, 1990).

INDEX

Of Related Interest...

Earth, Sky, Gods, and Mortals
A Theology of Ecology for the 21st Century
Jay McDaniel

This book won the College Theology Society's Best Book Award. Tom Berry calls it a "new context for ecological spirituality." The author pulls together the insights of process thought, liberation theology, etc. to present a call for a new piety responding to ecological consciousness.

ISBN: 0-89622-412-0, 224 pp, $14.95

Befriending the Earth
A Theology of Reconciliation Between Humans and the Earth
Edited by Anne Lonergan & Stephen Dunn

Thomas Berry and Thomas Clarke dialogue on the role of religion in ecological issues. "For people concerned about the direction of Christianity in the third millennium, this book is a must," says Michael Dowd. Geologian Thomas Berry and Theologian Thomas Clarke explore the principles and urgency involved for Christians. Includes questions for discussion.

ISBN: 0-89622-471-6, 168 pp, $9.95

In the Presence of Mystery
An Introduction to the Story of Human Religiousness
Michael Horace Barnes

A great book to help readers understand that the call to be human includes the religious response. The author's survey of history and cultures leads the reader to personal response. Highly acclaimed, this college text is an introduction to the story of human religiousness that goes to the very core of religious belief and practice, ranging from preliterate to modern culture.

ISBN: 0-89622-425-2, 344 pp, $14.95

Myths
gods, heroes, and saviors
Leonard J. Biallas

By looking into the myths and stories of other religious traditions, we bring a deeper commitment to our own. Morton Kelsey calls this book "a gold mine of material that can be used in high schools and colleges" with "stimulating questions and quotations that are provocative, searching and valuable in themselves."

ISBN: 0-89622-290-x, 312 pp, $12.95

Available at religious bookstores or from:

 TWENTY-THIRD PUBLICATIONS
P.O. Box 180 • Mystic, CT 06355

For a complete list of quality books and videos call:
1 - 8 0 0 - 3 2 1 - 0 4 1 1